Praise for
The Storyteller's Advantage

"Christina Farr has written an eminently useful and inspirational book—one that demystifies storytelling and can help anyone on their journey to break through the noise. Keep a notebook handy; you'll want to get brainstorming while reading."

—Sarah Frier, author of *No Filter*

"Today, the ability to tell a clear and compelling story is no longer optional—it's a defining factor in success. Christina Farr delivers a masterclass in the art and science of storytelling and proves how it is the thread that turns intention into impact. With insights drawn from the most compelling voices across industries, this book is equal parts practical guide and inspiring manifesto. This book is a gift for anyone who wants to sharpen their voice and tell stories that truly matter."

—Alyssa Jaffee, partner, 7wire Ventures

"At a moment when compelling and effective communication has never been more in demand, Christina Farr elegantly provides a roadmap for all of us to uplevel what we say and how we say it. This is must reading for anyone who wants their words to actually have impact and move audiences."

—Dr. Vin Gupta, former chief medical officer, Amazon

"In her groundbreaking new book, Christina Farr makes a compelling case that storytelling isn't just a nice-to-have skill—it's the competitive edge every business leader needs in today's crowded marketplace. Whether you're a founder who hasn't grasped the importance of a communications strategy or a business leader looking for the tools to build one, Farr's practical wisdom transforms storytelling from an intimidating art into an essential, learnable business skill—one that will serve you from the boardroom to the wedding toast."

—Soraya Darabi, founder and general partner, TMV

The Storyteller's Advantage

How Powerful Narratives Make Businesses Thrive

Christina Farr

EBURY EDGE

UK | USA | Canada | Ireland | Australia
India | New Zealand | South Africa

Ebury Edge is part of the Penguin Random House group of companies
whose addresses can be found at global.penguinrandomhouse.com

Penguin Random House UK
One Embassy Gardens, 8 Viaduct Gardens, London SW11 7BW

penguin.co.uk
global.penguinrandomhouse.com

First published in the United States by Basic Venture in 2025
First published in the United Kingdom by Ebury Edge in 2025

Typeset by Six Red Marbles UK, Thetford, Norfolk

Printed and bound in India by Manipal Technologies Limited

The authorised representative in the EEA is Penguin Random House Ireland,
Morrison Chambers, 32 Nassau Street, Dublin D02 YH68

A CIP catalogue record for this book is available from the British Library

ISBN 9781529146486

Book interior design by Amy Quinn

Penguin Random House is committed to a sustainable future
for our business, our readers and our planet. This book is
made from Forest Stewardship Council® certified paper.

For Wendy, the most gifted storyteller I've ever encountered

Contents

Contents

Introduction

Good storytelling can inspire, elicit action, persuade, and change minds. Few tools are as valuable—and accessible—for businesses in our global world, where millions of us live and conduct our work online. Because so many of us in our digital economy have bought into the slogan "Data is the new oil," most companies have come to revere numbers and to undervalue storytelling.[1] Most of us in our careers have received requests from managers to prove our progress in linear terms, ideally in the form of metrics that can be presented in charts and graphs. Storytelling can seem more subjective and its results less tangible. How do you know if it was a feat of masterful storytelling, a slick demo of the product, or a combination of the two that won over an intractable customer? Can any of that be proven? Perhaps not, but most of the leaders I have interviewed for this book would acknowledge that storytelling often plays a significant role. And yet, very few organizations provide resources and opportunities for employees to become better storytellers.

We seem to have forgotten that data, just like oil, is useless in its raw form. In fact, data is not the antithesis to storytelling. It is a potential partner or ally. Data scientists at the top universities are routinely learning storytelling techniques so that they can turn raw feeds of numbers into something emotionally moving, useful, and actionable.[2] Without the added layer of storytelling, data lacks meaning; most humans will struggle to interpret and digest, let alone remember, it.[3]

"You can be successful with a great product that finds an audience and gets in front of them," said Neil Lindsay, a senior vice president at Amazon, who runs the health group and previously ran Marketing and Prime worldwide. "You can be a *lot more* successful if you can amplify the truth about what you do and share the emotional benefit it can bring to people's lives."

Lindsay shared an analogy of buying any old jacket versus a Patagonia jacket. The two jackets might look and feel about the same, both functioning to keep you warm on a hike, but the Patagonia choice carries greater meaning because the brand has put so many resources behind sharing its story. Patagonia makes clear that it loves the wild parts of the earth. Its website includes multiple references to its mission of conservation, proudly proclaiming that we as humans must use our pioneering spirit to defend "our one and only home." The company has also put its money where its mouth is (as we'll discuss, one important aspect of storytelling involves backing up claims with action) by funding environmental nonprofits and climate solutions. Patagonia ranks as one of the most reputable brands in the United States, associated consistently with such positive values as favorable consumer experience and sustainability.[4] Hence, so many consumers continue to buy Patagonia jackets.

Human beings have been telling stories for millennia. Our brain evolved to process stories, to organize details into plots and form them into long-lasting memories. So storytelling should be a priority for every company today at the leadership levels, running all the way through the organization, across the legal, human resources, policy, product, and operations departments and not just public relations and marketing. As *The New York Times* puts it when speaking to potential advertisers, "Consumers, more than ever, want to have a genuine connection with the brands they so loyally support. However, consumers can't be loyal until they understand a brand's mission and purpose. Storytelling bridges that gap."[5]

Most companies I see today are falling short when it comes to storytelling. I say this confidently, as someone whose job for the past fifteen years has required them to spend a lot of time listening to poorly told stories. And I mean a *lot*. I would estimate that I have listened to 5,000 hours (equivalent to about seven straight months) of founders, CEOs, and company spokespeople trying to communicate what their products do and to win over potential customers to their business models, much of that in the form of PowerPoint presentations.

Being on the receiving end of so many company pitches was a big part of the job I signed up for as a business journalist at CNBC, Reuters, and *Fast Company* and later as a health and technology investor at OMERS Ventures, the private company investment arm of one of the world's largest pension funds. From there, I joined the strategy consulting and legal firm Manatt, where I continue to invest in and advise companies. Throughout my evolving career, as an advisor, investor, and journalist, I recognized that I was on one side of a transaction. In the first part of my career, I knew that most companies viewed me as a necessary tool in achieving a broader agenda to gain attention. In the second part, my value was connected to my access to funds, which could help fuel a business to the next phase of growth or keep it afloat until the business model started to work. Nowadays, I try to straddle both sides of the equation, helping founders and business executives use storytelling to achieve their goals, knowing that there is no better way for them to get ahead.

Looking back to all these pitches over the years, most of the encounters were unsuccessful in the technical sense—I did not write a check or put the company or its CEO in print. But occasionally I found myself truly riveted by the person sitting across from me and compelled to help. In those moments, the transactional feeling fell away. I wanted to root for those businesses, despite any skepticism I harbored going into the interaction. A switch flipped in my brain because I bought into the company's story on an emotional level. Each time that occurred, it reinforced something fundamental for me: Good storytellers will inherit the world.[6]

You might object that plenty of successful companies have bad storytellers at the helm, and you would be correct about that. But as we will learn throughout *The Storyteller's Advantage*, storytelling can be like gas poured on a fire. If the business is legitimate, a good story will help things progress much faster. Even with a dubious or poorly performing business, a good story—in the hands of a master storyteller—can rocket a company to stratospheric heights before the inevitable downfall. The major reason behind that is obvious: When a storyteller captivates their intended audience, be it a media personality, a potential customer, or a new hire, they have won over a key ally.

4

With enough alliances, companies can build up momentum quickly. Great team members flock to the business, investors pile in, and the press takes note. And yet, I've heard storytelling capabilities described in the pejorative, particularly in Silicon Valley, where I lived and worked for more than a decade. If a founder is described as a "good storyteller," the assumption is that the company is more hype than substance. As former Activision Blizzard communications chief and Shopify board member Lulu Cheng Meservey shared with me, negative sentiment toward storytellers is far too pervasive in the business world—and it should be the exact opposite. She believes that any company with compelling stories to share with the world could be "twice as successful," and those who believe otherwise are likely to be bad storytellers. "It's sour grapes," she said.

Delian Asparouhov, an investor at the venture firm Founders Fund and a founder of Varda Space, believes the technology industry could most benefit from great storytelling. The more technical the business, the more important the narrative is. "With a consumer social application, you can just ask someone to download it to get them excited about it…[but] with anything that touches on AI, or climate, or space, or new science, usually all you'll have is the story for years." Imagine Mark Zuckerberg pitching Facebook in the early days. He would only need to demo downloading the app. The companies building the truly breakthrough technologies—self-driving cars, artificial wombs, carbon capture, and so forth—have very little to go on but the story. These companies typically need to raise capital for a decade or longer but may have little to show for themselves in the form of progress toward their goal. To believe in a future where this technology is mainstream requires imagination. What builds imagination? A remarkable story.

So what kinds of stories are worth sharing for anyone, whether it's a CEO or a junior professional a few years out of school? Well, that is the very question we will explore throughout the pages of this book. *The Storyteller's Advantage* will share plenty of real case studies and examples of companies of all sizes that used storytelling in profound ways, both to overcome key setbacks and to shout from the rooftops about their success (without annoying anyone in the process). As we will discuss, being a great storyteller does not mean having a big ego, and it does not require constantly posting on social media. Plenty of founders, executives, and employees approach communications in an authentic way. At its core, storytelling only works when the storytelling is genuine—otherwise, the audience will feel as if they are being sold to and will tune out. "The best stories are the most authentic," said Lindsay, the Amazon senior vice president.

Here's the good news: Unlike most professional skills, storytelling does not require a huge investment of time or resources. Truly anyone, at all levels of an organization, can do it—with the right training and commitment. Contrary to popular belief, storytelling is not an innate quality that some people possess and others lack. Being good at storytelling requires discipline, preparation, and practice, like anything. And even the self-professed "experts" can improve their skills by refamiliarizing themselves with the basics or by soliciting constructive feedback.

Learning to be a better storyteller can also be fun and creative. Consider former Twitter CEO Dick Costolo, who credited a lot of his success to improv, a form of spontaneous, unscripted theater where actors make up ideas on the spot.[7] As he explained to *Bloomberg*, improv is like company building in that it encourages people to come together for a shared goal. The lesson here involves adapting in the moment to any new story, no matter how kooky or unexpected.[8] That is a valuable skill for anyone working within a diverse organization where many cultures, languages, and viewpoints vie for representation. For those who can't imagine themselves doing improv, there are plenty of other venues in which to practice sharing a story, be it LinkedIn, a conference, an internal team meeting, or an off-site presentation. My favorite medium most days is X, because I'm drawn to the idea of communicating in pithy sentences. My least is anything involving video, because I still cannot get to a place of comfort hearing my own voice.

We're all busy, with far too few hours in the day to refine our skills. So functionally speaking, how do we make storytelling a priority? For most corporate executives, anything that involves brainstorming, thinking, writing, and sharing ideas often takes a backseat to the treadmill of urgent meetings and projects. So I see many company leaders today thinking they can hand off the task of storytelling to someone else. Most companies outsource the narrative to a bewildering number of PR agencies and marketing firms that pull together scripted "talking points" and messaging documents. I cannot overstate this: That is not the same thing as storytelling. Those efforts often fall short because storytelling is deeply personal and requires a connection with the audience, be it a customer, an investor, or another key stakeholder. To truly work, it needs to be baked into executives' or operators' calendars from day one. They need to make time for it.

When I'm advising companies, I recommend starting with a simple, achievable discipline: Carve out an hour in the morning to read the news or practice jotting down thoughts in a free-form manner, even if these ideas will never be shared with anyone. Ask questions like "Why did I start or join this business in the first place?" From there, consider what you uniquely know and might share with others.

Becoming a "thought leader," the ultimate goal for most executives these days in their pursuit of storytelling prowess, will not be possible in a week or even months. And it certainly won't be made possible by outsourcing the job. As a friend of mine, communications professional Jacquelyn Miller, who formerly worked at both Google and Amazon, often points out, "Thought leaders have to have actual thoughts." As obvious as it may sound, that means having time in the week to think and process information. There's no shortcut, like commissioning a ghostwriter to put something together on an executive's behalf that an agency representative can blitz out to various press outlets. No matter how talented that hired writer may be, it is impossible to "think" another person's thoughts for them, and the result is often well crafted but generic. The same is true for storytelling. The right person to share the story is the one who lived and experienced it.

The heart of good storytelling isn't just the act of communicating the story. It's an appreciation for the audience. Storytelling is rarely effective when one side is interested in pushing their talking points or messaging versus finding ways to connect with the person or group they're talking to. That is where marketing departments at businesses globally should shift their thinking and their resources. We need to have fewer conversations about what we want to tell the world about the companies we work for and far more about what we can do to intrigue or support our audiences (with a focus on their needs, their goals, and their priorities). Thinking about the audience is a powerful way to stand out in the sea of content that has an explicit business agenda and seems to be written for no one in particular. Does anyone care that a CEO they've never heard of is going to empower us with a platform for data transformation in the cloud? Probably not, particularly without context about why it matters. The vast majority of content out there isn't storytelling. It's jargon soup.

Another hot tip? The internet has made it easier than ever to reach these audiences via an endless array of options from LinkedIn to Substack—but this also means there's no longer such a thing as true segmentation. If the goal is to speak to a customer, great—but anything that gets published online can be read by a consumer, the press, an investor, and so on. And those messages can fall flat—or, worse, get misinterpreted. Uncovering any information about a business only takes a simple Google search. The task now, as we'll discuss throughout this book, is to consider the needs of not just one audience but all audiences in tandem. Fortunately, stories are universal and have become more important than ever because they can help bridge the gap between those audiences.

In Part 1, we not only cover the stories most used in the world of business and unpack why they work, but we also hear the stories behind the greatest storytellers. Part 2 delves into the brands that are most effectively sharing their stories across a variety of channels and details how professionals can access storytelling in their own lives. And Part 3 provides an overview of some of the ethical dilemmas associated with storytelling, spotlighting those who have used it for evil, as well as of newer technologies that could hinder or improve these efforts, such as artificial intelligence. I will also touch on the pervasive biases that still impact storytellers—because it's about not only *how* we tell the story but *who* is telling it. Studies have found that audiences receive a story far more positively if it's shared by a white male rather than, say, a nonwhite female. So how do we overcome that?

Beyond hearing from the storytellers themselves—the CEOs and other business leaders who have mastered the skill—I'll suggest new styles of working and building teams that incorporate storytelling. In that vein, I will propose a new framework that I call "founder-led communications," which puts the founders and the creators back in the driver's seat when it comes to articulating their own story. That does not mean that the CEO should be the *only* one to take charge of the story—I'll discuss how to weave narrative into a company's culture and values so that everyone within the organization has a voice. My point is that leaders should avoid offloading responsibility too soon for communications and storytelling, before they've had time to test these out on key audiences themselves. Just as in founder-led sales—an increasingly popular technique that involves founders taking point on communicating with customers versus hiring someone else to do it—leaders have to master their own story before anyone else can. Once there's real evidence of traction, it might be time to bring on a team—but not before.

The Effect of Being Transported

Have you ever been in the presence of a truly great storyteller? Looking back on those experiences where I've encountered one,

I can recall the most minor details, including what restaurant we sat in, if it was raining, or what I wore that day. The exceptional storytellers I've interacted with include founders, senior executives, and CEOs, like Jensen Huang, CEO of Nvidia; Anne Wojcicki, CEO of 23andMe; Aaron Levie, CEO of Box; and Alexis Ohanian, founder of Reddit.

The first time I met Ohanian, at the South by Southwest conference in the early 2010s, I was a junior reporter at *VentureBeat* in my early twenties. I can still recall how crowded the bar was, the smell of beer mingled with sweat in the ninety-degree heat, and the hour I stood in the line to get in.

In our first one-on-one conversation, he shared the story of the original idea for Reddit: A food-ordering app he created with his friend and roommate, Steve Huffman, while they were at college together. That idea proved to be a bad one; it went nowhere. But he told me how a fruitful meeting with technology investor Paul Graham set the early team off in a new direction to create "the front page for the Internet."[9] That story nestled into my brain, as did many of the other anecdotes he shared, taking up permanent residence there. What was so effective was the vulnerable admission from Ohanian that his original idea had bombed. It made him unique, given that most people I met with in those days described their path as a series of unstoppable wins. It also made him human. Ohanian's story intrigued me, and we spent a couple hours chatting and hanging out.

That was one of my first professional encounters with a great storyteller, and it stuck with me. There's a reason Apple cofounder Steve Jobs, a skilled public speaker, once described the storyteller as the "most powerful person in the world." Most of us tune out when we feel pitched, but we become far more alert when we are in the presence of a good storyteller. We have all faced hardships and challenges. Hearing those stories from others reminds us of what we share, helping us form meaningful relationships in the process.

"You *have* to use stories when you're trying to inspire people," said Anne Wojcicki of 23andMe, a company that has sold at-home health and genetic tests to millions. Storytelling is a tool for companies to stand out at pivotal moments, including those inevitable hard times. Wojcicki has been through plenty of those. She's lost key customers, faced cyberattacks, handled pushback from federal regulators, had board members publicly quit, and weathered drastic fluctuations in her company's stock. She gets through all of that with the help of storytelling.

It has also had a direct impact on the metrics that matter to her and her business, which has reached some incredibly high highs and low lows (as of the end of 2024, Wojcicki is embroiled in a public battle to take her company private). One particularly important one: 42 percent of the company's employees have stuck around for at least five years, while an additional 4 percent have "boomeranged," meaning they have left the company and come back. The industry norms for a company of this stage and size is a tenure of less than four years.[10]

Wojcicki said that when she senses her team needs to feel motivated or inspired, she tells them a story. One of her favorites involves a 23andMe user who discovered via one of her company's tests that she was part Inuit. That woman was so touched that she quit her job and moved to the Arctic Circle. Three years later, she emailed 23andMe to say she had "found her true calling." This story also served as a not-so-subtle nudge that the team better not mess up when it comes to delivering test results: An inaccurate one could change someone's life in profound and potentially irreversible ways. But it was also a reminder that people take these tests incredibly seriously, and therefore the job of someone working at 23andMe mattered—at the very least, to this subset of users.

When all else fails, Wojcicki also tackles tough questions with her trademark humor and wit, another key component to good storytelling. When journalists called about the termination of a lucrative partnership after a sixteen-year run, Wojcicki shot back, "Would *your* teenager go for another sixteen years with mom?"

At the core of good storytelling lie humor, authenticity, simplicity, and surprise. This is easier said than done. I've personally read thousands of websites across every industry over the years, and the biggest compliment I can muster for many of them is "dry." The reality is that most of them are barely comprehensible. That's disappointing because, as the saying goes, there's only one chance to make a good first impression. Are companies doing that with a "solution" that "integrates with workflow in the cloud"? And don't get me started on the overuse of the word "platform" on corporate websites (what's wrong with just calling it what it is, such as an "app" or a "website"?). There are countless moments in the corporate world when brands could build strong connections to their customers and other key stakeholders but fail to do so. We'll discuss some of the most common marketing myths and misconceptions driving so much of this bland and emotionless copy—which I refer to as "corporate speak"—and how we can do better.

We Have Always Been Storytellers

Somewhere along the way, we've lost touch with the storytelling aspect of our fundamental nature. Human beings have always thrived on narrative, not on a stream of facts or statistics—and certainly not on corporate jargon.

Studies show that stories are powerful because they forge connections between diverse communities and because they convey culture, history, and values. Uri Hasson, a professor in the Department of Psychology and the Neuroscience Institute at Princeton University, has scanned people's brains to understand how we respond to hearing stories. He has learned that when told well, stories act as a bridge between people who might start out with different mindsets. As he put it, "If you start to get me, your brain starts to be similar to mine. . . . And if you really get me, we become more and more similar in our brain responses." In one study, Hasson and his team recorded brain activity in pairs of subjects as one told a story and the other listened. The greater the listener's comprehension, Hasson found, the more the two brains started to sync.[11] The scans showed that high-functioning areas of the brain, such as the frontal cortexes, became even more aligned when the stories came from real life.

Hasson told me that storytelling is most effective when people "click," which most often happens when the storyteller throws out the script and focuses instead on connecting with their audience. As he tells his own students, that does not mean winging it without any preparation. Hasson encourages his students to put themselves in the shoes of listeners or viewers and think about why they should care. "The audience wants to learn something, but there needs to still be a story with a beginning, middle, and an end," he explained.

As neuroscientists have found, stories are also powerful because they can stimulate parts of the brain associated with making predictions, which in turn encourages cooperation between two or more individuals. That cooperation occurs when neurochemicals are released in the brain, such as oxytocin, which is associated with feelings of trust, empathy, and reward. There's a reason why narratives are so helpful in inspiring people to donate to charity, for instance. They help us feel more connected to an individual or species or geography, even if we aren't directly experiencing negative impacts. And there's a growing body of evidence via brain-imaging studies that storytelling is strongly linked to memory, which explains why I was able to recount details of that meeting with Ohanian years later. For these reasons, storytelling can also become an ethical liability, as it can be used for good or for evil. In Part 3, we'll discuss how the CEOs of notorious companies like FTX and Theranos used their storytelling skills to perpetuate fraud and got away with it for years.

If CEOs were aware of the power of storytelling, no business would be reduced to jargon and slideware. Neuroscientists like Paul Zak, who teaches at Claremont University, now advise all CEOs—regardless of the stage and size of the business—to lead with a powerful story that includes some moment of setback to increase tension—and to do that before launching onto any deck. "In terms of making an impact," he writes, "this blows the PowerPoint presentation to bits."[12]

PART 1
WHY STORIES WORK

CHAPTER 1

The Founder as Chief Storyteller

The most powerful person in the world is a storyteller. The storyteller sets the vision, values, and
agenda of an entire generation that is to come.

—Steve Jobs, late Apple CEO

When Alexis Ohanian founded Reddit in 2005, he had a
vision to create "the front page for the Internet." It
might be hard to remember the web from back then, but it was
a disorganized mess, and many of the most popular websites we
rely on today did not exist. Ohanian and his cofounder, Steve
Huffman, set out to build a place where complete strangers could
go to discuss current events, politics, their spouses, their kids,
their cats, and everything in between.

Back in the early days of Reddit, the company's leadership
team were a bunch of twentysomethings playing multiplayer
video games like *World of Warcraft* until the wee hours of the
morning. Per Christine Lagorio-Chafkin's brilliant book *We*

Are the Nerds, the whole business idea came together through a series of happy accidents and some nudging from investor Paul Graham, who had encouraged the team to move away from a food-ordering app idea. Ohanian came up with the name "Reddit" at the University of Virginia's library after deciding between it and "Reditt"; he went with the former because it seemed easier for people to spell and say. Huffman and Graham weren't exactly fans of the name, at least not initially, but Ohanian said he put his foot down and went with it.

Because of the founders' lack of professional experience and the boldness of their vision, there were real reasons to believe that Reddit would not succeed. Most social apps were monetized via advertising, which the founders could only unlock by demonstrating strong user growth. So how would Ohanian, Huffman, and the early team get vast numbers of people to continue to flock to Reddit? Early on, Ohanian—who oversaw all things nontechnical—made the choice to dedicate a sizable chunk of his day to public relations and communications, taking on responsibility for activities that would help get the word out. For a consumer-facing company like Reddit, getting that right was crucial. An article or mention by an early internet influencer on a then-popular technology site like *Mashable*, *TechCrunch*, or *VentureBeat* (where I got my start as a tech reporter) could drive a lot of interest in what the team was building, leading to a key inflection point for the business. Reddit relied on retention—people using the site religiously while in line for coffee or sitting on the toilet—to be successful. And without a strong user-acquisition plan, they'd be stuck on the starting line forever.

So every day for about five years, Ohanian carved out a few minutes to personally cold email anyone with a platform, whether a blogger, influencer, or journalist, and ask them to meet and have a chat about Reddit. As the years went by, he came up with more creative ways to meet these folks in person. Periodically, for example, he'd go on what he would refer to among friends as a "fake media tour." Media tours were (and still are) a way for big companies to get their CEOs in front of the mainstream media. Typically, public relations teams with big budgets organize these tours. Flanked by an entourage of communications professionals carrying dossiers on the journalists, CEOs show up to newsrooms with steely resolve, ready to share their companies' wins and deflect any uncomfortable questions. On a personal note, I'd spot these dossiers while working at CNBC when they would slip out of the executives' folders by accident. Companies spend big money on these tours, which sometimes also culminate in fancy private media dinners.

Ohanian was far from a big shot—he was the founder of a website that for years very few people had heard of, and he had no budget for a PR entourage (nor did he desire one). So he would occasionally buy a bus ticket from his home in Boston to New York City and send a few reporters an email to say he was in town for Reddit's very official "press tour." He asked if they wanted to meet with him and nudged them to get on his schedule as soon as possible before all his slots got booked up. Ohanian initially thought no one would show up, but he soon realized that reaching out with a personal note—and a vibe that seemed more relatable and familiar than desperate—did the trick. Then he would sit in a café for a few days and chat with the people who turned up. There were no high-priced dinners with wine pairings, and he slept on friends' couches before taking the bus back home.

Don't Outsource Your Story

When companies refer to "PR," they often mean the function that drives buzz for the business by getting headlines. Many founders assume that hiring a public relations firm (or an on-staff PR lead) will quickly get them regular, glowing write-ups in *The New York Times* and *The Wall Street Journal*, which they can then share with their target audiences on Facebook or LinkedIn to drive demand and generate leads. Or better yet, they might get physical press clippings, which are a nice ego boost, even though fewer and fewer people read printed newspapers and magazines. These clips can be framed to adorn office hallways or sent to family members to stick on the fridge.

This way of thinking, however, leads companies to take a very hands-off approach to press coverage. As I've seen it done for years, the company hires an agency, points to a highlight or milestone it wants to promote (a product launch, a funding round, a key hire) or a set of "messages" it wants to impart, and then sits back and lets the agency go to work until the media ask for an interview. At that point, if there's any interest at all, an assistant arranges time via the public relations pro who is in touch with the journalist on the other side. This kind of arrangement builds in at least two or three levels of disconnect between the interviewer and interviewee. Then, at the time of the interview, the communications team attends the meeting and sometimes even chimes in with answers or comments. Usually there's also some heavy coaching going on behind the scenes to ensure that the founder or CEO is saying the "right thing" and not revealing private or sensitive information. The hope, from there, is that this will result in a rave article with all the talking points included.

This strategy is rarely effective, particularly when it's so hands off, which Ohanian realized from the start. He took a much more informal approach—but he also treated PR very differently than most founders and CEOs do. He viewed it as a strategic investment in the long-term success of his business, not a necessary evil to achieve a set number of press mentions per quarter. And he didn't treat his relationships with the media as purely transactional. Even if a meeting didn't result in a press mention for Reddit, he could categorize it as a win in other ways—and therefore as worth the time. As the company grew, he continued to view public relations as a priority—and something that he would personally manage rather than fully outsource to someone else.

Ohanian was also special in that he did not bristle at the idea of incorporating communications into his job description. Many CEOs will stress that they're too busy, given they're also on the hook to recruit, answer product questions, manage teams, and conduct meetings, among a host of other responsibilities. But I'd argue that communications should be extremely high up on any CEO's priority list, and Ohanian would agree. It's a catalyst to drive everything else. For example, winning over talent is typically far easier if they are aware that the business exists and perceive it as a cool company to join. While considering a role at a company that isn't yet a household name, it's downright useful to be able to email out a press article to friends and family members ("You may not have heard of it, but this start-up is the real deal!"). An emphasis on communications makes everything else that little bit easier.

So here's how Ohanian made every interview count:

- *He built a network and a following.* Reporters meet with a lot of companies and are trained to be on the lookout for stories that might pique the public's interest. Ohanian realized that speaking to people whose job it was to regularly network, assess companies, and interface with the public would be inherently valuable for him as a cofounder. And even though he wasn't yet a noteworthy CEO, Ohanian said he knew reporters would rather open and reply to an email from a CEO than a flak, an industry term for a communications professional.

- *He viewed journalists as a discerning audience—if he could win them over, he could win anyone over.* By paying close attention to the person's body language and other visual cues, he could determine if his story was resonating. Could he be telling it differently or better? If he could convince this naturally skeptical audience to care, might that help him be a better storyteller when trying to convince other important audiences too (when recruiting, pitching investors, making sales)?

- *He leaned into the "butterfly effect."* Journalists have big networks and are purveyors of information, most of it not conveyed in print. So meeting with them could open doors for his business. Case in point: Ohanian once had an extended conversation with freelance technology journalist Rachel Metz even though she explicitly told him that she would not be covering the company. Metz was nonetheless intrigued enough by the conversation to discuss it with her editor at *Wired*. That editor happened to be married to the director of business development at Condé Nast and promptly introduced Ohanian to her husband. That led to a licensing agreement, and eventually Condé Nast acquired Reddit. Years later, Ohanian often talks about this experience to remind people in his life that there's value in staying open-minded versus being extractive in all encounters.

- *He learned to listen.* In interviews with journalists, Ohanian learned to talk—but he also learned how to sit back and be quiet. He started to see a lot more value in these conversations when he stopped talking and instead asked the journalists earnest questions about how they did their job and what tools they used to succeed. Through that process Ohanian recognized a business opportunity *and* a public relations opportunity. Because there weren't many websites on the internet for reporters and bloggers to use to understand public sentiment around the news, Ohanian figured Reddit could fulfill that need. Sure enough, that led to a double whammy for Reddit: Members of the press used Reddit to help them do their jobs, turning their news organizations into partners, which increased their desire to write about Reddit in their stories.

Over time, Reddit became much more well known, eventually becoming one of the top sites on the internet. Ohanian's star rose alongside the site he helped create, particularly as he began to share more lessons learned and strategies for building companies. He is now an investor with his own venture capital fund, Seven Seven Six. He's also a sought-after public speaker, company advisor, and television commentator. And in 2017, he married tennis superstar Serena Williams. Ever the joker, after receiving a coveted invitation to the royal wedding of the decade from Prince Harry and Meghan Markle, Ohanian posted a video of himself at his home, adopting a fake British accent to declare, "You can call me Lord Ohanian from now on."

In Reddit's heyday, before Ohanian struck out on his own, many of his investors asked him why he bothered with Twitter and Instagram, as well as why he had so many meetings with the press. Weren't there more important things to focus on, like growing revenue? But Ohanian made it clear he did not consider the media work a waste of energy or time. All that brand building, which at that point also included his own presence on LinkedIn, Twitter, and other social media sites, created a virtuous cycle and added a halo effect around the company. "As your planet gets bigger," Ohanian told me, "you become more interesting to more folks in the media who wonder what you're up to, and then it just compounds from there to investors, potential employees, and beyond."

When considering investment opportunities now, years after Reddit became a success, Ohanian looks for founders who take the lead on their own stories. In his mind, those who take on this challenging work have an edge because they are willing to face rejection and pick themselves back up after each failure (the reality is that a lot of reporters, just like any group that receives a lot of email, will not always respond). When they succeed, they are creating their own halo effects, which is a crucial differentiator for any business.

Unfortunately, the list of founders serving as their companies' chief storytellers is not long. According to Ohanian, everyone wants to have a big brand, but very few will do the work; nor do they have the patience. Most well-respected people who have a big brand on the internet took years to build it.

He explained it to me when we spoke:

In my mind, generating press was not dissimilar from building community. Everyone wanted it, but no one wanted to do the work. I saw this outreach as "the work" because I understood that every person I met could be a Redditor. And a lot of the people who could use Reddit were in the media. So I had a great story to tell. I learned how to talk about the product [and] talk about the business. And now that I'm a VC, I give this advice constantly to founders: *Don't outsource your story.* Journalists would rather be talking to the actual builder than some middle person, especially before you get to the size when that's less practical. Just imagine you're a journalist with an inbox full of press releases and random requests. As a founder, you have to break through that. And [you have to] empathize with the journalist, because they're not getting up in the morning to write about a company that will probably fail and isn't even real yet. And yet, only about 5 percent of founders have an affinity for it. But I see that 5 percent doing better.

Because of his coaching, many of Ohanian's portfolio companies are among the best companies out there when it comes to storytelling, meaning they make it a priority in how they do business. Among them is Ro, which sells hair-loss supplements, Viagra, weight-loss medications, and other health-related products online and is valued in the billions of dollars. Ohanian also sits on the company's board of directors. Ro CEO Zachariah Reitano described Ohanian as the "master" when it comes to storytelling. Because of Ohanian's example, he keeps an open line of dialogue with his customers on social media, including taking the time to respond to comments. He also often writes lengthy pieces that accompany any new product launch so that people really understand his thinking and his views on the market. He recognizes that being misunderstood is a risk but that this tactic is essential to being ahead of the curve. The key is to be loved by users and to feel accessible to them. "[Ohanian] taught me that authenticity and honesty scales," he said.

In the next few chapters, we'll get into exactly what kinds of stories to tell and how—so stick with me! But before we get there, it's important that we reflect on a few of the macro trends that are transforming communications and making it more important than ever that founders master telling their own stories.

Storytelling in Founder-Led Sales

So how can you be part of that small group of elite storytelling CEOs who get the spotlight and have a seemingly magical power to pull people into their orbits?

It requires making a serious commitment to communications—namely, to finding the right forums to share the story and individuals to share it with. I'll acknowledge that it's a juggling act, given that a lot of business leaders today are already taking on more than they ever used to. The job of a CEO or any manager is a constant battle between doing the work and communicating about the work; between being head down and popping your head up to motivate the team or inform the outside world. Yet crucial functions are beginning to move back into the remit of the CEO. Communications is one of them.

Let's talk for a moment about a company-building method that took off in the 2020s known as "founder-led sales." This framework encourages founders and CEOs to take on sales and customer relationships as their primary responsibility in the early stages of the company's growth, rather than hiring a head of sales before the revenue engine is running. Only once they've gotten the business to real revenue is it time to consider hiring a sales leader to turn on the gas. The first step, though, is proving that the business should exist, and that's the job of the founder and/or CEO. In other words, don't hire a sales leader before the business has achieved product-market fit. Otherwise the company leaders could waste a lot of time blaming someone else for why the product isn't selling like hotcakes. Or worse, the executives might fail to recognize customer feedback that could have saved the business.

Founders who have embraced founder-led sales are finding that it's a critical learning experience for two key reasons: It's a way to refine how the sales story is shared with a potential buyer, and it forces them to sit back and listen. To effectively make a sale, it's critical that a founder ask questions of potential buyers and be genuinely curious about what they have to say. Is a real need being solved? Or is this just a cool product with no real buyer? Another benefit to founder-led sales: Founders doing this are forced to face rejection and get comfortable with all aspects of the sales process. In return, they'll find that their storytelling capabilities improve over time and evolve as the business changes.

As founder-led sales expert Peter Kazanjy wrote in *Founding Sales: The Early Stage Go-to-Market Handbook*, the art of selling as a CEO in large part entails product marketing and "evangelical" product management, meaning bringing a product to market and aligning it with a customer's needs. Those who get comfortable sharing the story will find that telling it has become second nature. In sales, the results are easy enough to quantify and reflect upon. Did the sale go through? And if not, is something about the story not landing? That might lead a founder to hop on the phone for an honest conversation with an important or potential customer and perhaps to tweak the strategy as a result.

Founder-led sales is now a cottage industry, with hundreds of consultants and coaches offering their support to founders as they navigate building customer relationships. After speaking with a half dozen of them, I learned that much of that coaching teaches founders how to get comfortable with storytelling. "People buy emotionally," said founder-led sales coach Grant Parker. "A customer cares about what will make their life better, so the best way to make a sale is to figure out what they want and then tell them a story that resonates."

Storytelling in Founder-Led Communications

Let's take this notion of founder-led sales one step further. Among the closest and most important adjuncts to the sales function are communications and public relations. But compared to sales, remarkably little has been written about why founders and business leaders across a variety of industries, and not just technology, can benefit by doing more communications. That's because it's so often devalued and outsourced relative to aspects of the business that are more directly tied to revenue, as we discussed above. But I'd argue that communications is just as critical as sales, particularly for a subset of businesses, and that there's just as much to gain from founders taking it on—as would Ohanian. He'd also argue that things have changed since 2005, when he worked to get Reddit off the ground. Breaking through the noise has become more challenging than ever for founders, but more opportunities also exist now than did back then.

In terms of what's become trickier, let's talk first about the changing media landscape. Journalists and bloggers are the folks most often associated with sharing the story of the company with the public. But their lives (and livelihoods) have fundamentally changed in the past few decades.

The short of it: Things are dire in the world of journalism (with a few exceptions—the biggest bright spot is probably in independent and "trade" media, which continues to show growth). From 2008 to 2024, newsroom employment dropped by 26 percent in the United States, according to a Pew Research Center analysis of data from the Bureau of Labor Statistics.[1] While newspapers have been harder hit than digitally native organizations, the industry overall is struggling. In 2023, the *Press Gazette* reported at least 8,000 cuts across the United Kingdom, Canada, and the United States. Some countries don't have much of a functioning free press at all.

All these cuts mean that it's harder and harder to get the attention of fewer and fewer journalists working full-time at news organizations. Many companies are preoccupied with generating media lists of important contacts. Those lists are growing ever shorter every year.

So how should companies adapt?

The first way is to right-size expectations around media attention, regardless of whether the communications function is insourced or outsourced. Communications professional Jacquelyn Miller, who's worked at start-ups as well as big companies, told me that when she pitched the funding round for a 2014 start-up called PillPack, forty-one reporters covered the news. Nowadays, given the lack of journalists covering start-ups, she said, the companies she works with would be lucky to get even *one* mention in a top-tier publication. I'll repeat that: The drop went from forty-one to one in a decade. And this kind of statistic was consistent for many of the communications professionals I spoke to. Making matters worse, there are now about six PR professionals for every one working journalist, a ratio that continues to get starker every year.

But all is not lost. The solution here for companies is to focus on quality over quantity, hire the right team and collaborate with them (versus outsource to them), and step up direct outreach.

I recommend that leaders should start by highlighting *no more than* three to five journalists covering their industry or sector whom they're eager to build a relationship with and to reach out to them directly in a thoughtful way. This should take a few hours and is no more complicated than sending an introductory email. Those journalists might not respond—and that's okay. It doesn't mean the strategy isn't the right one. And as Ohanian reminds us, handling rejection is part of the job of being a leader.

Understand that these outreach efforts are not about driving clicks and mentions. They're about building long-term relationships with a lot of give-and-take. It could take years for a journalist at a top-tier publication to want to write about a company or to find an opportunity to do so that their editors will approve (they have bosses and goals too). So I advise that company leaders reset their thinking and use the time to refine the story, notice how it's being received, and occasionally sit back and listen. The journalists who remain employed at respected outlets today have a clear mandate: Their job is to sit within the information flow and talk to lots of companies. Founders and CEOs should treat every conversation with them as a learning opportunity and not just spend thirty minutes reciting the litany of talking points.

The direct outreach approach also means the CEO forges a new relationship with the head of communications, assuming there is one at the company. Like the head of sales, this person should be brought on once the business is starting to show some traction with customers—and in my opinion, not before (except in rare cases, where that individual is a founder and/or functioning at that level). Finding that ideal moment to hire that individual is tricky, as is finding the right candidate. As a result, I've seen plenty of executives downplay the function or hire outside help when there's no real story to tell yet. I've also seen others who do it too late, simply because they don't prioritize the skill set enough.

Before onboarding the communications head and team, the founder should be proactive and build those key media relationships early, on their own, investing time in the process without adopting a transactional mindset. Once the story—and the business more broadly—seems to be working, then it's time to consider bringing that help on board. The exception here is a company that is doing something extremely complex from a regulatory perspective or in terms of the technology or science. That may necessitate bringing on professionals to ensure that the company isn't giving away key intellectual property or communicating in ways that no one outside a niche audience will understand. Even then, there are often reasons to focus on telling the story externally. There may be some risk of a competitor stealing intellectual property, but most of the time the differentiator is not the idea but the execution.

Communications in the typical, outdated org chart today

COMMUNICATIONS

Next, it's important to establish exactly where this person should sit within the organization. On page 34, you'll see a model typical of many large companies today. I refer to it as "outdated" because no company's organization model should look like this.

In many companies, particularly larger ones, the communications leadership reports to the marketing department and is a few steps removed from the founders and/or the CEO. As a result, they simply aren't aware of what's going on at the CEO's level because they aren't brought into key internal meetings. Instead, they are relegated to a function whose main job is to drive press mentions (the myth that driving press mentions is all the job entails is the root of the problem). This is a recipe for disaster. As Jacquelyn Miller, the communications consultant, explains, press mentions do not even drive growth. They drive reputation and brand (when an individual googles you or your business, what do they find?). That is a critical distinction, because most people assume that press is a catalyst for user growth and sales. But because most press is driven by what's topical, people tend to pay attention for a brief moment and then move on. The exception involves users who are already strongly considering making a purchase. A press mention can drive legitimacy, so buyers feel more comfortable with their decision. Given that, what's the head of communications doing under marketing at so many companies when their real function relates to reputation?

The strategy for building an external presence through communications should be oriented around connecting with the customer on an emotional level and finding ways to build goodwill, also known as building the brand. Communications should sit *alongside* the CEO and work cross-functionally with the entire executive team, including legal, business development, operations, and policy, helping them share what they're passionate about both internally and with the outside world. They should be the closest confidant and counterpart to the CEO, capable of answering questions about the business in excruciating detail—and, if they're ever stumped, able to get the right person on the phone within minutes.

When founders take charge of communications and *ally* with their head of communications, everything changes. This person—more a chief communications officer (CCO) than a director of communications—should respect journalists and have a keen sense of what's newsworthy. They should be plugged into everything at the executive level of the company. And they should be super knowledgeable about both the business and the larger landscape. They might even have an all-star team once the company is big enough. Like the CEO, the communications executive should not just be pushing for positive articles in good times and then lying or evading questions in bad times. They build mutually beneficial relationships with journalists because customers and other key stakeholders trust what they have to say.

In this model, the founder and/or CEO and CCO are allies on a mission:

- to build influence with target audiences via direct channels (social media, conferences, podcasts, newsletters, and so on) in order to drive both awareness and a sense of legitimacy in the market;
- to build relationships with the media, bloggers, and other key influencers;
- to use internal communications to help create a work culture that enables employees to show up to work with

a clear sense of the mission, even—especially—if that mission is highly capitalistic in nature. The operative word here is "clear," as many organizations today create cultures where communication breakdowns and misunderstandings are commonplace.

Where communications *should* sit in the org chart

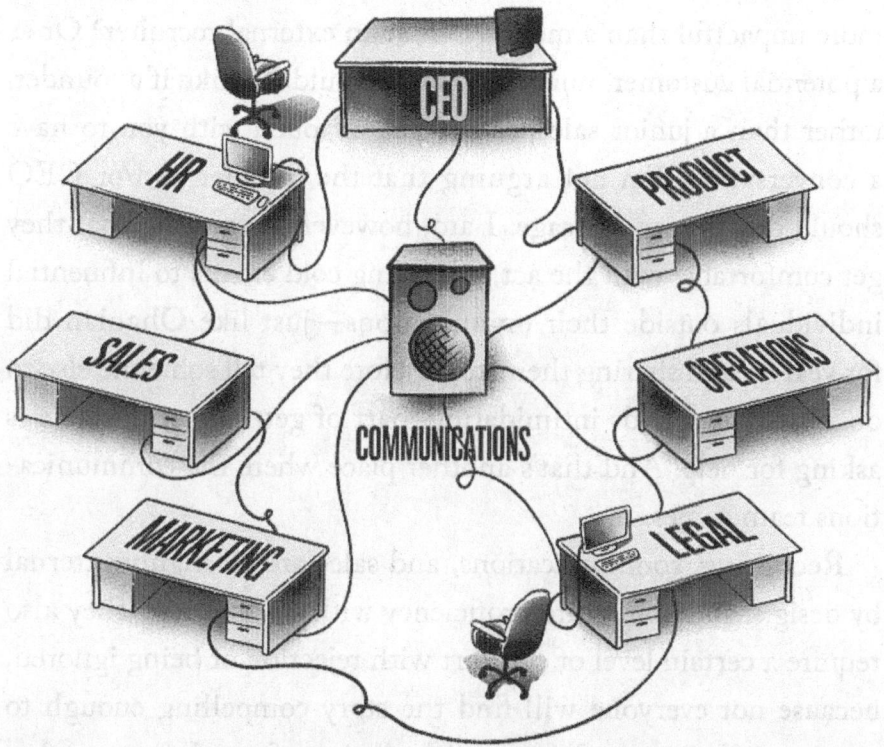

It's important to underscore that all of this works best when the company's leaders take ownership of the communications function and lead by example. I have yet to find organizations in which people further down the ladder feel inspired about external and internal communications if the CEO neglects them. If those organizations exist, they're rare birds indeed.

So here's a controversial idea I'd like to plant in your mind. Three of the most outsourced functions, particularly at early-stage companies, are recruiting, communications, and sales. I'd argue that with all three, it makes a very big difference when the founder and/or CEO takes ownership. Think about what it would mean if a CEO reached out to you on LinkedIn about recruiting you into a role at their company. Wouldn't that be far more impactful than a message from an external recruiter? Or as a potential customer, imagine what it would feel like if a founder, rather than a junior salesperson, got in touch with you to have a conversation. I'm not arguing that the founder and/or CEO should draft every message. I am, however, suggesting that they get comfortable with the act of sending cold emails to influential individuals outside their organizations—just like Ohanian did for years—and sharing their story before they tell someone else to do it. If that sounds intimidating, part of getting comfortable is asking for help. And that's another place where the communications team comes in.

Recruiting, communications, and sales are all highly external by design, and all require proficiency with storytelling. They also require a certain level of comfort with rejection or being ignored, because not everyone will find the story compelling enough to act upon. Having proficiency with all three from day one, rather than outsourcing them, is critical for modern start-up CEOs.

The Thought Leadership Problem

Here's an axiomatic statement: To be a thought leader, you need to have some original thoughts. Many CEOs do not reserve time in their day to think and instead outsource their thought leadership to third parties. This makes absolutely no sense. How can you be a thought leader if you're not willing to make time for thinking, let alone jotting down some thoughts? And why would you even want to position yourself as one?

It rarely works to pay someone else to simply write thoughts, although I can understand the appeal of handing the project off. It is very hard to represent someone else's views effectively. So, if there's no time in your day to write or think, scrap it and focus on something else. Or find a way to prioritize it and make the time. Start by writing, with no intention of publishing, until it becomes second nature. For many people, writing can become a process for thinking. For those who do feel comfortable sharing what they write, potentially becoming "thought leaders" in the process, there are more ways to put their thinking out in the world than ever before, including LinkedIn, Medium, or a newsletter platform like beehiiv or Substack.

Are you a ways off from putting pen to paper? I routinely suggest to companies that the team reserve an hour in the mornings to read over a cup of coffee and do a little writing. If that seems like too much, even an hour a week can make an enormous difference.

"Going Direct"

With all the backlash against mainstream media, some prominent tech investors are increasingly encouraging founders to build out their own channels of influence. That way, they can bypass the press completely—because, in their view, the press is inherently biased against technology companies. This is often called "going direct," a term that influencers and technology pundits discuss on social media.

No one is interested in covering your product launch? No problem. Build a huge social media following and share it with your legions of fans! It's that simple—or so the theory goes.

Given the level of effort required and the shrinking number of journalists available to pitch, some companies might be tempted to ignore the press altogether and focus on writing their own stories and sharing them on social media or on their own blogs. I agree with aspects of this way of thinking—but I'm not entirely on board. The mainstream media *is* shrinking, so there's wisdom in not being overly reliant on reporters to cover updates and milestones. But I also don't advise throwing the baby out with the bathwater. If there's a story suitable for *The New York Times* to cover, bring it to a reporter there. That kind of coverage can still be priceless, and high-quality journalism matters. It does, however, require investing time to develop and pitch newsworthy stories—and not all companies will have the capacity or the confidence to do that. In reality there are many ways to build a relationship with audiences, and the press should just be one of them. Let's talk about exactly when those moments might arise.

In the communications business, professionals will often talk about PESO: paid, earned, shared, and owned media. Here's how they break down:

- Paid media has historically been the focus of marketing departments and includes sponsored content, paid publishing, and social media ads.
- Earned media relies on journalists essentially as middlemen—you need to pitch them and "earn" coverage in their publications.

- Shared media primarily refers to partnerships, community building, and co-branding opportunities.
- Owned media involves no middleman, and that's why many CEOs prefer it: They can publish directly to channels that they own, which means they control the message, and that message is infinitely editable.

The smartest minds in communications believe that these activities shouldn't be siloed, but they do serve different purposes. Earned media, for instance, adds credibility to businesses, because a third-party arbiter with no skin in the game, such as *Bloomberg* or *The Wall Street Journal*, has taken the time to write a piece. That carries weight with people who don't know anything about the company and are looking to discern whether it's legitimate.

Owned media, meanwhile, is more effective for reaching people who already know the business and are following its blog or social media channels. Owned media is a great way to remind them of all the exciting things happening and to increase their interest in the company. Determining when it's appropriate to target earned versus owned media—or any other channel—requires an appreciation for what's newsworthy. It also requires determining the business's intended goals at that moment in time.

Many CEOs find that challenging. As the business grows and becomes more complex, they get deep into what feels like a bottomless pit of work. Some rarely come up for air to see that there are other things going on in the world, and they fail to appreciate that their company's latest product announcement might not be earth-shattering news to the person next door.

Admittedly, there was a period when the technology start-up press corps, in particular, did cover a lot of routine announcements. Back in the 2010s, the business media had a habit of covering every funding announcement, while the tech press was eager to cover product announcements, even from relatively young companies. So companies assumed that they could rely on the press to cover everything they did.

There are so many problems with this kind of thinking.

To begin with, the intended audience for whatever news (if it's even news) a company wants to share might not read *The New York Times* daily. So even if the press did cover that announcement, would it serve its purpose?

More foundationally, journalists aren't paid mouthpieces for companies. I cannot stress this point enough. It's not their job to cover everything that a company does (unless it's a massive company like Apple or Google and the reporter is dedicated to covering that company as their sole beat). It *is* their job to think about whether a piece of news is relevant to the audience they serve—and usually that audience is far broader than the market that a given company is talking to every day. Publishing that information should serve the public interest, not purely one company's agenda.

If we agree that the press shouldn't be the only channel to build awareness, CEOs will have to stop referring to every effort to communicate externally as "media relations." That's too limiting. In terms of the PESO model, it focuses exclusively on earned coverage and overlooks the paid, owned, and shared channels available. I often tell CEOs to stop thinking the press should be responsible for telling every company's story *for* them and start thinking about how they can tell their own story *alongside* the press.

As one of my favorite exercises, I invite companies to think about whether the average person walking down the street would be interested in the story the CEO is telling in the way they're telling it today. If the answer is no, that's a good sign that it's not newsworthy.

Of course, there are exceptions to this rule. For example, the trade press often goes very deep into specific niches like cybersecurity or health technology. Even then, the "average person" exercise is still helpful because the trade press is interested in news that's relevant to their target reader, even if it's a smaller and more informed group. So it's always important to make the story as accessible as possible.

Watching founders today, Ohanian feels almost envious that they have so many new tools at their disposal to connect with their target audiences. Back in 2005, when he was starting out, personal publishing companies like Medium, Substack, and LinkedIn didn't exist. It was traditional media or nothing. But now, with so many channels, it's much easier to find opportunities to get creative and reach target audiences where they are most likely hanging out in person or online.

Ohanian gave me an example of a space-tech company he invested in called Stoke Space. The founders asked Ohanian for advice on PR because they needed to get the word out to engineers to hire technical talent. Ohanian encouraged them to spend time on YouTube channels dedicated to space content, which aerospace engineers might be more likely to watch, and not to focus on mainstream media. On the other hand, if the company had a bigger story to tell about the future of human spaceflight, that would be a good time to talk to the press.

"It has never been easier for these founders," Ohanian told me. "They can succeed while being their authentic selves."

Yes, there is value in the go direct strategy. But building influence takes time. To offer an example, when I was working in venture capital, one of the companies that my firm invested in had a lot of commercial success. The company, Container Xchange, built a marketplace for shipping containers. Not exactly a story that would get most of the mainstream press riled up to pay attention. At the time, Container Xchange wanted to reach its customers, namely people in the shipping industry. Those people were increasingly spending time on LinkedIn. Because he enjoyed the format, Xchange's CEO, Christian Roeloffs, decided to record short videos on Fridays that he shared on his LinkedIn account. The videos included lots of analysis and data about container prices and the implications for industry professionals. Container Xchange's potential customers ate it up. His videos developed a small but dedicated following. I recall that it didn't take long for that to convert into new customer relationships— and from there, into revenue.

The key consideration for going direct: It only works when the executive or company in question is not fueled solely by a motivation to promote themselves. When was the last time you followed someone who only wanted to share how great they were? Reputation is earned when a company or individual uses their platform to *contribute* to their community by sharing learning and information versus to *broadcast* their own or their product's greatness. That's a big reason why plenty of low-ego people can thrive with the go direct strategy. Don't just talk about yourself and your company's achievements ad nauseam. Think about how to provide value to others. How can you help them achieve their goals? What information can you provide that they wouldn't otherwise have access to? That's a major reason why Container Xchange became a "must listen" for executives and operators within the shipping world.

Back to Ohanian, who is still putting his personal touch on communications. Even though he's an investor now, he's still a powerful storyteller for his investment fund. Like most investors, he spreads the word when his companies are ready to announce they've raised financing. But unlike many investors, he contributes something unique about why he chose to invest in that company. Typically, it's a highly personal story, which he shares on LinkedIn, including some of the key factors that got him to a yes. The idea is to share something personal with his audience that they wouldn't have heard about otherwise. For instance, if he's discussing a new investment in a business software company, he'll talk about the struggles he encountered when building tools for his own venture fund and how he overcame them. If he's talking about a new investment in a social media platform for collectibles, he'll take you on a video tour of his own office to show you all his favorite video games and trading cards. And if he wants you to try out a website for people to experience one-on-one coaching, he'll talk about the value that he's found over the years in professional mentorship.

You can do it too, by leaning into what makes you unique and by taking charge of your own story. Whether that's to "go direct," to build relationships with the media, or to pursue a combination of the two, there's no better time to do it.

CHAPTER 2

Plot Lines

> There is what I would call the hero journey, the night
> sea journey, the hero question, where the individual
> is going to bring forth in his life something that was
> never beheld before.
>
> **—Joseph Campbell, author**

When Aaron Levie came up with the idea for Box, a way to store, share, and collaborate on files with teams through a simple web link, he was a sophomore at the University of Southern California. He and cofounder Dylan Smith built the first version of the product while pitching venture capitalists, most of whom got back to him with a quick no. The duo's first real break came when the billionaire Mark Cuban responded to a cold email pitch by agreeing to write them a $350,000 check.[1] When the team released their software in 2005, they were initially targeting consumers, but those early adopters liked it so much they started using Box at work. At this point, things were going well enough that Levie decided to drop out of college to focus on running the business full-time.

By the end of the company's first decade, Box had made the transition to focus on larger enterprise accounts, raising tens of millions in venture capital to accelerate that shift. The company had made steady progress, growing to millions of paid users, who relied on Box at work (if you've ever received a link for a large file at work, you likely received it from Box).

Fast-forward two decades and the company is worth about $4.5 billion and publicly traded on the New York Stock Exchange.

But we're getting ahead of ourselves. If this sounds like a linear path to success, because a few young guys had a good idea, it wasn't. By the time Box shifted to focus on the larger clients, the market had plenty of established competition, with plenty of larger tech companies eyeing the opportunity. Dropbox, Microsoft, Amazon, and Google had all set their sights on the enterprise cloud storage market, alongside about a dozen or so venture-backed start-ups. Box at the time was more focused on corporate customers with specialized needs around privacy and security, like government agencies or hospitals, while Dropbox, its largest competitor, had its sights set initially on the consumer market. Millions of consumers also needed ways to share large files—albums of family photos and videos, large CAD files, and more—and access them via the web or the smartphones in their pockets.

So how to stand out? Levie didn't see a path to winning against his better-funded rivals by shelling out huge sums on a nonstop parade of booths, billboards, and television ads, thus committing himself to an ever-growing paid marketing budget to keep up with his competitors. He decided to play a different game, one that emphasized the company's strengths and downplayed its weaknesses. "There was this moment within enterprise software where we were moving from the 'old guard' to the 'new guard,'" Levie explained in an interview. "We had events and conferences and talked to anyone we could in the media to share this bigger message."

That new game involved a nimble campaign, led by the company's first head of communications, Ashley Mayer. From the outside, the main goal seemed to involve positioning Box in people's minds as the cool new player on the block. Mayer's thinking was less intentional than that. She encouraged Levie to be his erudite, thoughtful, occasionally nerdy self on stage, on television, and in one-on-one conversations with the press. Mayer realized that people did not want to feel sold to, so she never encouraged Levie to push talking points about Box's software. "One thing that was fun about Aaron [Levie] is that he would read a ton and he was all about business books," Mayer explained. "He was also writing all the time to get a handle on his thoughts [and] he loved to publish opinion columns."

Levie quickly became known in Silicon Valley for his witty aphorisms, his trademark sneakers, and colorful socks. According to Mayer, he had a particular knack for connecting the Box story to topics that people cared about while making them laugh. When Facebook bought WhatsApp for $19 billion, Levie joked to a *Wall Street Journal* reporter, "It makes you depressed if you're not selling at $20 billion. . . . I have a lot more work to do." And at a *Recode* event, on stage with veteran technology journalist Walt Mossberg, he cracked a joke about the company's funding story. "So, uh, we were just in college hanging around, and like all college students do, we were thinking, 'How do we do file storage in the cloud?'" Not one to be easily bamboozled, Mossberg shot back, "You're not profitable, right?" (For context, many of the venture-backed technology companies were nowhere near profitable, even when they filed for their IPOs—and there's often an unwillingness to acknowledge that fact.) Levie hit back with feigned awkwardness: "Uh, it depends on your definition, but no, we're not," he said, to chuckles from the audience. He ended the interview by describing Box as a platform and added, with a deadpan expression, "That's how you raise your valuation." And another round of chuckles erupted from the audience. (For many investors, the word "platform" was on trend in the 2010s, just like "AI" has been in the post-Covid era.)

Another example of connecting the technology and the product to larger trends: Even before the pandemic, Levie often talked to the media about how common it would soon be for people to flexibly work from home and access their work files and documents from anywhere. That would mean far less commuting into offices and wasting hours of time sitting in traffic. But, to make working from home viable, businesses would need to grapple with cybersecurity vulnerabilities, as well as with collaboration and communication across teams. In some circumstances hashing out a problem in person is easier. Most businesses need to plan and prepare for the next big trends related to the future of work, so it didn't take long before Levie's foresight made him one of the most sought-after voices in the industry. Television producers and journalists kept coming back to him, oftentimes in lieu of reaching out to his larger competitors, because they could rely on him to answer questions directly without overly promoting his company.

What Levie understood seems to evade most companies and CEOs: Be insightful and interesting, and connect the company to topical events that are relevant to the broader public. People will find out who you are and where you work not because you beat them over the head with your message. Instead, delight them, educate them—and let them be intrigued enough to *find out on their own* what you do. Sometimes there might be a natural moment to plug what you're building. But not everything needs to connect to an explicit product plug or a push for a sale.

By pursuing this strategy, Levie became the face of the cloud software "New Guard," earning regular spots on top-tier business media outlets like CNBC, *Bloomberg*, *Vox*, *Axios*, and more. Whether he pursued this strategy intentionally or otherwise, this New Guard idea is brilliant, particularly viewed through the lens of human psychology and neuroscience. It's grounded in storytelling principles and what we know about the brain. We've been gravitating to these kinds of stories for centuries. These kinds of "out with the old, in with the new" plots remain familiar to us through generations for the simple reason that they work.

Ironically, Box is hardly a start-up anymore. A newcomer might refer to them as the Old Guard, given how long the company has been around. But Levie is dead set on ensuring he's never viewed as the slow-moving incumbent, because in his mind becoming the establishment is the first step to irrelevance. So the trick becomes retaining a New Guard philosophy, even as you become an Old Guard company in terms of size and scale. Much has been written about this topic because it's so hard to pull off. In his essential work *The Innovator's Dilemma*, Clayton M. Christensen demonstrates how companies get disrupted and miss new waves of innovation because they fail to appropriately value new products and therefore fail to bring them to market. Christensen argues that management at larger companies has the capacity, but is not set up to do so. That's because new ideas often take time to generate the kind of financial returns that move the needle for a larger company.

To avoid falling on these landmines, Levie does a few things differently than most public company CEOs. Communication is critically important for him. He maintains a direct line with his audience via an extremely large X following. More than two million people (about the population of Nebraska) share and like Levie's dispatches about the cloud, the future of technology, and artificial intelligence. Because he still spends time on the platform, that helps him give off an air of accessibility, and it means he's constantly learning and tuning in to feedback from the industry. He has remained part of the discourse within the tech community, intimately aware of cool new start-ups and trends that people are talking about. How did I contact him for this book? I slid into his direct messages on X. That's how I've always been able to reach him since my days as a reporter at *VentureBeat* more than a decade ago. Even after Box went public, he shared that kind of open style with me and with many others.

When we talked recently, I asked Levie if anything had changed for him, considering how many employees work for him now and depend on him for their livelihoods. A lot of responsibility comes with that. And as a rule, publicly traded companies are far more scrutinized by Wall Street than their private peers, and executives can more easily get into trouble. Saying the wrong thing doesn't just mean a bad day for the comms team; it could impact the company's stock and reduce confidence in its leadership. But Levie told me that his X account would only be "10 percent" different if he weren't a public company CEO with the corresponding accountability or responsibility. "I've had to moderate a bit," he acknowledged. "But I still only say things that I believe."

The Power of the Underdog

You've probably heard the biblical tale of David and Goliath, or at least the rough outlines. If not, here's the gist: A heavily armed Philistine giant named Goliath challenged King Saul to send out a man to fight him. He repeated his challenge for forty days, but no one dared to take on such a daunting opponent until David stepped forward armed with slings and stones. Everyone thought David was crazy and certain to lose against such a brutish foe. But in a surprise attack, he hit Goliath on the forehead with a stone, and the giant keeled over and died.

The David and Goliath tale dates to the seventh century BCE, which shows humans have enjoyed stories of this ilk for at least that long—and possibly longer. We just love an underdog, hence our fascination with the New Guard even today. It's a big reason that millions of people around the world continue to tune in to watch sports. We're all searching for that magic moment when a team of players that no one thinks much of manages an upset that changes sports history. Countless films and television shows have been produced about the topic, reminding us that there are still moments in life when we can be genuinely surprised.

Psychologists have studied our underdog fascination and found that humans are wired to support the contender who is not the favorite. Something in our brains makes us override logic and bet with our hearts instead of following a more rational assessment of the odds. When a pair of researchers at Bowling Green State University asked study participants to read descriptions of two basketball teams playing each other in a fictional seven-game series, they rooted for the team described as the underdog a whopping 88.1 percent of the time.[2]

But what if the underdog started to win? Would that change anything? Well, the researchers also found that if the team a participant previously backed started succeeding, making the other team the underdog, alliances would shift to this *new* underdog. The researchers theorized that while humans appreciate a winner, we are more emotionally interested in a contest where an underdog has the potential to overcome their inferior status. One plausible explanation is that it is a way for us to hedge our bets and avoid disappointment. If the underdog wins, it's a great feeling. And if they lose, well, that's to be expected.

And yet an entire marketing industry has been set up to depict companies as winners, never as underdogs. Huge budgets go into campaigns that describe companies as the "number one leader" in their category of enterprise software or sparkling soda drinks. I have seen a lot of companies making up categories, just so they can claim to be the leaders in them. That impulse is understandable: People want to ally themselves with the idea of winning so that customers and potential hires choose them. It's also a way to attract investors at all-important capital raises. Leadership gets an ego boost out of it too. It's the same reason why many CEOs are clamoring to be on "40 under 40" lists.

But underdog status is not a bad place to be in terms of brand positioning. Studies have shown that people tend to associate underdogs with qualities like passion and determination. Under-dogs are also more often referred to as having "heart" or "hus-tle," while winners tend to be ascribed qualities like "talent" or "intelligence." There's nothing wrong with being referred to as talented, but most executives, particularly of the early-stage com-panies I know, would prefer to be associated with the former set of qualities, which imply that they worked both heroically and hard to achieve their success rather than having it come easy. Plus, underdogs are also more interesting to watch. Occasionally, a David gets to beat a Goliath. And when that happens, people really pay attention. It is far more entertaining to witness an upset in action than to watch a well-known winner continue to win.

My takeaway here is that any business can benefit from being perceived as an underdog and leaning into this kind of storytell-ing, at least in the early years. There are also ways to be both a winner and an underdog. A company might be an underdog in one area, such as a new product line that it's developing, but a winner in another. There's a reason why Levie's "New Guard" language worked so well. He was essentially positioning Box as the underdog against a far larger and better-capitalized foe, which included Dropbox. Both companies in media interviews are posi-tioned throughout the years as engaged in a "cloud storage war."

And yet Levie and his executive team at times also lean into language around Box being a "leader," such as in the field of cloud content-management software in order to lure their key customer: midsize companies and large enterprises.[3] Levie, in interviews with the press, openly acknowledges that his compe-tition is better when it comes to attracting that everyday user, but he stresses that his business has invested in building a product that aligns more closely with the highly specialized needs of its behemoth customers. And in that arena, he believes Box is superior. That strategy has been highly effective, proving that it is possible for companies to toggle between the two, particularly if they're thinking creatively and have a strong communications team. It's very possible to be both a leader and an underdog, which I'd argue is the most enviable place to be.

Bottom line: Humans are naturally inclined to like and want to ally with other humans perceived as bucking the odds. We like to root for the underdog. Always have, always will.

Pick a Plot

What other plots should companies know about? Well, as it turns out, the best stories are repetitive. Most Hollywood movies are just a variation on a theme. Even the greatest artists and writers in history, like William Shakespeare, stuck to a few favored plots.

Author Christopher Booker, who spent years examining stories in movies and literature, has identified seven common plots that show up most often. The seven basic plots have played a far more influential role in human history than most of us realize. These Booker plots are highly applicable to the world of business, and every budding storyteller should familiarize themselves with them.

Overcoming the Monster

Our hero or heroine needs to destroy a monster that is threatening their community. Sometimes the monster has treasure or is holding the princess captive. There are plenty of Disney movies with this plot, like *Beauty and the Beast*, originally a fairy tale, and most James Bond films involve the charismatic spy saving both a beautiful woman and the world. David and Goliath, of course, is a classic Overcoming the Monster plot. When companies like Box use language like "Old Guard" and "New Guard," this is also a subtle way of referencing this plot.

Rags to Riches

We love stories about heroes and heroines who are poor and downtrodden but have the potential for greatness. They overcome their humble origins to accumulate wealth and power. This, of course, is essentially the plot for the classic Disney film *Cinderella*, originally a folk tale, although fans of that film will know that it incorporates other plots, including Overcoming the Monster (the protangonist Cinderella eventually gets a kind of revenge on her evil stepmother). Moving on from the movies, Oprah Winfrey and Starbucks' Howard Schultz are both real-life entrepreneurs who have referenced how their early life experiences converted them into scrappy entrepreneurs with the necessary grit and determination to succeed. Oprah has opened up about being born in poverty to a single mother and being molested during her childhood, before landing her first job in radio while still in high school. Schultz was born to a receptionist mother and truck-driving father and grew up in the housing projects before landing his first job in sales. Both Schultz and Winfrey rose up the career ladder relatively quickly, recognized early on for their work ethic and talent.

The Quest

In this plot, the hero or heroine goes on a journey somewhere far away to achieve a great prize or accomplish a great goal. Hello, *Lord of the Rings*. There's also a more profound version in which the hero realizes that the object did not bring them happiness. I'm again reminded of Starbucks' Howard Schultz, a native New Yorker who described in media interviews how he found inspiration at the great coffeehouses of Italy before he returned home to become the CEO of Starbucks.

Voyage and Return

This plot is highly linked to the quest, so in a business context they're often used interchangeably. In this plot, the hero or heroine travels to a new world that feels strange but exciting. Eventually, they decide to make the precarious journey home as a changed person. A classic tale that follows this plot is *The Wizard of Oz*. One of the best known corporate examples is Apple's Steve Jobs, who was fired by the board from Apple before starting a new company, NeXT. He then made a triumphant return to Apple after the company bought NeXT. This is a story most of us know thanks to copious biographies written about Jobs.

Comedy

This is a more loosely defined genre that could include stories about relationships between people who undergo trials and tribulations but always manage to pick themselves back up in sometimes unexpected (and humorous) ways. Typically some form of healing and catharsis brings the plot to a neat close. This is essentially the arc of every romantic comedy that Hollywood ever made and every film starring Drew Barrymore or Rachel McAdams, including *The Notebook*. In the tech world, several books have been written about the complicated dynamics between PayPal founders Peter Thiel, Max Levchin, and Elon Musk. In a move that has become infamous, Musk was at one point ousted from PayPal by his colleagues while on his honeymoon, according to biographer Walter Isaacson. In the ultimate twist, despite all the infighting and early struggles, all three became billionaires in their next acts.

Tragedy

In this genre, the hero or heroine does not achieve their goal, and everything ends on a disappointing, sad note. The intention of tragedy is to invoke an accompanying catharsis, or a pain that awakens pleasure for the audience. Shakespeare is known for his tragedies, where the protagonists do not get a satisfying ending but are rather destroyed by their own flaws. Just look at *Hamlet* or *Othello*, plays in which a lot of people die and the hero's goals are never fulfilled (or are fulfilled in ways they never intended). Hamlet dies, and so does his entire family, leaving the crown to a foreign ruler. Companies rarely share these stories of their own accord, but one tragedy that springs to mind is the story of WeWork. The once-hyped real estate company was essentially dismantled in public view, because of both its hard-driving, hard-partying culture and the challenges with the business model. WeWork was valued by its investors like a technology company but was ultimately a real estate company. It never really had a clear path to profitability because it owned and operated expensive real estate, but it was valued like a technology company and expected to grow like one. The company, once valued at close to $50 billion, filed for Chapter 11 bankruptcy in late 2023. Storytellers don't have many reasons to lean into tragedies, with a few exceptions. A story like this is a powerful one and could be a cautionary tale for others. It might also make a competitor look better for having avoided a terrible fate by making more strategic and considered decisions along the way.

Rebirth

In this type of narrative, the hero experiences a transformation, spurred by some sort of realization or event that changes their perspective or their lifestyle. A classic tale of rebirth is "Beauty and the Beast"; another is Charles Dickens's *A Christmas Carol*. In "Beauty and the Beast," a beautiful and intelligent girl from a local town is lured into the lair of a beast. She learns in the process of getting to know him that he's actually a prince, and the process of falling in love converts him back into his true form. Likewise, *A Christmas Carol*'s protagonist, Ebeneezer Scrooge, is transformed into a gentler, kinder man after being visited by spirits from his past, present, and future. In the business world, Warren Buffett is a classic character who has experienced many rebirths—as an author, a proponent of value investing, a CEO, and a philanthropist—and much has been written about each chapter of his life. One of my favorite stories about his life involves the moment he transformed Berkshire Hathaway's approach to risk taking, recognizing over time that doing one massive deal would generate a faster return than doing ten smaller ones. He took the time to study the numbers, the businesses, and the people rather than looking for quick hits, and that turned him from a stock market afficionado into a true C-suite executive. And now he's consistently rated one of the most well-loved executives in America.

We've all heard versions of these seven plots at bedtime while reading books to our kids, or perhaps we recall them from our own childhoods. But in business the best storytellers have also frequently and intentionally exploited these plots to advance their goals. These storytellers have used these plots readily and interchangeably, moving from one to the next with ease. For them, a story can use multiple elements of any of these genres, depending on their goals. By learning from their example, we can do the same in our professional lives. These narrative types are known to most people, and that's precisely what makes them great.

The Importance of Company Lore

Every company should have a few stories that are shared regularly with employees internally (for instance, through employee orientations) as well as with the outside world. These stories should involve a crossroads or a seemingly insurmountable challenge, and ideally they should be linked to one of the Booker plots. Again, these stories shouldn't be purely linear in nature—they must contain some kind of setback. Otherwise, they are hardly stories at all.

You'll notice in Booker's seven plots that almost always the hero or heroine must triumph over a monster or enemy. We root for the hero because we relate to them and because the monster they're facing is a genuine threat. So I always recommend that business leaders think hard about a moment when the company almost didn't make it or faced its own version of a monster. The story should contain some degree of suspense or surprise—if not, it won't be particularly entertaining or gripping.

For employees, it's important to hear these stories—"company lore" connected to company culture—so they feel their jobs have meaning. It's a moment to recall that the leader behind the business is human and had to make some very tough decisions to get to where they are today. Such stories serve to make the founder or CEO seem relatable. We might even empathize with the stress or indecision they felt at that moment and the relief they experienced when everything worked out. Every company executive should have at least two or three of these company lore stories in their back pocket so that they can break them out instantly when asked.

I asked Levie about Box's company lore. He didn't hesitate to share two of his core stories.

The first involved the moment when Box almost got acquired, early on in its history. The acquisition offer reportedly would have made Levie and the rest of the founding team extremely rich. The details of that offer—the buyer and price—were never publicly disclosed, so we'll never know for sure. But rumors in the press speculated that it was higher than the company's then–$550 million valuation.

Faced with an extremely tough decision, the founders came together and discussed their options over a few days. Should they take the deal or walk away? They decided to turn down the offer because of what Levie describes as their "insanely long-term thinking." The Box founders had a hunch that the company would get a whole lot bigger, so taking the deal now would mean leaving money on the table. They unanimously decided to bet it all. And fortunately for them, as we all know, they won the wager. The company is worth many times that acquisition offer price today.

Returning to our Booker story plots, this story is a Voyage and Return plot, where the heroes are offered an enticing option in a new home but decide to return to what's familiar. It would not be such a powerful and pleasing story if they walked away from their best offer, never to see such a rich opportunity again. That would instead be a tragedy for the founders, the investors, and anyone with equity in the business. The decision proved to be the right one, albeit a difficult one to make at the time—if Levie had been wrong, he would have not only lost out on millions of dollars but also let down his employees. Most people join start-ups hoping for some kind of exit, opting to work long hours for lower pay for years in the hopes of an outsized return. Most companies are taking big risks in rejecting an acquisition offer, as they truly do not know whether another opportunity for a big payout will be on the table again.

Another story that Levie often shares with his employees involves the moment when Apple founder Steve Jobs launched the iPad in 2010. As soon as Levie got his hands on the device, he felt strongly that the tablet represented the future of personal computing. So he decided to make a big bet on the iPad and immediately pivoted the business, including his valuable engineering resources, to focus on building a native iPad app. If the iPad had flopped, it would have been disastrous for Box. But when the iPad launched and millions of people flocked to stores to buy one, Box was one of the first applications they could use to access and share documents. In its first year alone, Apple sold 7 million iPads; in its second year, Apple sold 32.4 million iPads; and by the end of its first decade, it boasted 350 million iPad sales. Box benefited financially from all of that. Levie uses that story to remind his teams that even as the company grows, they must stay lean and humble enough to know when it's time to bet the farm. Missing a major new wave of technological innovation is how the New Guard becomes the Old Guard.

The story plot that he's leveraging here is the Quest: Sometimes you must take a big risk without knowing the outcome and have faith that the rewards and riches will be there in the end. In both cases, Levie made the right decision—but as he shares the stories, he reminds his listeners (in most cases, his employees) that he understood the consequences of being wrong.

As an aside, company lore like this can set the stage for rationalizing decision-making that may not make sense in the immediate term. In Levie's mind, nothing as impactful as the introduction of the iPad happened until he saw Open AI's ChatGPT in action for the first time. Levie sees AI as a revolution with the potential to transform Box's business yet again, and the company has rapidly been working on new features. In the case of Box, that might mean marketing teams improving content with a few clicks or sales reps getting answers about customers from vast quantities of data in real time. So now he's allocating major resources to that trend, even as plenty of other businesses still grapple with the decision.

Consider any iconic story about a CEO or business that's well known to the public, and you'll find a strong link to one or more of the seven basic plots. Some business stories may involve multiple plots, which make for even better movies inspired by real life. A Rags to Riches plot might morph into a Tragedy—think of BlackBerry, the former king of the smartphone universe based in Canada, which was riding high until getting utterly crushed by Apple. In a functioning market, even the most successful companies eventually face disruption.

The Origin Story

For those looking for inspiration about what stories are most compelling, ask yourself this question: What prompted you to join or start the company in the first place?

The story that most often becomes company lore is the origin story, the moment that the company was founded. For Box, the origin story wasn't a particularly compelling one, because Levie remembers it as a slow and meandering set of experiences, many of which were not exactly pleasant—as he puts it, a series of "paper cuts." There was no big "aha" moment that would make for a good story.

But his competitor, Drew Houston, CEO of the larger file-sharing company Dropbox, does have an effective origin story, which has become his own version of company lore. Houston has shared this story thousands of times. When I sat down for coffee with his former head of enterprise marketing, Helen Min, she still knew every word of it by heart many years after leaving the company because she'd heard Houston share it so often. The story involves the moment when, as a student at the Massachusetts Institute of Technology (MIT), Houston realized he had left his USB drive at home. That incident sparked the idea for a cloud-based file-storage service, which led to the formation of Dropbox. As Houston explained, never again would anyone have to miss an important presentation because of a lost USB drive. In a way, that's an Overcoming the Monster plot, if you can imagine the monster as representing all the various ways that life can conspire to deny us access to our most important files. It's the nightmare when you're making that all-important management presentation, and the document is not there. Sometimes, in a business sense, the proverbial monster is that bad outcome or event that we have all encountered and would do anything to avoid reliving.

Dropbox, of course, was Box's biggest early competitor and remains so to this day. Levie joked with his self-deprecating humor that he's "jealous" of this story because he doesn't have anything quite so powerful to share.

As I looked across my network for more inspiring examples of origin stories, I found that almost all of them could fit into one of three categories or narrative arcs. These are not plots like the Booker frameworks, but they're variations on the hero or heroine's journey with a specific focus on their origins.

These include "The Comeback Kid," "The Brilliant Child," and "The Personal Experience," and they're most useful, as I'll explain, for helping people frame stories about how they joined or started a business.

The Comeback Kid

The Comeback Kid is a plot line that works well for founders who have struggled with a prior venture and are now back at it with a new idea that is bound to succeed. It's the Rebirth plot in action.

One of my favorite examples of a "Comeback Kid" whom I've interviewed in my career is Apoorva Mehta. When we first met, Mehta shared that he tried to start twenty companies before settling on a delivery app for groceries. Instead of hiding any of this, he wore his failure like a badge of honor. His company, Instacart, proved wildly successful, making its early investors, like Y Combinator, Andreessen Horowitz, and Sequoia Capital, a lot of money when it went public in 2023.

While it may sound counterintuitive, sharing stories of failure can be highly effective. Such stories demonstrate that the founder is truly committed, because they've faced a challenge, been defeated, and, instead of quitting, come back to try again. Studies have also shown that publicizing failures makes business leaders more approachable and successful at garnering support, because it mitigates negative emotions like envy. In fact, there may even be a risk in hiding failure. Sharing stories of moments that didn't go well are also an opportunity to return to the idea of the underdog, which, as we previously discussed, is a powerful but underutilized storytelling device.

When researchers at Clemson University studied transcripts of presentations given by entrepreneurs at Stanford University between 2001 and 2013, they found that failure had become part of the "social norm of entrepreneurship" and that tech founders mentioned the topic disproportionately compared to other types of business leaders. The word "fail" was mentioned over 600 times, appearing in all but 3 percent of the presentations.[4] In fact, failure was described more often than success. CEOs have also found ways to use new types of language to emphasize the positive aspects of failure in ways that are both temporal and scalable, like "fail fast" or "fail fast forward" and "leverage it." Words like "pivot" are also essential in demonstrating how entrepreneurs learned from prior failures, quickly moving in a new direction.

What types of founders are "Comeback Kids"? Well, anyone with a prior history of struggling to get ideas off the ground who remains committed to entrepreneurship and leadership as a vocation. Nailing that moment of realization is critical in leveraging this narrative. The audience must be left with the impression that this next idea will finally be the one that works.

The Brilliant Child

Another particularly potent story involves a founder who first got started building their company when they were precocious and young. I like to call this "The Brilliant Child" story. The business world, especially outside tech, loves this story, so it's no surprise that it pops up again and again across a variety of industries. In fashion, we often hear about iconic fashion designers, like Ralph Lauren and Alexander McQueen, who lacked the money to buy expensive clothes to keep up with the popular kids, so they crafted their own custom outfits. In the entertainment industry, we hear stories of talented ingenues who were plucked out of relative obscurity, like Ava Gardner (the spotlight found her after her photograph was displayed in her brother's photography studio) and Lana Turner (spotted as a junior in high school). Not to mention Harry Potter! J. K. Rowling notoriously submitted to a slew of publishers before hitting success. The Drew Houston USB drive story is another classic example of a Brilliant Child story, because he was a bright young college student at MIT when he first turned his idea into action.

These types of stories are compelling because we love the notion of an entrepreneur somehow destined for success. There's also some kernel of truth here. There's a body of research demonstrating that adolescents who are particularly gifted in certain areas will often wind up going into those fields as adults. Some of us are naturally suited to starting and leading companies, and that can show up at a young age. Findings from a recent forty-five-year study from Vanderbilt reveal that gifted teenagers' preferences and values, present already by age thirteen, accurately predicted the types of careers in which they would make their mark.[5]

In the tech sector, we've all heard stories about brilliant business leaders who dabbled in code and other scrappy ventures from a young age. This camp includes Facebook's Mark Zuckerberg, Pandora's Tim Westergren, and TaskRabbit's Stacy Brown-Philpot. Brown-Philpot got inspired to start TaskRabbit after becoming the "CFO of her paper route" in Detroit when she was only ten years old.

Should you share a "Brilliant Child" story? Well, a good question to ask yourself is this: If you look back on your early years, did you feel a pull to the problem that you're trying to solve as an entrepreneur? Did you feel drawn to work in a specific field from a young age? Or were you gifted at a particular subject in school—one that has since made you stand out as a leader?

To nail this narrative, describe how your early years made your path as a founder seem almost inevitable. You'll give investors the impression that you were destined to be the one to solve the problem. But a word of caution: If overdone, these narratives can be a bit annoying, particularly if the storyteller has a lot of ego.

While there's a lot of value in mentioning that you've harbored a passion to solve a problem from a young age, take pains to avoid coming off as if you're some kind of wunderkind "chosen one."

As with all things, humility and self-awareness are key. Sharing a failure story, by the way, might also be an effective strategy to balance how you come across!

There's one exception here—if someone else tells your story for you. We were all drawn to the actor Jesse Eisenberg's portrayal of Mark Zuckerberg in the movie *The Social Network*, even as his character was hardly likable. No one could deny the young Zuckerberg's brilliance, as he sat hunched over in his dorm room coding until the wee hours of the morning. Zuckerberg's company undoubtedly gained prominence in the wake of the film, even if he may have taken issue with it. Dozens of articles penned by fans of the company argued that the depiction was wrong. Either way, the film undoubtedly built up a mythology around the Facebook founder—and that propelled the company to even greater heights.

The Personal Experience

A third and final trope involves a founder who's had a profound personal experience with the problem they're trying to solve. We see that a lot in mission-driven industries, like ed tech, climate tech, or health tech. I invest in and spend a lot of time meeting companies in the health-tech space, so I personally hear from a lot of founders who have lost a loved one to a disease or who became caregivers when a loved one needed help. Some founders have been patients themselves, sometimes with serious, chronic conditions. These experiences made them want to build a better health-care system for others. One example of that is Glen Tullman, the CEO of Livongo, a company that sold for more than $18 billion to Teladoc. The original thesis came from his son's diagnosis with diabetes.

The deep personal experience demonstrates that the founder is connected to the success or failure of their company on an intimate level, and it indicates that they have some close-up perspective on the problem.

The deep emotional connection helps build trust that the founder has the passion needed to see the company through to success. A lot of research has been conducted on the question of why most start-ups fail. One of the major reasons, as uncovered by Harvard Business School professor Tom Eisenmann, is a lack of passion.[6] Entrepreneurs must have a burning desire to solve the problem they're tackling; otherwise, they'll give up in the face of the inevitable challenges. So emphasizing the personal connection to the company's mission through the story signals to the investor that the entrepreneur has the passion it takes to succeed. That is what makes this particular story so effective.

When that desire is coupled with deep preparation—in the form of the right team, the expertise necessary to solve the problem, and a deep understanding of the market—the combination can be powerful.

The Reluctance to Be Authentic

The screenwriter Robert McKee spent his career weaving stories that could transfix audiences. In his later years, he became a storytelling lecturer and coach. His students include more than 65 Academy Award winners, 200 Emmy Award winners, and countless other leading lights in film and TV. He has also shared with business leaders his insights about how to leverage the storytelling lessons he learned in Hollywood. His lecture series, "Story in Business," has been well attended by CEOs across a wide variety of industries.[7]

As McKee has observed, most corporate leaders, even in super-competitive industries, do not tell their own stories well.

"They strategize with numbers, not narrative," writes McKee. Despite all the evidence we've heard about why storytelling works, CEOs will deprioritize it.

McKee believes that CEOs are biased to prefer data over stories because data is quick to parse—they can glean meaning from data with what he calls "the flick of an eye." Business leaders can use data to make a point to their teams without having to dedicate much time to communicating, and their days are busy enough that it just seems more efficient.

I'd add that many business leaders are reluctant to share their stories because they don't want to get too personal. Sometimes that stems from innate modesty or shyness. Sometimes it comes from a well-founded desire to stay out of the spotlight: For example, a female CEO might prefer to keep a low profile to avoid the inevitable controversy and added scrutiny that every high-profile woman leader in business gets subjected to eventually (a topic I'll cover in more detail in Chapter 9). Maybe they just want to keep their personal life separate from their public life.

That's a shame, because most companies do have stories to share that draw upon some of the common plot devices and themes we discussed in this chapter. Storytelling is especially valuable for early-stage companies that don't have much in the way of data to point to. But it's also critical for bigger companies, because the stories can give shape and meaning to the numbers and charts.

Even publicly traded companies like Box and Dropbox must sell a vision to Wall Street about a future path of greatness that may not be obvious today. In this regard, facts alone often fall short.

That's why every business leader—whether founders or executives at established companies—should take the responsibility of storytelling seriously. Even for those who are reluctant to get "too personal," there's a strong argument for taking charge of the story. By embracing it and telling it yourself, you can control the narrative more effectively, focusing attention where you want it. Decide what aspects of your personal story you're willing to weave into the corporate story. Use the seven plots and three kinds of origin stories elaborated above to craft a story that will resonate with your target audiences. Do this effectively, and these stories will feel deeply personal to your audience, helping them form a connection with your brand and your products. That will help both you and your company to be more successful.

The seven basic plots will propel any company forward, and they're easy to remember. Likewise, entrepreneurs might find value in sharing a story of failure, a personal anecdote, or a moment where they felt predestined for success. Levie from Box will always make time for storytelling for one simple reason: He wants his company to be super successful. "There isn't a single company we can point to that was able to scale and have a massive dent on the world without figuring out the essence of that one big story," he said. "Every company needs to find out what that is."

CHAPTER 3

The Big Four Storytelling Secrets

The privilege of a lifetime is to become who you truly are.

—Carl Gustav Jung, psychoanalyst

Our story was about failure," said Jonathan Bush, the former CEO of Athenahealth, a health technology company that went public in 2007. Bush is one of the most candid executives I know in the world of business. His style might not work for everyone, but it works for him for the simple reason that it's authentic. Authenticity is one of the most important traits that any decent storyteller possesses at their core, the first of what I call the "Big Four." The prior chapter explored the plots that make sense. In this chapter, we'll examine how the best storytellers in the business operate via a series of traits they have in common.

Back to Athenahealth. The company started out in the late 1990s, cofounded by Bush—a cousin of former US President George W. Bush—and Todd Park, a health-care consultant turned entrepreneur.[1] The two men had previously worked together at the firm Booz Allen Hamilton and later came up with the idea of running their own centers for women's health and birthing. It didn't take them long to realize that operating a medical clinic was a lot harder than it might seem, given the billing complexities, the labor shortages, and the documentation burden on the customers. Bush and Park pivoted the business to selling software for medical practices, which they saw as the greater need. At the time, clinics were increasingly looking to invest in tools to modernize their medical record systems and move away from paper, making the timing ideal for a scrappy new player to move in.

But there were also headwinds for Athenahealth. It was not the only company to seize on that particular moment to build software for hospitals and clinics. That scrappy Athena team faced incumbents, as well as a dozen or so newer competitors, some with far more funding and larger commercial teams. Bush and Park knew that to stand a chance, they had to get creative in how they pitched potential customers: thousands of doctors' offices. As Bush started conversations with these physicians, he leaned into a compelling narrative: the initial failure that led to a key insight. He spoke about pivoting away from running a medical practice and into software instead.

Bush recognized that the story, though not a positive one, was a powerful way to acknowledge how hard his customers' jobs were. So, in sales meetings, he led not with the product—technology to streamline the operations of running a clinic—but with the story.

"We told them that we were a bunch of former consultants running an independent medical practice...and within a few years, we ran it into the ground," he recalled.

The story was effective because it surprised its intended audience: Most sales calls do not start that way. Bush didn't sugarcoat or gloss over the defeat when asked about it by potential customers, which further disarmed them. He dwelled on it. "Never mind a fart in church," he told me years later, with his trademark, occasionally crass humor. "We admitted to pooping our ass."

During my career, I've spoken to dozens of executives and founders who have prided themselves on their storytelling capabilities. And after all these conversations, the best storytellers lean into what feels authentic to them. As cheesy as it sounds, the fastest path to becoming an effective storyteller is to be yourself. Levie from Box, whom we met in Chapter 2, also prides himself on his sense of humor. Like Bush, it's authentic to him. Levie tends to lean to the self-deprecating, while Bush surprises his audience into laughter by never holding back. And that may mean making a vulnerable admission, as long as it's authentic.

If you follow Athenahealth's trajectory, you'll find it didn't end well. Bush's run as CEO resulted in an activist investor targeting the business and booting him out. So, you might argue that his decision to be himself, rather than a buttoned-up corporate executive, was a bad one. And you'd have some justification in making that point. But I contend that Athena was far more successful than most businesses, making it through to an IPO and beyond. And it's had staying power, even after several decades in business, so it's still worth examining what Bush got right in those early days to make that business stand out in a crowded space.

Those of us in the industry recognize that for a long period Athena was the darling of the health-tech industry, and Bush was a poster child for the space. Most companies dream of getting the kind of attention Bush received, but few do. The press loved putting him on television, moderating panels with him, and featuring him at their events, because they could always count on him to entertain the audience. Most other CEOs in the space would bore them to tears. Back in my reporting days, I remember him showing up to meetings with no agenda or scripted notes, unlike most of the executives I met. John Hallock, Athenahealth's former communications lead, told me that he once handed Bush an extensive dossier with dozens of pages of information and a list of prepared talking points to get him ready for an interview with a journalist. He took one look at it and joked, "How many trees did you have to cut down to make this?" Hallock doesn't hold a grudge.

If you don't yet believe in the power of authenticity, ask yourself this: Have you ever liked Mark Zuckerberg more than in his current incarnation as an unapologetically quixotic billionaire, farming artisan beef with his daughters in Hawaii, building an octagon in his Palo Alto backyard in case Elon Musk again challenges him to an MMA cage fight, and ditching his gray tees and hoodies for gold chains and Sherpa coats? The moment he threw out the heavy coaching and the script and leaned into being himself was the moment we started warming to him for the first time.

"Instead of trying to appease everyone like he used to do, Zuckerberg has decided to go full 'weird rich guy,'" *Bloomberg* technology editor Sarah Frier, who covered Facebook for years, explained to me. "And somehow that has seemed more authentic and appealing to the masses. People who hated him for years have started to root for him."

With that in mind, I'll note here that the case studies I share throughout this book on companies like Facebook and Athenahealth are meant to inspire, not to be copied. What's authentic in one high-powered executive won't necessarily be so for you—in fact, it almost certainly won't be. Not everyone is comfortable substituting careful planning with off-the-cuff commentary, but it works for Bush because it comes naturally to him. And most of us aren't endearingly weird billionaires like Zuckerberg. You need to find your own voice.

Authenticity, hands down, is the trait that the best storytellers I've interviewed have in common. It gives audiences a sense that they're connecting with a real human, not just a collection of slogans or safe messaging points developed by a marketing department or an AI chatbot. That's why it's the first of the four core traits required for successful storytelling. Along with authenticity, three other traits have come up repeatedly as I've interviewed dozens of storytellers. Here's an acronym to remember them: SOAP. *S* is for surprise, *O* for openness, *A* for authenticity, and *P* for pathos (in other words, having empathy for the audience of the story). I call them the "Big Four," but if it helps, feel free to remind yourself to use SOAP.

Openness, or transparency, may seem closely related to authenticity. But they're not one and the same. People who are transparent are not always authentic, and vice versa. Those who show both qualities can maximize trust with their audience, which is beneficial in good times but especially so in turbulent ones.

And let's talk about the twist. The element of surprise is essential. There's a reason we all gravitate to books and films that include an unexpected element. "Storytellers should tell the audience something that they don't already know," said Tim Brown, one of the country's foremost user-experience experts and chair of the global design firm IDEO. An unexpected revelation can elicit all sorts of emotions from the listener, as well as keep them interested in the subject for longer. Most of us will not put down the murder mystery until the big reveal (some of us can't help ourselves and skip straight to the last page). Either way, it's engrossing.

Great storytellers must also have empathy for their audience. I cannot emphasize this point enough because it is so often lost in the corporate world. It requires thinking about whom you're speaking to and what the audience might hope to gain through the interaction. Most of us walk into networking conversations thinking about what we hope to get out of them versus approaching the person we're meeting with curiosity.

We'll go into each of these in more depth in the following pages. So let's dive in.

The Value of Authenticity

Heidi Zak was a competitive gymnast from the age of eight through high school. In her twenties and thirties, she built a career in finance and technology, got married, and had two kids. As she juggled her personal and professional pursuits, Zak prided herself on her athleticism, even completing a half marathon while seven months pregnant. Suffice it to say, she had no aspirations to become a Victoria's Secret angel in her spare time, gliding down the runway in oversized wings, five-inch heels, and a cleavage-enhancing bra. Zak, like many women, gravitated to brands that spoke to her need for simplicity, style, and comfort.

When it came to her undergarments, she wanted to feel supported. A bra should reflect her lifestyle, and not the other way around.

So, in 2013, she started a company, ThirdLove, to design comfortable bras for real women, including those with stretch marks and lumps. From the early days, Zak described her company to friends and colleagues as the "antithesis of Victoria's Secret." She leaned into her identity as a working mother and an athlete with aspirations to stay fit and healthy as she aged. That message resonated with consumers, many of whom could relate to Zak's no-nonsense aesthetic. After its first decade in business, the company grew to be valued at $750 million, with news outlets ranging from *The New York Times* to CNN raving about the wearability of its bras.

All was going as well as it could, given the challenges of getting any new retail business off the ground. And then, the critics came out in force. Former Victoria's Secret marketing executive Ed Razek targeted ThirdLove directly, publicly commenting that his company's sexier bras were customers' "first" love. He also noted that Victoria's Secret's attempt at a television special featuring plus-size models had fallen flat with consumers. Customers wanted fantasy, not reality, Razek pointed out, implying that they would not purchase products from ThirdLove.

Zak was livid and initially unsure about how to respond. Was speaking out worth it? Would there be negative consequences associated with it? Ultimately, after talking it out with her close confidants and advisors, she decided to hit back by taking out a full-page ad in *The New York Times*, accusing Victoria's Secret of "selling a male fantasy to women." In the piece, she wrote, "Each time I read it I'm even angrier. How in 2018 can the CMO of any public company—let alone one that claims to be for women—make such shocking, derogatory statements?"[2]

It was a bold move. When I asked Zak about the decision to fight back against a much larger competitor years later, she told me she decided to lean into how she genuinely felt. Very few companies had taken a step that bold at the time, so she recognized that she would be going out on a limb. Zak also knew that Victoria's Secret could have retaliated by telling its manufacturers not to work with ThirdLove. That could have stalled her business virtually overnight, if she couldn't scale manufacturing capacity to meet customer demand.

"I was truly worried about it before I put it out," Zak told me. "There was a lot of discussion internally about whether to publish it, because open letters weren't a thing at the time. I feared it was too aggressive. But at the end of the day, every word I wrote was connected to what I was building, and it felt like the right moment and time to say it."

Her gamble was a big success. The mainstream media rallied around Zak, describing the ThirdLove brand as "feminist" and "inclusive."[3] The ad also put ThirdLove into the headlines for several weeks straight, increasing awareness of the brand and boosting sales. According to Zak, that made the ad one of the most important catalysts for turning the business into a household name.

For Zak, speaking out by placing the ad was the right thing to do because Victoria's Secret had undermined her core customer. She asked herself before she decided to publish, "Why did I start this company in the first place?" She felt in that moment that she had to defend the average American woman, who was not buying into the male fantasy when it came to making an underwear purchase. For business leaders, it's critical to weigh the potential costs before taking the leap on a risky decision, but as we will note throughout this book, too many companies are far more cautious than they need to be. Too often they overlook the risk that customers and other key stakeholders can forget that you exist.

In fact, I believe companies in the future will be on the hook to take on more risks. Why? Because it's become more challenging than ever to stand out by playing it safe. And because there's never been a good story that did not involve some kind of tension or conflict. It doesn't always need to involve a bigger competitor, as in the case of ThirdLove, and it needn't entail taking on immediate business risk. Conflicts can also be subtler, such as an internal struggle over an operational decision or a fight with the unacceptable status quo. Either way, there needs to be some moment of setback to make the narrative interesting. No one wants to root for a hero who's experienced nothing but success.

Saying yes to opportunities to be authentic, especially when doing so involves saying something powerful or taking a stand against a competitor, is a method we know works. There may be risks, but let's not forget that there are also ample rewards.

The Power of Openness

Many authentic people are open. Others may feel that being thoughtful about what they share is most genuine. Perhaps they're introverted or have been burned in the past. Many of us are afraid of the consequences of saying the wrong thing, particularly in the cultural moment that we're in. And that's okay. CEOs should be encouraged to be themselves. I see problems arise, however, when people who would otherwise be open and transparent feel the need to hide what's really going on because their companies have told them to do so, particularly when there isn't a strong reason. I've seen many companies with legal and public relations departments seemingly set up for the sole reason of saying no. They advise against the leadership team sharing information with the public and even limit internal communication to a "need-to-know basis." I have encountered countless times when this has fallen flat. People will often fill an information void with their own narratives, true or otherwise. And worse, I've seen CEOs being less than truthful because they're concerned about spilling the beans on a topic they don't have official sanction to discuss.

One notable example: Facebook's Mark Zuckerberg once told the tech reporter Casey Newton about the promising test flight of Aquila, a drone with a wingspan larger than a jet that Facebook was working on. Newton reported what Zuckerberg had said—that the test flight was a success—but later *Bloomberg* uncovered that the drone had in fact crashed. Newton later described feeling like an "idiot" for trusting the company's version.[4] That led to coverage about the company's salty, low-trust relationships with tech journalists, a precursor to much of the bad press that followed.[5] Whether in life or in business, trust, once broken, cannot be easily repaired.

Those who choose the opposite path—the path of openness—are ahead of the pack. Corporate ambivalence toward openness (or even the truth) has been so prevalent for so long that leaders who take the opposite tack—embracing transparency—are finding success when it comes to attracting customers *and* retaining talent. When the company Slack surveyed its own employees on the subject in 2018, it found that 87 percent said they hoped the culture of their next job would be transparent, just as Slack's company culture is known to be. The company has spoken about transparency as the next wave in corporate evolution and provided guides to its customers on how to use it to thrive. It lives up to its own code by sharing a "Transparency Report" that includes requests it has received for customer data from law enforcement and government entities. According to Slack's report, transparency is crucial because it builds trust and strengthens accountability within organizations.

One fascinating case study out of India involving a little-known company called HCL Technologies makes the case for open communication strongly. When Vineet Nayar took over as CEO in the mid-2000s, the company was a sleepy IT services firm surrounded by faster-growing competitors. But under his leadership, the company experienced a period of low employee churn and unprecedented growth. That prompted him to write a book about the changes he made while in the driver's seat. Despite opposition from parts of the company, he described opening up the firm's financial performance data to every employee and creating a portal where employees could ask candid questions of the CEO and other leaders. Nayar also allowed managers to submit their business plans to the entire company rather than just to the leaders.

During his tenure, the company grew its market cap and its revenues, prompting Nayar to become a big advocate of approaches that involve transparency with employees from the top down. As he explained later, once people saw the company executives' willingness to be open with their teams, they started trusting their decisions. Nayar also said he flipped the hierarchy so that senior leaders were accountable to employees and not the other way around. He described a cultural shift during his tenure, which opened up a lot more avenues for innovation and progress, leading to larger and larger software contracts that propelled the company forward. Transparency not only keeps employees around; it makes a workforce a destination for top talent. And that in turn drives commercial success, even in challenging, competitive markets.

Likewise, in tech hubs like Silicon Valley, where I worked and lived for years, there's an increasing trend among technology companies for CEOs to share their own (sometimes deeply critical) performance reviews with their teams. I've even seen cases where CEOs have shared these reviews online for anyone to see, such as Dan Siroker, who tweeted, "Lots of people told me I was crazy to post our Series A pitch deck publicly on Twitter. But, one of our cultural values at RewindAI is transparency so I did it. Turned out great. Now I'm doing something even crazier. Here are my last five 360 performance reviews as CEO."

Employees I spoke with for this book described finding that type of sharing encouraging because it indicates that their CEO's performance is also scrutinized; leaders should be consistently learning and improving, even if it means hearing critical feedback. Everyone is held to the same standards of accountability. Best-case scenario, it results in a culture where more candid review cycles become the norm. Rather than a box-ticking exercise, the review cycle could become a moment for teams to step back and find opportunities for improvement, on both a group and an individual level. And that could be a lever to improve company culture and productivity over time, as well as to ensure there are more A players around the table.

A caveat worth stressing here: Those who choose to embrace transparency need to do so consistently. A leader who offers to answer questions from employees at the next all-hands meeting should not limit them to softball questions with prepared answers that feel like spin. Or an executive who agrees to speak to the press should not respond only to questions about what's going well. Many executives will expect to be publicly lauded when they do something right but will sneak away and hide if asked hard questions or when something doesn't go as expected. This might help them avoid confrontation, but it can also erode trust.

Indeed, openness does have its limits, particularly for those who struggle to project competency and confidence. A recent study found that lawyers and teachers interviewing for jobs who were honest about their personalities and work styles, including their very real limitations, were more likely to get offers. That does not include admissions like "My weakness is I work too hard and care too much." But that only held true for applicants whose résumés had been rated in the ninetieth percentile or higher. Because their strengths were already evident to the hiring committee, sharing their weaknesses made this group seem accessible and likable without provoking any concerns about their ability to do the job.

What does that tell us about company culture? Being authentic and transparent should not mean sharing only our flaws. It's a balance. Sharing difficulties judiciously, within limits, can help build trust. It works best if the negatives are embedded within a strong overarching story with a positive message. As the organizational psychologist Adam Grant puts it, "Authenticity without boundaries is careless. When we broadcast our limitations, we need to be careful to avoid casting doubt on our strengths."

The Element of Surprise

One of my favorite marketing campaigns comes from a company you'd least expect: a bank. The Canadian subsidiary of TD Trust back in 2014 arranged for special ATMs in its Montreal, Toronto, Calgary, and Vancouver locations to "thank" customers by spitting out a $20 gift. Some customers, whom the bank deemed especially worthy of recognition, received larger cash gifts. The exchanges were all planned out ahead of time. When a preselected customer showed up at the ATM, the machine began talking to them, even recognizing them by name, and captured the interaction on video.

This campaign got national attention after the videos appeared on social media. Some received millions of views. The element of surprise in this campaign was central: No one expects to show up to the ATM and receive a free cash gift. We go to ATMs to take money out, often experiencing some anxiety about what's left in our bank account afterward. Furthermore, most people don't associate banks with the spirit of generosity, so this campaign upended expectations across a variety of fronts.

Such a simple and effective campaign. You might think that giving away free money isn't much of a storytelling tactic; of course, 30,000 people would be psyched to receive $20 when they didn't expect it. But the money was merely a prop for the bank: It served a larger story about unsolicited generosity. And the campaign shifted the public's perception of the bank at a time when trust in financial services was at an all-time low. The concept may have been expensive relative to typical PR campaigns, which don't tend to involve major cash rewards. The bank in this case must have shelled out hundreds of thousands of dollars. But it generated massive publicity—both in the form of mainstream press attention and social media views—and helped shift the narrative extremely effectively. The campaign was such a hit that in 2024, the bank followed up by creating a special ATM at its Philadelphia location that issued dog treats instead of cash rewards![6] Woof.

It's not surprising that surprise is such a potent way to keep audiences on the edge of their seats. Most films will include some kind of plot twist to ensure audiences don't tune out somewhere in the second half. If you know exactly what's going to happen next, you're probably watching a terrible, low-budget B movie. In the corporate world, we too often forget to find ways to deploy this tactic, even when there are plenty of creative ways to do it. One way is with unexpected rewards, as TD Bank did with great success. Another is with a kind gesture to a customer, like having a high-powered CEO take a few minutes out of their day to write a personal note. Apple's Tim Cook is known for this, writing responses to users who take the time to send him letters, which most of us would assume he's far too busy and important to take the time to do. Apple is the largest company in the world by market cap.

Tim Brown, the IDEO chair, has spent his entire career doing user-centered design research on behalf of brands and finding ways to incorporate surprises. His method involves studying how customers engage with products, then taking what he's learned back to the company to design solutions grounded in what customers really want—and might not know (yet) that they want.

Brown gave me an example of a recent project where a client asked IDEO to design better toothbrushes for kids. Instead of creating something technically perfect in a lab, the designers instead watched hundreds of kids brushing their teeth. They gleaned that these kids struggled to hold the toothbrush on their own but really wanted independence from their parents or caregivers. That pivotal insight was surprising for the toothbrush company that commissioned the work. The company hadn't realized how difficult it was for kids to wield their toothbrushes. This led to a new design that was far more comfortable and natural for a young kid to hold. That kind of story could even be part of the company's brand marketing—a tale about how they designed this toothbrush with kids (and not their grown-ups) in mind.

Brown thinks that companies should be thinking about two kinds of "reveal" or "aha" moments, both for customers and internal teams.

- The first is "the insight" about users that may seem obvious but flies under the radar or isn't talked about enough. The toothbrush handle is a good example of this kind of surprise. It's that moment where you might say, "I didn't know that about some or most people, but it totally makes sense."
- The second is exploration of a potentially revolutionary new way of thinking about the world and how it operates—that moment where you might say, "Huh, I've never thought of it that way before!"

For a client in financial services, IDEO asked dozens of people to draw what sprang to mind when they thought about money. One person drew a giant pile of stuff, showing the association between money and purchases in their mind. The client was surprised by that response, expecting people to think about money in relation to where they lived, how much they earned, or potential opportunities to save. That led to a revelation that most people lack a "smart money" mindset unless someone has taught this to them, an education that's hard to come by in schools. So that client built a solution whereby young people could show up to enjoy dinner and discuss things like retirement plans and living on a budget—which would present its own form of surprise. Because it's not too often these days that we get a free meal to talk about spending less money versus buying more products.

What makes for a surprise or delightful feeling in a campaign? In the IDEO example, that meant defying expectations by creating safe forums for people to discuss personal finances—a topic that many people are uncomfortable discussing out loud.

"There are so many rich places where the surprise can be very powerful," said Brown.

Empathy for the Audience

In my journalism career, it never ceased to amaze me how many CEOs came into meetings ready to pitch me as if I were a sales prospect. It spoke to a lack of empathy for my role and professional goals. Before you step into a meeting with anyone, it's important to think about what the listener really wants—which will be fundamentally different based on who they are and what role they have. Let's look at it through the lens of a few powerful stakeholders: a journalist, an investor, a customer, and a potential recruit.

How are all these audiences different? The answer requires an understanding of what their jobs entail and how they define success. This is where empathy comes into play. As a storyteller, it's important to adapt the story to meet the needs of the audience or to ask questions to learn more about their level of knowledge or their mindset on a given topic before diving in. Knowing about your audience doesn't in any way undermine your authenticity as a storyteller. It's perfectly possible to balance both mandates: being true to who you are, while also considering the person on the other side. That holds whether your audience is sitting next to you over coffee, across from you in a boardroom, or in the audience of a packed stadium.

"The story needs to be different depending on who you're telling it to, depending on who they are and their belief system, and you've got to care about syncing with that person," said Uri Hasson, a neuroscientist and psychologist at Princeton University. "We always think there's a way to tell a story that is universal, and we miss that."

As I mentioned earlier in this chapter, our internet era means that stories meant for one audience aren't necessarily going to be limited to that audience alone. If you say one thing to a journalist in an interview but something else entirely on your recruiting site, there's nothing stopping the reporter from noting the discrepancy. That can become embarrassing or worse, depending on how badly you're contradicting yourself and how substantive the contradictory information is. You need to ensure that anything you say or publish is consistent with your overall story, then find a balance between consistency and tailoring your story for each audience. If it sounds complicated, it's not. Just remain authentic and transparent and make certain that any story you tell is not wildly contradictory of what you've said before or offensive to any of your audiences. Don't forget to use SOAP!

In one-on-one conversations, taking time to understand the audience is crucial. With that in mind, let's look at the various stakeholders who will at some point be your audience and consider what version of the story they'd find most compelling. The challenge is that every individual and group is different, so there are no hard-and-fast rules. But this framework is intended to start you off.

What Investors Want

Let's tackle the "money people" first. It may seem daunting to pitch an investor, especially if you've watched an episode or two of *Shark Tank*. But take it from me, they are an easy mark compared to most other stakeholders. It's true that most investors will turn you down, because they can't invest in everyone they meet. The good ones will give you a quick response, enabling you to move on. But it is also the investor's job to take chances and occasionally say yes.

If you're pitching this audience, you need to convince them of two things to get them on board:

- You and/or your team are the right ones to build your company.
- Your company is targeting a large enough market, meaning it has a chance to generate a big enough return to make an investment worthwhile.

Investors, whether they admit it or not, are looking for a reason to believe in you, and they're looking for reasons to like you. When Laura Huang, a researcher from Harvard Business School, surveyed dozens of venture capitalists to understand how they decide whether to invest in one company versus another, she kept coming upon the notion of a "gut instinct." As she dug in, she found that most investors were looking for a connection to a founder, which was usually grounded in the founder's ability to tell their own story, not in any particularly sophisticated analysis of the financial prospects. She also found that this wasn't necessarily a bad thing. By relying on financial analysis alone, investors will be unlikely to see something that others will miss in the numbers, so gut instinct helps this group identify powerful stories and storytellers. (And powerful stories, as this book shows again and again, are crucial contributors to success for early-stage start-ups.)

For most founders, the ideal framework for a pitch should include these elements:

- An anecdote about a personal hardship or series of "trial-and-error" attempts that led to some moment of inspiration; that is, the "big idea" that solves a great problem identified by a company or team
- An explanation of how this big idea will make the world a better place
- A call to action around what this big idea will replace
- The steps the team will take—or already has taken, if it's a later-stage business—to get there, along with an explanation of how they'll combat key risks and challenges along the way

Investors recognize that the individual on the other side of the table is ultimately asking them for money. But the best pitches make them feel more than that. They want to be an ally on the journey. Hence a VC will most commonly end a call by saying, "Let me know how I can be helpful." My advice is to take them up on it! That's how to convince them to bet on you as opposed to one of the five other entrepreneurs they've met that day.

What Customers Want

For any business, landing a first sale (and continuing that trajectory) is of monumental importance. That's particularly true for young companies. Customers are taking a big risk when they buy an unproven or relatively new product or service. I cannot overstate this. As the old saying goes, no one ever got fired by choosing IBM. Choosing to buy from a well-established company helps guarantee the availability of ongoing support and the product's likely longevity, if not its excellence. By contrast, buying from a start-up is inherently risky.

In my years as an investor, I have spoken with plenty of buyers. What comes up repeatedly in these conversations is their need to believe that the risk is worth the reward. An incremental improvement in their bottom line is not enough; they're better off just sticking with the status quo and avoiding the switching costs and risk. Like investors, customers want to hear the big vision about what the technology or product can do, but they often want to be asked first about what they're looking for before the salesperson launches into the pitch. They do not want to hear someone educate them on something they already know.

Articulating downside risk can be very powerful. Customers will likely have a list of factors in their heads for why a product or service won't work. It's their job to be skeptical and to think ahead. Explicitly describing challenges as well as any strategies to combat or mitigate them can be helpful in allaying concerns. That builds trust and drives confidence.

What Users Want

This is a particularly tricky one, as the words "customer" and "user" can mean many things. By user, I typically mean the person using the product. Customers are often those buying the product—and the two are not always the same. In this case, I'll refer to the user throughout, whether or not that is the customer. Be it with a user, a customer, or both, the best strategy involves simple, precise, and direct communication, and I'll elaborate on why with a case study.

When the cybersecurity company CrowdStrike made global headlines in the summer of 2024 for a power outage, one of the largest in history, many communications professionals found its statement lackluster. Lulu Cheng Meservey, the former external affairs and communications chief at Activision Blizzard, spoke out publicly, describing the response on X as "WEAPONS-GRADE CORPO SPEAK."

The several-paragraph statement, which included sentences like "The issue has been identified . . . and a fix has been deployed," took no responsibility, according to Meservey. It was written throughout in the "passive voice," a grammatical construction that shifts the focus of a sentence from the subject to the recipient. The company also failed to say it was sorry or to provide clear direction to customers needing support. Those impacted by the outage included banks, hospitals, and airlines. The cost to Fortune 500 companies alone was more than $5 billion in direct losses, according to one insurer's analysis.

CrowdStrike CEO George Kurtz shared the statement in full on X, as outlets across the world raced to pick it up. After several months of questioning and criticism, a senior executive did eventually apologize.

Again, keep the language simple and bring users along for the ride. When things go right, let your customers know in a way that doesn't come off as overly self-promotional. Box's Aaron Levie from Chapter 2 is a perfect example of that, taking time out of his day to communicate directly with his users on X and informing them about broader topics in the zeitgeist—and not just his company's latest feature update. When there's a tough moment, apologize directly rather than using phrasing that absolves anyone of responsibility, like "Mistakes were made." In general customers do not want to engage with a brand that speaks like a robot, bombarding them with nonsensical corporate speak. I've never found evidence that anyone gravitates to that, let alone makes a purchasing decision because of it.

We'll dig far deeper into this topic in the coming chapters, particularly as we delve into "story-driven brands."

What Journalists Want

Not all journalists want the same thing: It very much depends on the beat they cover and the type of publication they write for. So, before speaking with any journalist, spend at least fifteen minutes on Google doing some homework about the stories they've recently written and the audience that the publication targets. Do not rely on anyone else to do this work for you, including ChatGPT!

If you want a more general rule of thumb, here's how Sarah Frier, the senior technology editor at *Bloomberg*, summarized what she (like most journalists) is looking for:

> In the broadest simplest terms, I want to learn. I want to understand it so deeply that I can explain it to someone else. That means if it's an announcement or piece of news, don't bullshit me, don't obscure the information with jargon, don't lie, don't just repeat the press release or corporate mission statement, because then I will just have to keep pressing you or others until I can learn the real motivation, real before and after picture. Because I have a responsibility to my readers [and] they trust me.

A few things to stress here. The journalist's responsibility is to readers and not to the person pitching them. So if you do not say anything interesting, they are by no means obligated to give you airtime. Many companies may feel that playing it safe and being defensive is the safest, perhaps because of their distrust of the press, but that strategy is not going to work for journalists. An executive interviewed for a story who doesn't say anything interesting probably will not be quoted.

While we're on the topic, context matters. A journalist, or anyone for that matter, will have difficulty grasping a company that doesn't fit into a preexisting market and can't be sized up against other bigger or smaller companies. I often see entrepreneurs and sales teams reeling off lists of things that are great about them, without explaining why they're better than what's come before. They'll say they offer "flexibility" or a "better experience," for instance, but compared to what? Very few ideas are truly novel or exist in a vacuum. Likewise, as we explored in prior chapters, the term "leader" is prevalent, but very few companies can back that up with real data.

Another handy tip to keep in mind: Most journalists, whether they'll admit it or not, are also looking to entertain their readers. To do that, they'll need spicy details. There's nothing wrong with that—unless of course, those anecdotes smack of lies or hyperbole. Do them a favor and share some insider moments that'll make people feel like they're in the room. In Frier's book on the history of Instagram, *No Filter*, those juicy details make the book sing. You learn that the idea for adding filters to photos came from the company CEO's then-girlfriend during a vacation in Mexico. Only after he saw her using these filters did he have the realization for what Instagram could and should be. "Then sitting on one of the outdoor lounge chairs with a beer beside him and his laptop open, he set about writing it into reality," Frier wrote in one of her opening pages. Those everyday moments transport the reader, connecting them with that moment in time and with the story being told on paper.

Relatedly, journalists are also often on the lookout for human-interest angles. I cannot stress this enough. It's no coincidence that many journalists choose to begin their news articles and features with a personal anecdote. One of my former editors—Matt Rosoff, who's had a long career in tech journalism—went as far as to stick a Post-it note on my desk with the line "People, Not Things." As humans, we are wired to be interested in other humans. Stories about humans will always generate more reader interest than stories focused only on some product or technology. Every time I hear a businessperson tell me that they want their product to speak for itself, I remind them that's not the way the world works. Products are usually not all that interesting to read about. What is compelling? Humans and the things that make them tick.

One last note about journalists before we move on. Journalism is not the same as marketing or public relations. Reporters are not paid mouthpieces for your company, so anyone who can help journalists cut through a company's "official" line is adding enormous value. Yes, that's a double-edged sword, since it means there's an incentive for the journalist to dig under a company's official messages. But I've seen firsthand how executives who are honest and direct with journalists will get far more positive attention than their competition. Better yet, they'll simply be left alone, because there's no juicy story to reveal.

A friend of mine, Alex Benson, recently took over as CEO of his company, inheriting some challenges in his new role in refining the company's scope. So his first act was to write a LinkedIn post titled "Introducing the Next Chapter" all about his intentions for his tenure and doubling down on a business model that he could see working while deprioritizing others. "While new market pursuits are always exciting (and attractive) they can also be distracting to what really matters," he wrote. "Like others before us, we stumbled here." Benson received plenty of public and private comments admiring his honesty, without any backlash.

Likewise, when Naomi Allen, CEO of Brightline, a kids' mental health company, made a difficult decision to conduct a layoff in light of a changing strategy, she penned a refreshingly honest blog post about it. In that post, she described the conditions leading to that moment and signed off by offering to help those impacted by the restructuring, who "are hands down some of the most talented professionals I've ever encountered in my career." She continued, "With their permission we've developed a list of the talented individuals at all levels from our clinical and corporate enterprise teams who are looking for their next roles and opportunities. If you are hiring, I would love nothing more than to make an introduction." Most companies would have downplayed this information, but Allen was open about it. Her post garnered tens of thousands of views in the first twenty-four hours and dozens of positive comments.

Again, there's no better defense against a negative perception of a brand or founding team, both internally and externally, than simply telling the truth.

What Employees and New Hires Want

Employers sometimes forget that the people they're interviewing have other options. Choosing the right role is imperative for any prospective employee. It's time-consuming, challenging, personally frustrating, and risky to look for a new job, so most people want to land in a role where they can stay for a few years or more. And they may also be looking to find personal fulfillment at work, as well as community and friendship.

Recruiters are some of the best storytellers in the business because their job is to convince people to leave their (oftentimes stable) roles. It's no surprise that most recruiters start their conversations with curiosity, by asking questions to determine if the person they're talking to is indeed poachable. If that's a yes, their next set of questions involves determining whether a potential recruit is a good fit for the role. It's their job to sell the new opportunity—ideally with a story that touches on the key elements that the recruit is looking for. In my industry, health technology, one of the top recruiters is also one of the most successful investors: Trevor Price. Price ran a recruiting firm (Oxeon) for years and started up a venture fund (Town Hall Ventures). He chalks up his success in both endeavors to his curiosity, his appetite for information, his network, and his storytelling skills.

One final note here on Gen Z. Increasingly, with younger candidates, recruiters tell me that employees want to believe in the company they're joining. Mission and purpose are everything. Studies from consulting firms like Deloitte have shown that Gen Z values salary alone less than any other generation in history.[7] So, a recruiter who fails to mention the company's "why" or doesn't zero in on a relatable personal story may not get past the first call.

Bottom line: Every time there's an opportunity to leverage storytelling to get ahead, think about the audience first. How can you tweak the story to ensure that it's more relevant to them? And if you're not entirely clear walking into the meeting or the interview, it never hurts to ask. Taking a moment to ask questions before diving in lets the audience feel that the encounter isn't purely transactional. Investors, employees, and customers are not going to walk into an interaction with the same intentions. To land each of these stakeholders, it's important to consider what their respective goals might be. As the executive coach and longtime technology executive Ellen Petry Leanse describes it, an ideal question here might be "What does great look like for you? Can you explain that to me?"

For an instant improvement in your storytelling skills, familiarize yourself with the "Big Four." These include authenticity, transparency and openness, empathy for the audience, and the element of surprise. A good story should feel natural for the simple reason that it's true. But that doesn't mean you can ramble without any concern for story structure—consider plot devices, as we discussed in the prior chapter, as well as elements like surprise—and pay attention to the audience. Consider the case of Nayar from HCL Technologies. Those who can wield all four skills in the workplace will have untold advantages over their peers, even bringing back sleeping companies from the brink of obscurity and moving them into a new era.

PART 2
STORIES THAT SELL

PART 2

CHAPTER 4

Storytelling Is for Everyone— Not Just CEOs

Great stories happen to those who can tell them.

—Ira Glass, radio personality

Claire Vo is the chief product officer at LaunchDarkly, a company that builds tools for software developers to help engineering teams be more productive. She's had a diverse career, working in a variety of industries, from medical technology to business software. For the past decade, she's made a name for herself as one of the most prominent product storytellers on the conference circuit and on social media. On X and LinkedIn, the social apps where she spends most of her time, thousands of people follow her for insights. LaunchDarkly also benefits from that. Because Vo is a known quantity in product circles, her team has an easier time bringing in and retaining talent. For years now, her social media presence has helped generate a halo effect for the companies she's worked for.

"Having a visible technical or product leader can be really powerful for companies," Vo explained. "That's especially true for people who are thinking deeply about the actual craft, and who can build a narrative around that." In other words, Vo's social media presence makes it easier for her to connect with people who similarly care about improving their product chops—their "craft"—and that serves to expand her network and burnish her company's reputation.

The bulk of social media content generated by employees falls flat because it rehashes pre-written messaging, with plenty of hashtags, sometimes generated by sales and marketing teams and fed to employees to copy and paste into their social feeds. Vo's posts bear no resemblance to that. No one is telling her what to say or writing on her behalf. She uses storytelling as a vehicle to share what she's learned in her career. Most of her stories combine humor and lessons learned with a tone of vulnerability. One she often shares involves how she became obsessed with technology and coding at an early age but opted to get a liberal arts degree instead. That education taught her about the power of a good story, and she's grateful for it. Another involves her struggles earlier in her career to feel like she belonged, particularly as she got promoted into more senior roles, and how she learned to walk into a room with confidence. These days, she doesn't spend as much time hoping that others will validate her professionally.

These personal stories have a powerful effect on her audience. Because they feel on some level that they know her, Vo feels they are more likely to trust the products that she's building too. And because they respect her acumen as a product leader, they assume she must have made a smart choice about the company she joined.

Her company also gets a brand boost from her visibility, which is a major win for its sales and marketing division. Since embracing social media, Vo has been featured in posts celebrating women in technology. She's been interviewed for her product prowess in popular newsletters with hundreds of thousands of subscribers, such as *Lenny's Newsletter*, which LaunchDarkly's customers are likely to read. And she's been featured on countless popular customer podcasts and blogs, which is good for sales.

Vo's example proves that you don't need to be a CEO or even a manager to benefit from storytelling. Those early in their careers can do it too. To get an idea of where to start, hop on X and browse the conversation around #producttwitter. This hashtag is intended for anyone who works in a product-management role or aspires to do so, primarily (but not limited to) those in the technology industry. Hot tip: There are similar hashtags for virtually every role and sector—#marketingtwitter, #salestwitter, #engineeringtwitter, #climatetwitter, #AItwitter, and #healthcaretwitter to name a few. And that's just on X, as there's an ever-growing list of alternative social media apps. Introduce yourself, and you'll likely gain a bunch of new followers in no time.

Vo is emblematic of a new trend among talented employees in today's workplace. Outside the CEO or the appointed spokespeople for the business, a new generation of up-and-comers are building up their own brands in ways that serve their long-term career goals as well as their companies' interests. As I've discovered in my own research, a lot of this activity is happening because the employees have taken the initiative themselves, not waiting to be told to do so by senior leadership. Indeed, many of them are doing it without explicit permission: Plenty of the people I interviewed said management doesn't officially condone these activities—but isn't saying no to them either.

I'll note that there are ways for employees to share stories in closed, private forums, but for the purposes of this chapter I'll spend a lot of time talking about social media, because it remains a hot-button issue for many companies. For better or worse, we live in a digital world, and companies increasingly operate this way too, particularly those that are fully remote.

One of my favorite little-known examples of successful employee storytelling is from Mitel, a telco based in Ontario, Canada. The company kept a relatively low profile until a new chief marketing officer, Martyn Etherington, came along in 2012. Etherington, during his three-year tenure, encouraged his employees to be on social media, and he drove the following way up. When he started, around the spring of 2012, just 30 employees were actively talking about Mitel on Twitter, LinkedIn, or Facebook; by November of that year, that number had skyrocketed to 1,600. Etherington knew that many companies acted in the opposite way, even downright banning social media at work, but he felt strongly that his more open approach would give the company its best shot of competing in a crowded business software market.

Mitel was an early pioneer, but these days it's not uncommon for companies to disseminate playbooks to their employees on how to use social media. Many companies recognize now that people will post about their personal lives, so it's not uncommon to see people adding to their profile that opinions are their own and not their employers' to reduce liability. There are limits to that though, as many companies will discourage or downright prohibit posting about controversial, sensitive, or taboo topics, particularly if they're in professional services or any industry where that might result in lost customers or revenue. When it comes to posts related to professional milestones or developments, there's an increasing trend for companies to be highly encouraging.

Based out of Europe, one company called Synesthesia has a dedicated Slack channel where employees can see, discuss, and amplify each other's posts. Training sessions and manuals on how to do social media right are still commonplace across companies, but there are also now software products dedicated to supporting employees in sharing their companies' messages on social media, including EveryoneSocial and Bambu. PwC uses community-management software to share approved social posts that employees can reshare on LinkedIn and X, according to former communications director Kathy King. Being such a large organization, PwC doesn't have time to do one-on-one training with everyone. But King said employees understand that they should work with the communications teams when posting and stick to the high-trust "do no harm" mandate.

Case studies like these are inspirational because they show how successful employee storytelling can be, particularly when employees share anecdotes rather than copying and pasting from templates. But most companies haven't demonstrated anywhere near that much proficiency, and even fewer have prioritized it meaningfully. I see that many Fortune 500 companies today have some kind of official brand profile on LinkedIn and X run by a team of social media managers but little employee engagement beyond that. Some of that comes down to a lack of guidance and education, but there are also more guardrails at publicly traded companies because of Securities and Exchange Commission (SEC) rules and fluctuations in stock prices.

Social media still gets a bad rap in a corporate context. Because of that, employers might have a big opportunity here to encourage their workforces to use social media in ways that aren't purely a distraction and time suck. It's true that opening the door to social media might compel people to browse recipes and watch TikTok dances during work lulls, but there's also the potential to leverage these platforms to build an authentic connection with users and customers. In Vo's case, it also helped her company retain and attract talent, as well as build its brand among its customer set.

From what I've seen, the benefits far outweigh the risks of someone wasting a bit of time during work hours or straying from approved messaging in a counterproductive way. There are also golden opportunities for individuals like Vo to begin with a social media presence and, over time, build a reputation as a true expert in their discipline or industry.

So where to start when evaluating how to use storytelling in any role? Let's explore that.

What Are the Categories of Storytelling for Employees?

Here's how I'd break down the ideal buckets of storytelling for people who are not the CEO or an officially designated spokesperson, whether they are junior employees, mid-level managers, or senior executives within the organization. The intended audience here is not the company's leadership, as they might have a different set of rules about what they can post, particularly if they run a publicly traded company.

These buckets might not align 100 percent with official company messaging, although they can if the marketing team formalizes them into a program. Either way, pursuing storytelling in these categories will have a positive impact, both for the individual and the company, when done thoughtfully and with purpose.

- *Thought leadership* involves sharing a perspective about a theme or sector that is insightful and informative and, ideally, hasn't been widely articulated before. Bonus points for a spicy or controversial take that's still permissible. (For those posting who are employees and not the CEO, I'll stress here that it's probably not worth getting fired over a take that's *too* spicy, so use your best judgment, keeping in mind the company's guidelines.) Storytelling can play a major role as I've found that the most powerfully articulated pieces begin with a personal anecdote that illustrates the larger point.
- *Insights and advice* about a specific craft, such as the tweets on #producttwitter, remain extremely popular in industry subgroups. On LinkedIn, which is at its core a tool for recruiting and job-related updates, content about recruiting and workplace culture can do particularly well. Stories—for instance, about how an individual navigated a tricky situation in the workplace or parlayed learning a new skill into a promotion—can humanize advice and make it actionable.
- *Nonwork experiences* that have impacted an individual personally as well as professionally, such as navigating pregnancy and the postpartum period or caring for an

aging parent, can be extremely powerful for any audience to learn from.

- *Career realizations* referring to big on-the-job milestones, such as a decision to change job functions or become a manager for the first time, are extremely useful for an employees' peer group. I recommend concluding stories, like Vo often does, by sharing lessons learned in the process.

- *Breaking into an industry* is seemingly a niche topic, but I've seen plenty of junior-level investors, medical residents at top hospitals, and journalists build social followings by sharing how they were able to land their jobs. When they supplement that by posting links to open roles at other organizations, they make it easier for people who are involved in a job hunt to follow in their footsteps. Those individuals might also have success sharing the inside scoop of what it's really like to work in a specific role, because it's often a mystery to those who haven't done it before.

- *Breakdowns of complicated topics* are a personal favorite of mine. It can be a great fit for those who work in fields like artificial intelligence, medicine, robotics, or anything else that's complicated and very technical. Consider finding ways to share what you do while making it accessible to people. My favorite example here is Ryan Petersen from the company Flexport. While not a junior employee—he's the CEO—he is the most adept of anyone I've seen at explaining wonky supply chain logistics in ways that are exciting for the mainstream, often by starting out with a story, for instance, an observation about the lack of ships in a port might be the starting point for a detailed discussion of supply chain logistics globally.

Employees pursuing one or more of these strategies might experience some hesitation or pushback from the company—namely, the communications team. But I've seen plenty of individuals navigate that successfully and emerge on top.

Brian Chiglinsky, a former speechwriter who worked with the federal government, described how Andy Slavitt, the former head of the Centers for Medicare and Medicaid (CMS), had an active presence on Twitter with hundreds of thousands of followers. Due to the culture of CMS, Chiglinsky told me, that "made a lot of people nervous." Slavitt went ahead and continued to build an engaged following by sharing stories from his job or making health policy more accessible, which his followers appreciated. The administration followed his social media account closely. When the tables turned and the Republicans "came into office gunning for the Affordable Care Act," Chiglinsky recalled, Slavitt became a huge asset rather than a potential liability.

"It was enormously helpful to have a leader who had built an authentic public voice while others worked behind the scenes with lawyers," he told me. "What might have caused a little stress in message discipline pre-2017 ended up being an important part of the strategy to save health coverage for millions of people."

Slavitt proved to be an influential voice in health reform. But to be fair, there are also counterexamples where a communications team's worst fears are realized. For some businesses, tracking social media conversations alone is a massive headache that involves reallocating resources away from more important activities. Imagine having to monitor the social media output of thousands or even tens of thousands of employees, particularly if you're concerned about things like breaches of confidential information, offensive speech, or even illegality. In highly regulated sectors like health care, finance, and law, that is a very real concern (of course, services and software have been released to do just this, but it's rarely a perfect science).

Furthermore, any writing or posts shared by employees can blow back on companies—even if they aren't shared outside the company at first. Remember the case of James Damore, a Google employee who wrote a memo about the company's "ideological echo chamber" in response to its diversity program? Among other things, Damore wrote that biological differences can explain male-to-female disparities, and he shared that in his experience women tend to be more social, artistic, and prone to neuroticism. While Damore never published the memo publicly, a coworker leaked it to the site Gizmodo, and the press blowback was both swift and furious. Damore was fired as a result. One could easily imagine a scenario where something like this happens again to another company, except the employee posts their wild theories on LinkedIn or in a Substack newsletter.

Similarly, dozens of cases have since hit the news in which people have been fired for their social media posts, including consultants who revealed confidential new clients on Instagram and schoolteachers who shared stories revealing their hard-partying ways. In a classic example from 2016, a Yelp employee was fired for posting about her low pay package.

In follow-up posts, she shared that it happened because she breached her company's terms of conduct by discussing her compensation publicly.

Yet, regardless of all these risks, I still side with the camp that feels it's better for companies to be tolerant (or even encouraging) of employees trying to build an audience externally. But every company is different. So here are the two questions I'd ask before making a final determination: What does the company stand to lose and gain from its employees taking on more public roles? And how can companies mitigate the risks while maximizing the benefits?

I'll start by listing some of the positives that I believe workplaces should consider, because I believe they outweigh the potential downsides. I say "workplaces" rather than referring to a specific role, as communications, talent/human resources, legal departments, CEOs, and other functions should reflect on these issues:

1. *Building trust with the public:* We live in a time when executives are expected to be visible, and that expectation is increasingly trickling down to more junior staff. The public is more likely to trust a company when they see good people working there, and that's even more true if they interact with those good people and see that they are real and relatable. A company that comes off as a nameless, faceless brand doesn't exactly inspire confidence in its target audiences. Communications experts tell me that there's more encouragement than ever before for noncorporate spokespeople to get out there. "Increasingly, a diversified bench

of storytellers is being driven from the top, with boards and CEOs placing a high priority on these practices as core elements of a corporation's mission and values, and key lenses for decision-making," said Anthony Steel, head of Steel Communications.

2. *Building trust internally with employees:* Companies that encourage their employees to have a voice and support them in the effort inspire trust in both directions. It's meaningful to employees when their managers show that they trust them to make good decisions rather than micromanaging. When managers say, "We trust you to build your brand without crossing the line," it goes a long way toward encouraging and retaining talented people with big aspirations—the kind of people companies should endeavor to keep around for as long as possible. Baylor University, in its 2023 analysis of the topic, describes micromanagement as a major culprit in "eroding trust and creating an atmosphere of anxiety" in workforces today.

3. *Hiring:* When a well-known individual in a company reaches out to a prospective hire and says there's an opening on his or her team, that has an impact. Hearing from someone you admire is far more effective than having a random recruiter reach out about a role at a company you've never heard of. A potential recruit who has been following this individual for a while might even feel a little starstruck. That's what can happen when operators become storytellers and, ultimately, influencers within their own fields. It's hard to understate how powerful this is for recruiting. It helps the employee build value and increase their following,

and it improves the company's chances of bringing in the best talent, so it's a win-win.

4. *Fundraising:* Investors will look at the most high-profile operators' social media feeds for "signals" about which companies are the strongest talent hubs. In theory, talented people have lots of options and could work anywhere—so why that company? If an employee has a large social media following, that's a potential signal that the company they work for has something going for it. That person is more public, so likely has visibility into a lot of different companies in their industry.

5. *Building buzz:* My friend Jody Tropeano runs content and programming at one of the biggest health-care conferences in the country, HLTH. When she's looking for new talent to come and speak, she works through the long list of applications on her desk. In selecting the best speakers, she looks at their social media feeds. Have they shared anything insightful or provocative of late? Are they tapping into the zeitgeist? One way for companies to get more exposure is to encourage their teams—and not just the CEO—to share their views publicly. Likewise, I have my own podcast and newsletter, *Second Opinion*, and the first thing I do when considering a new guest is determine whether they've said anything interesting or insightful lately on social media. That's a decent indicator that they'll be a spicy guest, which will drive following for any media property.

This kind of encouragement from the top creates a culture where talent at all levels feels supported, and that decreases the likelihood of turnover at the organization. "Giving people opportunities to rise and shine will encourage them to stay," said Sarah Jones, a health-care executive who's been involved in the conference circuit for most of her career.

This all sounds like a no-brainer, but surely there are other risks we haven't discussed. Let's walk through them, and I'll also share a few thoughts on potential mitigation strategies.

Leaking company secrets or harming the business: An employee could share something online that harms the business's objectives or reveals company secrets. I can't think of too many super-public examples of employees spilling company secrets on social media, but it certainly happens. Elon Musk is a high-profile case study on what not to do. After he posted information that was material to Tesla's stock price on Twitter, the SEC fined him tens of millions of dollars. That said, he's also one of the kings of social media, so perhaps in his case he viewed the risk as worthwhile—and even tens of millions is a drop in the bucket for him.

How to mitigate the risk: An employee going rogue on social media is always a possibility, but you can reduce the risk by simply making clear where employees should draw the line. There's also common sense. Companies can make clear where they draw the line at offsites or all-hands meetings or on Slack or Teams. Employees should be made aware of what they can and cannot share. Other companies might guide their employees to avoid stepping into topics that are overly political, although that can be harder to do given that employees (in the United States, the United Kingdom, France, Spain, and many other countries) have the right to make political statements on their own time, outside work. Many companies will take this a step further by publishing a code of conduct on their internal websites, which includes anti-discrimination policies and needs to be baked into any officially issued social media guidance. Workforces can and should be inclusive of different viewpoints but also draw the line when a type of speech is harmful or offensive to an individual and/or group.

These topics are certainly complex, but I'd argue that most of these questions are primarily related to fringe cases. Most people can either effectively follow very simple guidelines or don't need them at all. And banning social media altogether is not very realistic given the social-media-saturated world that we live in. Pew Research Center found that most people will use social media at work, most commonly to take a break to scroll mindlessly or connect with friends. But social media use is not just recreational; staying in touch with others in the field or connecting with experts also contributes to employees' productivity. So rather than banning social media use outright, most companies would do well to think about how to set clear guidelines, then regularly offer educational sessions and training to employees on an opt-in basis in case of any confusion.

Leaking talent: If talented individuals at an organization are more exposed to opportunities because they've successfully built a brand and a following on social media, they may get poached by competitors and leave.

How to mitigate the risk: There is not much you can do to prevent talent that wants to leave from doing so. In my opinion, talent leaving should be encouraged. One example from my own network is Dhruv Vasishtha, a product leader in the health-tech space, who became so well-known on X for his perspectives on the sector that he landed a coveted venture scout role at one of the top venture capital firms, Bessemer Venture Partners. Vasishtha will now invest alongside Bessemer in companies that he networks with. He told me that the opportunity would never have come about if not for his social media presence, because it helped him expand his network and share his point of view in ways that would not have been possible without it.

Companies that lead with a high-trust culture will also find they're better able to retain employees. One study on the neuroscience of trust found that employees at high-trust companies reported enjoying their jobs 60 percent more and experiencing 40 percent less burnout at work. And that plays a role in reducing turnover.

Are These Activities Even Allowed?

Even if employee activity on social media isn't officially sanctioned, many communications leaders will see the value. Sarah Jones, a health executive who's long maintained an active social media profile, said that the smaller companies she's worked at have tended to be permissive and unconcerned about her public presence. The vibe she got from them was along the lines of "Sure, good luck."

However, larger companies may take a more conservative approach, explicitly requiring approvals before employees can share professional stories publicly. When Jones landed at a public company, by way of an acquisition, she learned that firsthand. She suddenly needed to find someone on the marketing and communications team to greenlight the materials she wanted to present at an upcoming conference. Making matters worse, getting that approval sometimes took weeks, but the conference required an immediate yes or no. That meant she had to slow down her public appearances and other brand-building efforts while working there.

Jones said that other employees in the same boat shouldn't see it as a total loss. She recommends finding opportunities to showcase communications skills to smaller groups or teams at work. That could take the form of an internal presentation. For some employees, a more restrictive company policy is also an opportunity to hit the pause button, do some thinking about the true value of having a public presence, and consider which are the right stories to share in the process.

If this isn't an appealing strategy, Jones warns that not every battle can be fought and won inside companies. Sometimes culture is unmovable, at least without years and years of effort, and there may be a better fit elsewhere for someone whose passions include having a strong public presence.

How to Take That First Step

Despite the myriad benefits, most people who aren't in leadership roles or on executive teams don't take the time to build their own brands. So let's take a step back to consider why more employees below the C-suite aren't leveraging social media platforms to tell their own stories. From conversations with dozens of people in my network about this topic—folks who continue to be passive listeners or avoid the spotlight entirely—it appears that this reluctance comes down to a few factors:

1. They lack experience and comfort with the medium.
2. They fear what their bosses and peers will say.

3. They are concerned that their thoughts and insights aren't interesting enough to deserve attention.

4. They lack positive examples at work of individuals who are successful on social media.

5. They've been told not to.

Dealing with the first three points often comes down to starting small and taking manageable steps forward. That might mean setting realistic goals for experimentation with storytelling in a variety of formats: giving talks, sharing low-risk posts on social media, or addressing a group of peers and then seeking feedback. For the fourth point, the next step might involve looking further afield—for instance, finding individuals in similar roles at different companies who are prolific on social media and following them to watch how they do it. Over time, engaging with those individuals one-on-one by responding to their content might be a valuable way to build a professional network. Getting started will take some trial and error and some deep thinking to figure out what to say and what to be known for and why. From there, you will need to take time to reflect on what a potential audience would find valuable to learn.

Take the marketing executive Jenna Hannon as an example. Hannon had worked at a variety of high-growth companies in her career, including a formative experience at Uber. But she had kept a relatively low profile for a variety of reasons, mostly because she had no clear reason to build an external brand. Her thinking changed when she decided to start a company of her own.

Her start-up was in the field of financial software, so she tasked herself with getting on the phone with as many chief financial officers as possible for user research. Before she even started, Hannon was concerned that CFOs who looked at her profile on LinkedIn might reject her request for a thirty-minute phone call. They didn't know her personally, and she had no background in finance. Her hunch proved correct. She struck out on most of her requests to connect, mostly getting ghosted or receiving a polite but firm "No, not at this time."

So how could Hannon get these CFOs on the phone? During a walk around her neighborhood, she recalled thinking to herself, "I worked at Uber, one of the fastest-growing companies of all time, and I helped launch one of their most exciting business lines." Hannon was one of the earliest employees at Uber Eats, the company's food-delivery business now used by millions of people. She saw an opportunity to build up her profile in a novel way and make herself far more interesting to these hard-to-get CFOs. So she got home and spent hours writing up a post about the process of starting Uber Eats and all the setbacks her team faced along the way. She recollected how few people from Uber wanted to work on the Eats team at first, how it started with low expectations, and how powerful its growth marketing engine became. Her post started off with a deceptively simple title:

From \$0 → \$1B
My story at Uber Eats

She included a photo at the top showing her former Uber company badge, and she made the post super easy to skim. As a marketer, she knew that many people would read her post quickly via their smartphones, probably while juggling myriad other tasks, so she wanted it to be as accessible as possible.

As soon as she hit "publish," she went to grab coffee with her boyfriend. Within seconds, Hannon started to feel her phone vibrating in her pocket. She turned to him and said, "I think I just posted a banger." While she sipped her cappuccino, her LinkedIn continued to blow up, with hundreds of comments and likes.

After letting the whole thing simmer for a few days, she went back to her original CFO outreach campaign. Within days, her hit rate skyrocketed: Most of the executives she reached out to were responding.

What I appreciated most about Hannon's strategy was that she took a moment to really reflect on what was unique about her background. She also considered the potential audience she was trying to reach: CFOs. If she wanted to learn from them, what could she share in return? Hannon could plausibly imagine a CFO being curious about the inside story of Uber Eats, and her theory proved correct.

That's the power of storytelling: It can incite curiosity to turn a no into a yes. For those considering a similar strategy, start with a question like the one Hannon pondered on her walk: "What insights and what professional experiences do I have that others do not?"

A Caveat: Pick Your Format

The last thing I'll share is that storytelling truly does work best when you lean into what feels natural. The leaders you met throughout this chapter preferred different mediums. Hannon gravitated to LinkedIn. Vo shines on X, in part because she's become very adept through years of practice crafting short-form stories. Jones is a natural on stage, so she focuses on the conference circuit.

I see authenticity break down most often in the moments when the individual feels pushed to do something that does not feel natural to them. Authentic storytelling, or really any form of communication, is most effective when the medium and the message are both a good fit for the person making the delivery. There is no need to be a jack of all trades to succeed in storytelling. If you take away one lesson from this chapter, let it be that the best storytellers are most effective *because they do it in their own way.*

CHAPTER 5

Management by Story

Why is culture so important to a business? Here is a simple way to frame it. The stronger the culture, the less corporate process a company needs. When the culture is strong, you can trust everyone to do the right thing.

—Brian Chesky, CEO of Airbnb

I n June 2005, Steve Jobs kicked off a commencement speech at Stanford University with this iconic opening: "Today, I want to tell you three stories from my life. That's it. Just three stories." He went on to reflect on some of the most important themes of his life, reminding the graduating students in the room to follow their own path instead of the one that's expected of them. Do that, he advised them, and it'll all make sense in the end. Because he was nearing the end of his life, this advice seemed particularly poignant. If you haven't watched this video online, do it now; you'll thank me later.[1]

To recap it for you, Jobs's first story involved his decision to drop out of college, in part to ease the financial burden on his parents. Because of his abiding love of learning, he stuck around campus for another eighteen months to audit classes that inspired him. He did that with no motivation other than to pursue his interests, knowing it would not make him any more employable once he started to look for a job. His school—Reed College in Portland, Oregon—had a well-regarded calligraphy course, so Jobs stopped by. The course fascinated him, and it turned into a lifelong obsession with calligraphy that became one of the major sources of inspiration for the graphic design for Apple's personal computer that launched in the 1980s. Apple fans widely credited the Macintosh as the first machine with truly beautiful typography, and it was an instant hit.

For Jobs, a seemingly random series of events turned out to have a great deal of significance. The lesson: Make decisions without a clear purpose in mind, purely for the sake of learning or joy, and that decision may become useful in unforeseen ways.

The second story involved the moment the board of directors fired him from Apple. The experience could have demotivated and destroyed him. But instead of moping, Jobs picked himself back up and decided to start over with a new venture called NeXT. He described the years that followed as among the most creative periods of his life. You probably know what happened next (no pun intended). Apple later acquired Jobs's new company, which brought him back into the CEO seat. If he hadn't been fired, Jobs never would have needed to start over. And if he hadn't started over, he may never have ended up back at the helm of Apple at just the right moment. He concluded by advising the students in the audience, "Don't settle." Jobs may not have had the option, given that leaving Apple wasn't his choice at the time.

But he learned, and imparted to his audience, that life is too short to stay complacent. With his return to Apple, Jobs took nothing for granted, swiftly shutting down projects that weren't performing, aligning teams into one functional department to destroy silos, and focusing on the company's core strengths.

In his final and most powerful story, he described his cancer diagnosis and his growing recognition that his time on earth was limited. All of that meant that he no longer needed to sweat the small stuff, spending time on minor things that he didn't care about. He advised the students not to waste time following someone else's dream.

Many of us are already familiar with these three stories. They're legendary, even years after Jobs's death. And, full credit to Jobs, these stories barely scratch the surface of what you think you know about him. You've probably heard stories about the former Apple CEO from dozens of biographies, biopics, and media articles. His name is synonymous with an obsessive attention to design, exacting standards, and a relentless focus on delighting users. Countless stories in biographies about him recount how he would get irrationally angry with colleagues at the office for failing to meet his expectations, and his commitment to his work came at a personal cost. We know he prioritized work for long stretches, damaging personal relationships, including with his daughter Lisa.

If you're aware of all these stories about Steve Jobs, a person you've never met, that's intentional. Jobs was an extremely powerful storyteller, and he leveraged narrative as a vehicle to communicate ideas. Rather than just telling people what he believed, he demonstrated it constantly through personal stories. By all accounts, the tactic was highly effective. Users understood that the moment they opted to purchase an Apple device, they were signing up for both quality and attention to detail. Likewise, Apple employees understood exactly what the job entailed as soon as they put on their badge. If you didn't agree with that, there were plenty of other places to work.

My friend Robin Goldstein worked at Apple for over twenty years, slowly rising through the ranks and eventually finding herself in the legal and regulatory department of the health team. She's the type of person you'd expect to thrive at Apple: A huge proponent of storytelling and a published author on the topic, Goldstein gets her kicks out of tackling hard problems with the entrepreneurs who come into her orbit. She's been trained in the school of user-centered design, a set of method-ologies related to approaching problems with insight into user need (the opposite of building a technology because it's cool and then figuring out what it can be used for). Some of her more fre-quent prompts to friends and colleagues in her orbit, including those who dive straight into the technical or scientific weeds of their business, typically include "But why are we doing that?" and "Whom are we building that for?"

While at Apple, she primarily worked under Steve Jobs, although she also stuck around for the early years of the Tim Cook era. She didn't spend much time with Jobs one-on-one, but she was struck by how much storytelling drove Apple's culture daily. Somehow, people at all levels of the organization under-stood what was on-brand for Apple and what was not. Apple HR seemed to understand that simply handing employees a checklist of values at orientation was unlikely to motivate them: It needed to give them stories they could believe in, so they could orient themselves to the Apple culture quickly.

Goldstein relates one moment she'll never forget. One afternoon, a few years before her 2017 departure from the company, a group of her peers assembled to discuss a health-monitoring feature for the Apple Watch. The question came up of how to balance user experience with a variety of legal and regulatory hurdles. As Goldstein recalls, the long-standing employees from Apple got to work discussing how to collaborate with regulators to make that (not yet released) new feature frictionless for consumers to use, without requiring a doctor's sign-off. Something like that had never been done, and it would not be easy.

Once the group started getting into the challenges, one of the lawyers (a new employee at the company) scoffed at the hurdles associated with the project. He then uttered the fateful words "Users will just have to live with it." There was a collective gasp. This attitude was *not* Apple. And it would never be Apple.

That lawyer didn't last long at the company.

Why did Goldstein and her peers understand what was expected of them in that moment, years after Jobs's passing? Because that team had heard countless stories about the primacy of user experience. They innately knew getting the feature right was worth spending the extra time, even if it had never been done before. They'd all heard how Jobs himself would spend weekends at appliance stores, studying the white, clean lines of the Cuisinarts, looking for inspiration to make the Apple user experience that little bit better. As Goldstein puts it, these cultural values ensured that "all of us employees recognized that we were rowing the same boat in the same direction." There would never be a time when the user experience wasn't pristine—and if that happened, Apple would have failed.

This phenomenon is what I like to call "management by story."

I spoke with another longtime Apple employee, Randy Nelsen, who transitioned from NeXT and later to Apple University, the employee education arm that Jobs set up in 2008. The aim was to inform employees about Apple's history, technology, and culture, as well as to teach employees this concept of "management by story"—or, as Nelsen referred to it, "management by culture." The two terms mean essentially the same thing, although storytelling is a vehicle to share cultural values. Apple University targets managers, and most attendees are directors or vice presidents and above.

"A deep test for employees was the question, 'What are you doing when we [leadership] aren't around?'" Nelsen recalled. "The idea was that every employee would know what to do, because attention to detail was everything."

How was storytelling useful in creating "management by culture"? Well, it was crucial to Jobs because he wanted to create a company where everyone, at every level of the organization, both understood and internalized their shared goals. No one was paying lip service; this approach had to be both authentic and real.

These techniques were powerful as Apple was building and scaling its business. I'd argue that these kinds of techniques are even more important today. Since Apple first became a household name, selling its devices to millions of people, companies of all sorts have become even more diverse and global than ever before. Now they must get everyone rowing the boat in the same direction amid language barriers and cultural differences, with teams constantly shifting between real-life interactions and Zoom. Not an easy task!

Apple is one of those companies today, with employees based around the world. At the time of this writing, its website featured profiles of a dozen or so employees from different offices and retail locations, all from a variety of roles, levels, and backgrounds. Navigate through each of these profiles and click on a photo to learn more about the individuals' stories and backgrounds. Linked to each? One of Apple's corporate values. One example is a hardware engineer who chose Apple because of its commitment to user experience (a value). Another is a program manager who faced super-tough obstacles to create more sustainable products but persevered nonetheless (another value).

Apple's approach works because it brings these values to life by linking them to *real people with real stories*. I cannot tell you how many company websites I have reviewed that merely list their values in a press release or on a web page rather than connecting them to any real humans at the organization. We sometimes forget that most companies (unless they're shell companies) are collections of real people pursuing shared goals, not sets of abstract values. These values can also be subtly incorporated into internal communications strategies, for instance in how the company encourages employees to approach projects or even how it names its conference rooms.

Another of my favorite examples is Amazon, which strongly values written documents instead of presentations. So it encourages employees, instead of producing PowerPoint decks, to present each new product idea in the form of a press release, which often includes a quote from an imaginary customer or from a business leader about how this new product will move their company forward. These values can show up in ways big and small—but they shouldn't live in the form of a list that people gloss over and immediately forget.

Don't Just "Tick the Box"

Today's increasingly polarized world is forcing many business leaders to think far more deeply about how to communicate what they stand for. Do they support a political candidate? Where do they side on a particular issue? Is there anything they should say about a war happening in another country? This is some of the most difficult work that a CEO, head of communications, or head of people will navigate in their tenure, and for that reason, it's critical that they spend real time thinking about how to tackle it.

Taking a step back and communicating with employees (otherwise known as internal comms) often gets deprioritized at many companies. And these very same companies are then surprised when employees lash out because they're not satisfied. Successfully launching an internal comms program doesn't just mean sharing positive press and mentions about a company from the internet and asking employees to like or reshare them on Slack. It means starting with the basics and asking hard questions, like

- What do we stand for and what would we take a stand against?
- What is our mission, and whom are we serving?
- As we scale, how do we retain our values?

- How would a new employee understand our values, especially at a time of high turnover?
- How would our values land with people working across diverse geographies and operating in hybrid environments?

One approach that companies have taken is to start with a set of corporate values. In some cases, that's a box-ticking exercise. In others, it involves deep work to consider what the company truly stands for and then figure out ways to ensure that shows up every day. These statements are then often shared both internally and externally.

While it might seem like a recent phenomenon, the trend of publicly issuing corporate value statements has been around for a long time. Some of the first-known examples date back to the 1940s. One of the earliest examples was written by Robert Wood Johnson and submitted to the Johnson & Johnson (J&J) board in 1943. Known as the J&J credo, it describes how the company has a responsibility "to the patients, doctors and nurses, to mothers and fathers and all others who use our products and services."[2] Other key ideas included in the credo involve J&J fostering an inclusive work environment and remaining committed to supporting good works. Most companies today have followed J&J and have their values laid out somewhere, usually on their website or on job boards.

As an aside, if you find a company compelling—whether you're a prospective customer or prospective employee—I recommend taking a closer look at their values. Most are generic, but in some cases you might be surprised by what you read. And that provides a strong insight into what the company truly cares about.

The exercise of coming up with a company's list of corporate values can be useful, if done thoughtfully and intentionally. Most companies today will do this and revisit the list at somewhat regular intervals to ensure the values are still relevant. For most CEOs, discussing corporate values has even become a preferred topic of conversation. I've seen many companies use any PR opportunity to discuss their values, whether an interviewer asks about them or not. CEOs have also written dozens of business and management books on the topic, with a wide variance in quality.

So we can all agree that CEOs like to "talk the talk" when it comes to their values. Far more questionable is whether they actually "walk the talk."

Researchers from the Sloan School of Management at the Massachusetts Institute of Technology (MIT) have spent years systematically studying this very question. From those efforts, the researchers built a data-driven analysis called "Culture 500," which includes an interactive tool, meant to reflect "how companies measure up on culture in the eyes of employees." That research is updated on an annual basis, as more companies develop value statements and share them with the world.[3]

Teams of MIT Sloan researchers have found that certain values tend to come up on company websites more than others. Terms like "innovation," "customer," "respect," and "integrity" are particularly popular with companies today. Less common terms include "grit" and "authenticity." As discussed earlier, most storytellers will agree that "authenticity" is the most important trait in determining success or failure, so I was particularly fascinated to see how rarely it gets mentioned.

Researchers from the university then cross-referenced the most used terms against more than one million Glassdoor reviews to see if employees agreed that the company's culture aligned with its stated goals. The results were disappointing. They found zero correlation between the companies' professed cultural values and employees' experiences of how well their companies lived up to those values. I'll repeat that: zero correlation. The report concluded that articulating these values is a waste of time unless they're specific, actionable, and grounded in context.

Apple stands out as better than most because it ties its values to the everyday experiences of real employees, using storytelling as a vehicle. Another company that does it well, according to the researchers, is the biotech giant Biogen. Rather than just referring to itself as "pioneering," it describes what pioneering means in practice, because the term can mean different things to different people. Pioneering, to Biogen, means that employees shouldn't refrain from asking tough questions and should test each other's assumptions. It also refers to being a pioneer in new treatments, such as in disease areas like multiple sclerosis and Alzheimer's disease. To reiterate its commitment, the company uses the term throughout its messaging, including in press releases to announce new medical breakthroughs, as well as on its website to describe its mission and culture.

Another company that stands out is Netflix, which describes "courage" as a core value (not a particularly common one). On its website, the company elaborates on exactly what courage might mean in daily working life. Being courageous, according to Netflix, includes being open to failure and taking risks when you've got high conviction, even if a higher-up disagrees. At Netflix, one encouraged practice involves putting an item on a meeting agenda to ask for direct feedback from the group. People can be polite and not reveal what they really think; that slows down important work or creates waste because teams spend time on work they don't believe in. Per Netflix, feedback must be actionable and accessible, allowing the person on the other side to accept or disregard it. The key for these companies is to include operative definitions of these values, explaining at every opportunity what they mean in practice.

The companies that most successfully live their values also find ways to praise employees for showing up. I'll give you an example from my own dinner table. My husband worked for several years for a developer tools start-up called Elementl. I put him on the spot while writing this book by asking him about whether he had any recollection of his company's values and if he could share them with me. He listed a few without hesitation, including "executing with fierce urgency" and "aiming high." I was curious and surprised. He told me he was able to recollect them not because he's employee of the year but because his company had a regular "all-hands" meeting for everyone at the company. The CEO, Pete Hunt, would share a story about one thing that went well that week—and then tie it back to the company's values. What did an employee or team do that week that involved "aiming high"? Did they secure a key customer that no one expected to land, or did they hire a sought-after engineer?

Providing context around the story can also help when it comes to articulating values. Jeff Gothelf, a speaker and organizational designer, wrote an illuminating case study for *Harvard Business Review* about how he helped a large enterprise client move over to a goal-setting framework based on objectives and key results (OKRs). OKRs are all the rage these days. If you haven't been exposed to them in your workplace, you're a rare exception. In short, the framework involves setting clear goals and then directly measuring outcomes. So how do you get a team onboard with OKRs? Gothelf's case involved a large company with 10,000 employees. He encouraged the leadership to do something called "contextualizing the decision." That meant taking a beat and answering questions like "Why is now the right time to move to this modern style of work? And how will it make things better for employees?" Executives should consider and address a few other important questions: "What prior failures or missteps prompted this decision? And what will be better about this, versus the old way?"

This kind of storytelling is crucial, or a big decision might end up feeling to employees like a "random, top-down management initiative," explains Gothelf. And yet, many companies forget to provide this context, opting instead to simply issue vague directives and expecting everyone to fall in line.

What Are You Against?

Most CEOs today can articulate what they stand *for* in the form of corporate values, even if they're not always successful in meeting those standards. Considering what they would stand *against* can be even more powerful for leaders and employees. If the company says it values transparency, what does the opposite look like? And how has that played out in real life? Sharing these stories with employees and potential hires can be a powerful motivator for them to look inward and change their behavior. These case studies are also a way to examine if teams are actually living up to the company's values. Considering what you're against may seem too negative, but the world's most effective storytellers use this device every day.

Goldstein, the former Apple employee, now advises start-ups tackling the most ambitious, thorny problems in our society. One company she works with designs self-driving cars. That company was thinking through its own corporate values, so she suggested that the leadership team read a 100-page report relating to a competitor, a subsidiary of General Motors called Cruise. A third-party legal firm created the report in the wake of a hit-and-run incident that involved a pedestrian struck by a Cruise robotaxi and dragged twenty feet. The case made the headlines in late 2023 and throughout 2024, and things quickly spiraled in the wrong direction for Cruise.

The report looked for mistakes that resulted in the accident and evaluated the company's handling of the incident. It found that the company's own reaction made things worse, setting off a chain of reactions that left it exposed and vulnerable. After its own employees lost confidence in how its executives handled the situation, cofounder and CEO Kyle Vogt agreed to step down. In response to the handling of the accident, one Cruise employee even sent a text to another stating, "Leaders have failed us."

What exactly did Cruise do wrong? The press at the time pointed to a series of technical errors, including the vehicle's inability to accurately detect the pedestrian's location. But there were also major issues with how the company handled the incident from a communications perspective. That boiled down to what the report's authors referred to as Cruise's "self-inflicted wound." The report indicated that the Cruise executive team was far too focused on shifting the media narrative to side with them and specifically on shutting down the question of whether the collision was the company's fault. Instead, Goldstein said, leadership should have acknowledged what happened and committed publicly to working with regulators to ensure it would not happen again. Goldstein recognized that there are going to be accidents as this recent technology comes to market—even if companies have done thousands of simulations. There will still be edge cases that test the limits of any self-driving car—and some of them will lead to terrible tragedies.

After reading the report, Goldstein's clients came up with a new set of values that could help them avoid making the same mistakes that Cruise made. They realized that trust is paramount when it comes to novel technology like self-driving cars, because consumers don't yet know what to think about them. Transparency also needs to be a value, because a lack of information can mean that people fill the void with their own ideas. And collaboration matters, because so many stakeholders need to get on board for this technology to go mainstream. So, for her client, that report provided the impetus for at least three corporate values: trust, transparency, and collaboration.

Contrary to popular belief, CEOs do not need to stay relentlessly positive and optimistic or to pretend that bad things don't happen or that the competition doesn't exist. Talking about what has gone wrong or what is broken can be a powerful place to start. Bottom line: If you know what or whom you are against, can you frame that in terms of a story? And from there, can you determine what your values are?

Taking a Stand

For CEOs, it's not enough to spend time thinking through your corporate values in isolation. Many employees now expect their business leaders to have a point of view on the macro issues of our time, including all the important socioeconomic trends happening in the broader world. According to research from the communications firm Edelman, 54 percent of employees believe that CEOs should address political and social issues, including those that are considered controversial. This is one aspect of the job that most CEOs today dread the most.

That's because it can put company leaders in a tricky position, which is why a select few—including Coinbase CEO Brian Armstrong—have gone in the opposite direction, publicly stating that they will not address these topical, macro issues at all under any circumstances. When Armstrong did that, he took a risk, as most CEOs still quietly manage these decisions on a case-by-case basis. As he said many times, there was huge fear of potential backlash from the technology industry and the media. And to be fair, there *was* quite a bit of backlash. Armstrong's critics in the media described the move as a sign that Coinbase was purely interested in making money and had no social mission at all.

But Armstrong stressed several years later that he made the decision because he had done his own internal research and spoken with employees. Per Armstrong, many employees shared with him that they appreciated not having to hear about divisive issues at work. Armstrong stressed in podcast interviews that it was not just the white men who felt this way. His stance enabled his employees to focus on getting their jobs done and make a clearer distinction between their personal lives and work. Considering those conversations, he felt strongly that he had done the right thing for both him and his business.

How does all this connect to storytelling?

Although tricky to navigate, these moments can be the right time for CEOs and managers to share their own stories with their teams and remind people about why they joined in the first place. Samir Zabaneh, the CEO for TouchBistro, a Toronto-based software company, told me he does take the time to reach out to employees when something arises in the news, including political events and tragedies, to let them know that the company will do what it can to support the communities that are impacted, typically in the form of volunteer work or a donation. He shares that he understands how these issues might impact people on an emotional level, because they impact him personally, and that people can't simply show up to work and turn their feelings off. That also is a key moment to explore TouchBistro's mission—to build software to help restaurant owners run their businesses, including those all over the world who might be impacted by wars, climate-related disasters, and other global events.

One company I spoke to candidly about this topic was Equip Health, a fast-growing start-up in the health-tech space based in San Diego. Equip is building a virtual clinic to help patients get treatment for eating disorders. Its CEO, Kristina Saffran, started the company after her own recovery from an eating disorder in her teenage years.

Saffran recognizes that many of her employees joined the company because they wanted to make a positive impact in the world. So she has felt pressure over the years to speak up on topics in the news that she and her employee base care about. Women's health and reproductive rights are high up on that list for many of her employees.

After plenty of struggle, she landed on this position: Equip's priority is to help patients with eating disorders. That's the mission of the company, period. If it fails to do that, then it has no reason to exist. She also knows that patients from across a diverse socioeconomic spectrum have eating disorders. Their families are also vital to their recovery process, which makes things even more complicated. Imagine a scenario where a patient is a major supporter of reproductive rights, but their parents are fervently antiabortion. Would this impact that patient's ability to seek care from Equip?

"As the daughter of conservative parents, I always think about the fact that my family likely wouldn't have brought me to a treatment center that was outwardly political," she told me. "Pulling that forward to other families, well, that was an unacceptable outcome to me."

Saffran's solution is a story, and a very personal one. So, when something arises in the news, she will often share with her team about her own experience struggling with an eating disorder and how she met families in residential treatment facilities with many different political and religious views. She implored her employees to put the patients first, because many of them had few alternatives to turn to.

That story and message have been highly effective at Equip, even in moments of intense pressure. Very few employees have left because of Saffran's decision to stay quiet on certain topics. She also knows that teams will change and that people will come and go. So, whenever something arises in the press, she takes the time to think about her response. If she comes to the same conclusion, she makes it a point to keep sharing her story with her team. They may not agree with her decision, but Saffran says that she's heard widespread feedback that employees respect her thinking *because* they understand it.

There's no one-size-fits-all solution—and these topics are complex—but I particularly appreciate Saffran's example because she brought her decision back to a personal story. And that's what resonated with people.

Leveraging the Founder Story

When a company is establishing its international communications strategy, one of the most important stories leaders can share with employees is the original founding story. For-profit companies including Nike, Workday, Salesforce, and Apple, as well as nonprofits such as Habit for Humanity, Everytown, and charity: water, have all shared their founders' stories to sustain the corporate culture over time.

Scott Harrison's story about why he started charity: water is particularly profound, and it is often shared internally. A former party promoter, Harrison powerfully describes how he took a trip to Uruguay in 2004 and found himself at a nightclub during an active shooting. That deeply traumatic moment inspired him to do something quite different with his life. Soon thereafter, he started volunteering with a Christian charity, which sent him to Liberia. While he was in Africa, Harrison realized he could use his social capital in New York to help raise money to provide clean water for people in developing nations. According to the World Bank, around two billion people globally do not have access to safely managed drinking water services. The nonprofit has now raised hundreds of millions of dollars to develop hand-dug and drilled wells, filtration systems, latrines, rainwater catchments, and other solutions for sanitation in developing countries, and videos released every year show donors how their generosity is making an impact on real peoples' lives.

Knowing that Harrison changed his life so profoundly has inspired people both inside and outside his organization. His story is a reminder that anyone can feel inspired to do something for others, no matter where they come from and the life experiences they have had.

In the for-profit world, the Salesforce founding story lives on the company's website to remind people of its humble origins. Back in 1999, four friends living in a one-bedroom apartment created a prototype to do sales force automation for companies in their network. These entrepreneurs decided that their guiding mantra would be "no fluff," focusing their work solely on "what they believe is important and necessary" and trying to do everything "fast, simple, and right the first time." The early team became known for wearing Hawaiian shirts (a tradition Marc Benioff, the company's longtime CEO and one of its founders, continues to uphold), and they appointed a dog to the C-suite as their chief love officer.

Both Salesforce and charity: water may be big brand names today, but it's useful to constantly remind people working there that these organizations at one point were little more than ideas on a napkin. It's inspiring—and we all want to know about the men and women who started these companies long before they were big successes. This type of story can help people build empathy for those who have become extremely well known and relate to them on a personal level. Marc Benioff may be a billionaire many times over, but knowing that he's super into Hawaiian shirts makes him seem more down to earth. And, as I've shown throughout this chapter, these stories may also help instill values in the company in a memorable and relatable way.

Those who don't have a marketing background should still work through the exercise of thinking deeply about their company's origin story and figure out how to communicate that with their team and the wider world. Eventually, a version of this founding story should exist on the company's website or intranet so that it can serve as a constant reminder of the original purpose. As companies get bigger, this clarity of vision can easily fade, and people can lose sight of the bigger mission. Stories like these can play a pivotal role in reminding employees about what matters.

Benioff now uses the founding story to remind himself of his connection to his employees and the mission. The number one piece of advice he offers other CEOs who are scaling their companies is this: "When a CEO reaches that pinnacle of their career, and yet they actually think they are not part of a total ecosystem, then my job is to hook them back up. That's it. That's what I do. I have had to navigate a lot of complex situations as we've grown this company from an idea to almost 100,000 employees. I've gone through all of these crazy things that can happen to you— maybe not everything, but the vast majority. *What I find is that when I'm talking to CEOs who are in trouble, it's because they've lost that connection.*"[4]

Take it from Benioff: Never get so detached from the business that you become inaccessible and forget who you are. Companies will only thrive when the CEO and the other key leaders are connected to their own teams; otherwise, they'll lose sight of what really matters. And there's no better means of staying connected than sharing a strong story.

CHAPTER 6

Story-Driven Brands

Stories constitute the single most powerful weapon
in a leader's arsenal.

**—Dr. Howard Gardner, professor of cognition
and education at Harvard University**

Bobbie, the organic baby formula brand, started off with a
mission to help families globally to feed millions of babies.
But the original idea came from just one Irish-born, US-based
mother, Laura Modi, after a lengthy struggle to breastfeed her
first child. At the time, Modi was working at Airbnb as a director of hospitality and host experience. While pregnant with her
first baby, she would have described herself as an upbeat and
optimistic person. But after her first daughter was born, she felt
like a failure. Breastfeeding was unexpectedly difficult for her, as
it is for many new mothers. After trying on and off for days, she
was desperate.

Modi, who is now a mother of four, will never forget the
moment when she rushed to the local pharmacy, jostling her

infant in her arms while frantically searching the aisles for formula. She vividly recalled feeling horrified after scanning the backs of the tins and finding ingredients like palm oil, corn syrup, antibiotics, and fillers. She wouldn't ingest these ingredients herself, never mind feed them to a newborn. Modi saw a huge opportunity to develop a formula with clean, organic ingredients that moms like herself could feel good about giving to their babies. If formula wasn't a parent's first choice, she wanted it to at least be a close second.

At that moment, Modi wasn't looking for an excuse to quit her job and jump into starting a baby formula company. She had zero experience in consumer-packaged goods. But she had worked at Airbnb for more than five years, which taught her how to build a strong consumer brand in the face of stiff competition. "Airbnb was taking on an industry that hadn't changed in centuries," she told me.

Similarly, just a few players had dominated the formula world for decades. It was gigantic—$70 billion globally—but notoriously difficult for new entrants. Most manufacturers had zero incentive to work with a company with comparatively small order volumes. Despite these challenges, Modi realized the time was right for a formula brand that spoke to mothers like her. She believed a brand that put a strong message at the core of everything it did, making use of a direct kind of consumer marketing not possible a few decades ago, had the potential to break out.

That Bobbie message went something like this: *You are not alone. You are doing your best. We are here to help.*

Here is the crucial distinction between Modi and most of her more established competitors. Bobbie isn't a formula company with a different kind of brand. It is a motherhood brand that happens to sell infant formula. This approach has given Bobbie a remarkable advantage: its brand story.

"We knew that we had to go against every marketing standard to make this work," said Modi. "Medical sales were not going to work, and we also did not have millions to pump into paid marketing. We had lofty goals to compete in a market that's a duopoly, and everything was against us."

Seven years after Modi started Bobbie, in 2023, the company announced plans in Washington, DC, to increase formula access by investing $100 million in the wake of nationwide shortages. That same year, the company raised $70 million from investors and acquired a twenty-six-year-old pediatric nutrition company—Nature's One—to triple the size of its operations. The company told reporters at *TechCrunch* that it had reached $100 million in revenue and was experiencing six times the growth of the rest of the formula market. For an industry dominated by companies like Abbott and Nestlé, this was notable. And few companies have broken out since, except for British-made Kendamil.

Even outside the formula market, Bobbie has become known for throwing out the PR playbook. A press release announcing the Nature's One deal features the two CEOs locked in a fierce bear hug, with the copy emphasizing that Modi is a "mom first, CEO second." Likewise, Nature's One CEO Jay Highman described himself as a "dad of two." Even more surprising, Modi acknowledged the limitations of relying on any one formula maker, even as she celebrated the step in the right direction: "I won't claim Bobbie is the cure-all solution." Most press releases are so mundane they get ignored by their target audience. But Bobbie's got notice and pickup from publications like *TechCrunch* because it was so against the grain. "The creative is just so strong," raved Jacquelyn Miller, a veteran communications professional, who has been following Bobbie's story for years.

Marketing Standards

Bobbie's success illustrates why a powerful story is so important to building a company's brand. Within modern marketing departments, there's a lot of tension between two methodologies: brand-driven marketing and performance-based marketing. I'm oversimplifying the distinction slightly, but for the sake of those without a marketing background, let's break it down.

Brand marketing, the classic form of marketing that's been with us for over a century, highlights the values, strengths, and emotional identity of a brand. It creates a feeling of goodwill and is critical in building consumer trust over time. An example of that might be a brand putting together an event that is topical and inspires fruitful dialogue or an ad that speaks to a broad aspiration without making an explicit sale. Nike is the master of brand marketing and a precursor to newer companies like Bobbie. The company was a pioneer in using sports influencers and developing ads that could connect fitness with an emotional experience. Nike made clear that the brand is all about standing *for* something. Its ambassadors include Colin Kaepernick, who sacrificed his football career to protest racism and police brutality in 2016. Nike, in the wake of an ad featuring Kaepernick, may have received backlash and incited controversy, but the company was also praised for the move. One analysis tracking the company's stock estimated that the Kaepernick ad campaign converted into over $43 million in media exposure for the brand.

Performance marketing is newer. Only appearing in the past two decades with the rise of the internet, it is essentially a type of advertising where ad buyers pay affiliates (ad platforms) based on results. It focuses on leads, conversions, and sales. Common performance channels include social media and influencer marketing, display ads, content marketing, search engine marketing, and sponsored content. There are different ways to measure the success of these campaigns via a variety of monitoring tools on the market, including things like cost per sale (you pay the affiliate when there's a sale) or cost per click (you pay them when prospective customers click on links). Performance-based marketing focuses on specific, measurable outcomes, and that's a big reason why it is so popular today. With the advent of the internet, marketing departments have shifted a greater and greater percentage of marketing dollars into performance-based marketing, where they can demonstrate a clear return on investment, instead of brand-driven marketing. Brand and performance marketing might share similarities, but, as we'll get into, the teams measure success vastly differently.

Some of the obsession with performance marketing is driven by CEOs who view marketing as an extension of sales. As Nick Zeckets, CEO of marketing software company Air Traffic Control, explained, "CEOs today are constantly looking for data, like 'oh, site traffic is up this month' and putting pressure on their chief marketing officers to deliver that." But that kind of data for most companies is essentially meaningless, according to Zeckets, because it's unclear what it converts to. Instead, investing in their brand by sharing substantive content that informs, entertains, and educates provides value for companies. That builds up goodwill for a brand among consumers. It can take months, however, for this kind of effort to translate into measurable key performance indicators (KPIs), and a lot of companies don't want to do the work or lack the patience for success over a longer time horizon.

Neil Lindsay, a senior executive at Amazon with a background in marketing, said that measuring KPIs is appropriate for companies and teams. But the real opportunity in brand marketing requires having confidence in the story and the "persistence and willingness" to continue telling it, particularly because not every story will land with target audiences at once.

Many marketers will find that challenging in practice, particularly if the CEO is not on board. "This is why marketing teams struggle to do the kind of work they know will move the needle," Zeckets explained. "They are being held accountable to sales metrics, but their best work doesn't happen on those timelines—and a lot of it is down to a lack of belief in the value of the brand."

The distinctions, however, are not entirely black-and-white. The two functions have some overlap—both, for instance, might involve publishing content. But performance-marketing teams are more likely to focus on short-form content that can be consumed on the go and drive hits to the website. Brand-marketing content might be longer form and higher quality, leading readers to form a more positive opinion of the brand. Both types of marketing might leverage influencers. But performance marketers would be more likely to pay influencers for a sponsored post that pushes their audience to buy a product, whereas businesses focused on brand marketing might look for influencers who authentically love their products and encourage them to post in their own way. Likewise, performance marketers might be looking for influencers with the highest follower counts, while brand marketers might be looking for individuals who deeply resonate with their mission.

The most consistent advice from the marketers I spoke with is to use both for varied reasons. But the most progressive marketing executives with the strongest backing, including from the CEO, are increasingly valuing brand-based marketing because these effects compound over time and drive profitability. After several decades of focusing on performance marketing, many companies are realizing that they still need to build powerful brands to sustain their businesses. While performance marketing is about trying to capture someone's attention once they know what they're looking for, brand marketing is about creating the kind of awareness that generates demand. That can be particularly important for companies that are creating new categories of products that people don't necessarily realize they want or need, like organic powder formula with European-style recipes.

Marketing leaders I spoke to have also found that brand marketing engenders a halo effect. If people have a positive perception of a brand's attributes (say, its focus on innovation), they might assume it has other positive attributes too (like good customer service).

Big companies can afford to have programs devoted to both performance and brand marketing, and they often have teams dedicated to each. But start-ups, particularly early-stage ones, don't have that luxury. These companies are under pressure to do more with less and to spend their capital strategically. Even if they can spend a lot on paid marketing, doing so may not make their business look attractive to potential investors. That's because spending a lot on advertising suggests that acquiring customers is very expensive for the start-up, and if the company can't retain customers for a long time, that's even more problematic (this is linked to a calculation known in investor speak as the long-term value to customer-acquisition cost, or LTV:CAC, ratio). In recent years, it has also gotten more expensive to run performance-marketing campaigns, particularly on social media sites like Facebook.

A decade ago, most budgets were allocated predominately to performance marketing, with a sliver going to brand. Now that seems to be shifting in the other direction. As the saying goes, necessity is the mother of invention. Because of the increased costs associated with advertising on social media, many companies, big and small, have been investing in telling their brand story: what makes it unique and what values it provides its audience. Some have been seeing those efforts pay off. Airbnb, Modi's former employer, reported its most profitable fourth quarter ever after shifting away from performance marketing and toward its brand. Instead of trying to buy customers, its CEO, Brian Chesky, said the company wanted to educate them about what his company stands for.

Airbnb, to its credit, has prioritized its brand from the start, making clear that it cares about providing customers with a sense of belonging—not just an affordable place to stay. But it has remained obsessed with its brand, alongside companies widely praised for their efforts to reach customers, like Tesla, Apple, and Trader Joe's. One of its largest branding initiatives in 2023 involved a series of animated short films, one of which included a group of friends on a relaxing, child-free vacation. The group encounters a hotel pool filled with screaming children and leaves to find solace at an Airbnb. This story is eminently relatable, even for those of us with young kids (myself included).

Airbnb may be growing well, but its prospects looked dire as travel bans took effect worldwide during the pandemic. The company's chief marketing officer, Hiroki Asai, described that period as a moment to contemplate what Airbnb's future could look like if brand and design were at the heart of the story.

I've seen similar results from smaller companies too. Kira McCroden, former head of communications for Modern Fertility, helped build a brand selling hormone tests for women in their twenties and thirties to get a better sense of their fertility. She said that Modern Fertility heavily invested in brand marketing in the early days, focusing primarily on informing women about a more proactive approach to family building. Earned media was a huge part of its success, as the company found that reporters leaned into this bigger story. It didn't hurt that Afton Vechery, who started Modern Fertility in her twenties, felt deeply and personally connected to that mission. Vechery spoke often in the media about the cultural transformation that made it possible for her and her friends to talk about their fertility in ways they had not been able to in decades. The company later got acquired by Ro, a company that sells a broader array of health tests, for $225 million.

"The golden rule for small emerging companies is that you are only as interesting as the bigger topical theme that you connect to," said McCroden. "That's how you build a brand."

The Importance of the Founder's Story in Brand Marketing

Most of the brands we know and love have a face. And that face is usually the founder and/or the CEO. Figures like Apple's Steve Jobs, Nike's John Donahoe, Epic Systems' Judy Faulkner, and Amazon's Jeff Bezos represent the older generation of founder-led brands. Today, there's a newer generation of brand faces, like the Collison brothers from Stripe, Bumble's Whitney Wolfe Herd, Bobbie's Laura Modi, and Glossier's Emily Weiss. These are all CEOs whose own brands have been tightly integrated and aligned with their companies.

The big question that we need to ask ourselves is this: Is that association helping or hurting these businesses? Is there a key-person risk? We discussed some of the best examples of founders who have used founder-led communications to get ahead, including Reddit's Alexis Ohanian. But companies also take risks when founders drive the brand and the businesses without checks and balances. Theranos's Elizabeth Holmes and FTX's Sam Bankman-Fried are prime examples of that, as we'll get to in Chapter 8. Putting founders out there as the face of the brand also makes replacing them hard if that's in the best interests of the company. Does anyone have any idea who took over WeWork as CEO after Adam Neumann stepped down? I bet most of us do not.

That said, it's not easy to build a brand in the early days without a strong leader's voice. Eventually, as things snowball and the company (hopefully) grows, a range of executives on the team will have their own stories to tell, and they should be encouraged to share them. But in the very beginning, there's often little beyond the founder and their vision. That's a risk that companies should be willing to take—and, in many cases, have no choice but to accept.

Conveniently, these people, for better or worse, tend to be inherently interesting to the outside world. On some level, we all want to learn why someone decided to quit their day job to build something new—and risk it all in the process. Why is that? My theory is that many of us secretly or openly harbor a dream of doing the same thing but don't follow through. These people are also risk takers, and we tend to be drawn to hearing their stories, particularly in our younger years.

I'll never forget my first interaction with a well-known entrepreneur as a teenager. Martha Lane Fox, founder of Lastminute .com, stopped by my school because she was an alumna. I'd never met anyone so compelling, and I hung on her every word. I remember even now hearing her talk about starting her business a decade or so prior, how she put herself out there by attending every networking event and conference so that she could raise money. It's hard to know for certain, but I suspect her visit is one of the reasons I moved from London to Silicon Valley, the heart of innovation, without knowing a soul in California. When we encounter people like this, who are so tenacious and unwilling to take no for an answer, most of us can't help but wonder what drives them and whether we have what it takes to replicate their success. A founder's enthusiasm for what they do is the biggest thing any young company has going for it. It's not something that can be easily handed off effectively and completely to anyone else, as I outlined in previous chapters, no matter how much a founder might wish to do so.

Returning to Bobbie, the mom-founded formula company, there's no doubt that Laura Modi is an important face of her business. And as a mother with a full-on career, she's ideally suited to talk about the pregnancy and postpartum experience. But it's not only about her. In my opinion, the ideal brand-marketing campaign leverages the founder and their story, while simultaneously making the brand about something bigger.

The difference between the two is subtle. As the communications specialist Drew Kerr explained, there's a difference between the story and the mission. Founders are very well suited to telling the story (Modi's rush to the pharmacy to pick up formula for her baby), while brands—and that includes the broader team—should stand for that bigger mission.

In Bobbie's case, the mission is clearly to feed babies while shaking up stigmas attached to formula feeding (the company uses the hashtag #bottleboldly throughout its social media efforts for that reason). The company has tapped celebrities like Tan France, a dad via surrogacy, and the plus-size model/twin mom Ashley Graham to champion the idea that there is no one right way to feed a baby. These well-known individuals can be a voice for that mission, while also making the brand seem more relatable. In a powerful visual statement for *Vogue*, Graham was photographed with her eight-month-old twin sons, feeding one from the breast and one from the bottle simultaneously.

Companies that can seamlessly toggle between story and mission are in a golden spot. One or two voices can build to become many, starting with a chorus of other executives—and eventually customers. Celebrities and influencers can also represent the customers' voice, particularly if they have an authentic story of their own to tell. As the movement grows, the founder should stay accessible and visible to their customers. That's how brands avoid becoming nameless, faceless corporations. People want to see that leaders are still relatable, good people who remain interested in their customers and will continue to do the right thing. Social media, which gives followers access to celebrities' and executives' everyday moments, is a powerful vehicle for that.

That brings me to Bobbie's ultimate stroke of brand-marketing genius: its "Our Story" page.

Many businesses use this space on their website to remind us of the credentials of their executive team. Not Bobbie. Instead, the brand features a video that starts off with a shot of Modi snuggling her adorable sleeping baby, describing the latch of the baby to the mother's breast as "so cute." In the next cut, presumably filmed a few days later, we catch her in an extremely vulnerable moment. She winces in pain as her newborn screams on her breast. "To know about us, you need to know about our journey," the caption reads. The rest of the video depicts a series of mothers and babies, including employees who are also mothers (among them, Bobbie cofounder Sarah Hardy), as well as customers. The video culminates with a voiceover explaining how these first months hold moments of immense joy but also hardship. The whole thing is achingly raw, and the mothers in the video start tearing up because they have been given a chance to speak about how challenging the first year of a child's life is. From personal experience, I can say that there is nothing less real than the glamorous photos that influencers share with their newborns. Most of us are tired, cranky, covered in spit-up, and figuring it out as we go, but we feel pressured by society to say that we've never been more in love. That may well be true, but we've also never been more overwhelmed.

In an age when everything is filtered, it's incredibly appealing when brands help us lean into those real, gritty, human moments. We live in a world where true vulnerability and authenticity are increasingly rare—and as a result, they've become the most valuable currency there is. Modi understood that when she made the decision to portray herself as a CEO—and as a mother wrestling with breastfeeding late at night with deep bags under her eyes from lack of sleep.

As we see in the Bobbie video, the storytelling aspect of a brand-marketing campaign should involve two critical pieces: an individual's story—ideally the founder's—and a larger mission that may include the customers and the broader team.

But there's one more step: How do you turn that into a movement? Situating the brand within a broader context gives it meaning beyond the company's own marketing goals. Modi, as an example, has chosen to speak out about the lack of paid maternity leave in America. She does that even though it's the very reason that formula is necessary for thousands of mothers and families (although there are plenty of other reasons for that). One in four women in the United States returns to work within two weeks of giving birth. These mothers do not have the resources and the luxury to breastfeed for a year or longer. Likewise, in America, very few companies provide comfortable, safe spaces to pump, let alone encourage mothers to take the time off required. (And access to those spaces is often correlated with income: Public health studies have found that the more money you earn, the longer you are likely to stick with breastfeeding.) If these policies changed, in theory fewer families might need formula—although there will always be a need for it. But this is a calculated risk Modi is willing to take. That is another reason Bobbie is not just a formula company—it's a brand that supports babies in their first year and beyond and happens to sell formula.

Women and families in America may not feel supported or empowered. But Bobbie turns that around by making them heroes. Good marketing should ideally tie back to customers by highlighting the problem that a business has solved for them—a problem that they are not alone in having. That's what Bobbie accomplishes in its "Our Story" video, leaving viewers with hope that their challenges are being heard and that they are not alone.

By talking about issues bigger than the product, brands have the potential to inspire customers and advocate for real change. This is a trend that industry experts refer to as "purpose-driven" marketing, and I view it as an increasingly essential part of brand marketing. This kind of marketing used to be tied to a company's social or philanthropic efforts, totally separate from its money-making agenda. Now, though, purpose-driven marketing is increasingly a core part of companies' financial performance.

Much of this ties back to the idea that people want to work for purpose- or mission-driven companies. They also want to feel good about their purchasing decisions, buying from companies that stand for more than just profit. More than eight in ten executives now believe that a keen sense of purpose drives employee satisfaction and boosts customer loyalty, according to findings from *Harvard Business Review*. The former CEO of Best Buy, Hubert Joly, shared that defining purpose at his company had "boosted the company's share price about tenfold since 2012." Best Buy, after much deliberation, came up with its purpose: "Enriching our customer's lives through technology." Joly said this purpose wasn't empty; in fact, it allowed Best Buy to justify entering new markets that were making a positive impact, such as a new health-care business focused on helping elderly people age at home. That both supported the company's bottom line and allowed it to serve its customers in new ways.[1]

Consumers are rewarding purpose-driven brands. A global study from the communications firm Zeno in 2020 found that customers are four to six times more likely to purchase from, as well as protect and trust, companies they associate with having a positive mission. The research found that audiences expect the brands they support to have a perspective on issues they care about. Campaigns that lean into this are having outsized success. When design and communications agency Ogilvy & Mather started working with Kotex, the tampon and liner company, it realized that many of the company's customers lacked basic knowledge about their sexual health. Ogilvy's team created an award-winning campaign called "Generation Know" to teach women about their vaginas. This campaign was so effective that it led to an 18 percent increase in Kotex sales.[2]

Purpose-driven brands need to ensure their claims are credible versus cosmetic. Those that do not will be called out. One notable example is The Wing, a women's coworking space with a brand oriented around female empowerment. But after years of rapid growth and plenty of spotlight, the company's CEO, Audrey Gelman, was forced to resign amid allegations of racism and a toxic workplace culture. Employees noted that Gelman only practiced what she preached (creating a "utopia" for women) with a cohort of specific women, namely white women. *The New York Times* spoke to twenty-six former employees who described how their initial enthusiasm had turned to anxiety and disgust within a matter of months—all made worse by the fear of losing their jobs.

When CEOs attach their companies to a higher purpose, they must work extra hard to act to embody it. Acting one way in public and another in private is simply not an option. The rewards of being out there are greater—but the bar is also higher.

The Emotional Sale

After watching Bobbie's "Our Story" video for the first time, I felt a rush of gratitude. Finally someone had given voice to how I'd been feeling for years as a mother who struggled to breast-feed her two babies and turned to an intensive regimen involving exclusive pumping. And my next impulse was to buy Bobbie's formula.

This impulse, firmly rooted in emotion, has been studied for decades. Psychologists, academics, and CEOs all tell us the same thing. Companies that tap into people's feelings will see a bump in their returns, as well as an increase in customer loyalty and retention. But how much? Is there any way to measure that?

Well, as it happens, customer intelligence experts Scott Magids, Alan Zorfas, and Daniel Leemon teamed up in 2015 to probe this question and dig a level deeper. For *Harvard Business Review*, they took on the following questions: What are those emotional motivators that lead to a sale and why? Can we effectively rank them? How do these behaviors work? The authors recommended that companies take the time to figure this out and provided a methodology for doing it.

First, they suggested that companies inventory their customer data to look for qualitative descriptions of what motivates their customers, then do the necessary research to understand why. They suggested that companies figure out the motivators specific to their highest-value customer group, then commit to forging an emotional connection with customers via every function, not just the marketing department. The authors recommended thinking about this exercise as a "science—and a strategy." Most brands have yet to do this work, but employing methodologies like this one is a necessary first step.

In surfacing these emotions, however, companies should be careful about taking customers' feedback at face value. The author Simon Sinek argues in *Start with Why* that brands should think about not only the what but the why. His book has motivated companies to avoid pitching their "better mousetrap"— meaning how they are better, faster, or cheaper than the competition—and instead to ask why customers buy their products in the first place.

That's an important first step, but humans may be more complicated than that. In a piece for *Psychology Today*, the science writer Abigail Fagan makes the case that a lot of people will say they like popular brands, such as Nike or Apple, because wearing a pair of Air Jordan sneakers or using an iPad makes them feel cool. Let's not take that at face value. Deeper emotions may lie beneath. Why do we like feeling cool? Could it be because it creates a sense of community? Humans are a social, tribal species, so that feeling could be extremely powerful for many of us. It's one we actively seek in our daily experiences. And it's probably a big reason we keep coming back to the same brands repeatedly, allowing them to stand the test of time.

Airbnb understands that well. By combining a product people want with an insight about how to tap into customers' emotions, Airbnb has shaken up even the entrenched, competitive markets of luxury travel. Its slogan is "belong anywhere" for a reason. The vision to create connection is present throughout all its messaging and the way it designs experiences. The company encourages meetups for its hosts; it thinks about belonging in terms of how it rewards executives; and the focus on belonging even shows up in philanthropic work, such as its $100 million Community Fund, which provides grants to organizations supporting communities globally. As CEO Brian Chesky put it in a Medium post, "People thought Airbnb was about renting houses. But really, we're about home."

Forging an emotional connection with the customer is an effective way to build trust. But for many brands, that takes a major investment of time and resources over years. The global communications firm Edelman found that trust is increasingly important for consumers, even as it is on the decline. Trust is down for politicians, media, and other institutions, as well as brands. And yet, if harnessed, it can do incredible things. When consumers trust a brand, according to one survey, they are 59 percent more likely to buy its products—even if they are more expensive than a competitor's.

If brands can maintain trust, they can transform consumer behavior. It once seemed inconceivable that anyone would trust a website to connect them with complete strangers for the purpose of staying in their homes. Now this is a normal occurrence that no one questions.

Trust can do more than that. In the case of Bobbie, transparency and authenticity (a precursor to trust) helped the company overcome its worst moment—a crisis that frankly would have killed most companies. That occurred in 2019, a few weeks after launch, when Bobbie's product was recalled by the Food and Drug Administration (FDA).

It's impossible to overstate how bad that is. As a parent, would you be able to look past that? The situation may have come off terribly for Bobbie, but it was more nuanced than it seemed. The problem had stemmed from an article that referred to Bobbie's formula as "infant formula," versus "companion formula" or "toddler formula," before it had been approved to use that label. After acknowledging the misstep, Bobbie hit the pause button on its strategy and leveled with its customers about what had happened. It forged stronger relationships with manufacturers, added a regulatory expert to its team, and secured new funding from an investor. Modi spoke to the press to explain why the product was in fact safe for consumption. Within about a year, Bobbie's product was back on shelves after the FDA agreed it met requirements. Within months, it had secured its position as one of the fastest-growing infant formula companies to enter the market since the 1980s.

Recognizing that trust can only be earned and regained through openness, Modi continues to share updates publicly with Bobbie's user base. Case studies and press articles have now been written about the company's recovery, because a lot of businesses in the same position would not have survived. And because of the team's resilience, Bobbie's formula was back on the market in time for an important tailwind: the nationwide formula shortage. While other companies were running out of inventory and pharmacy shelves were running dry, Bobbie was able to acquire a company to shore up its manufacturing capabilities to meet the demand as best it could.

By understanding how a customer feels when making a purchase, brands can weather their ups and downs. Don't forget to share the whole story, not just the conclusion. People connect better to brands that have experienced moments of hardship, and the best stories have a beginning, middle, and end.

The IKEA Effect

Why does the "IKEA effect" work? Well, Gallup research has found that emotional factors drive about 70 percent of decision-making for consumers, whether rational or otherwise. Behavioral economists like Daniel Kahneman and Dan Ariely have spent their careers studying consumer buying behavior. As it turns out, we tend to make quick, intuitive decisions when it comes to what we choose to purchase, and much of that is driven by our emotions versus our rational, data-driven brains.

Ariely, a professor at Duke University, calls this phenomenon the "IKEA effect." It may be annoying and time-consuming to assemble furniture ourselves. Cheaper furniture that requires no investment in labor might be available. And yet we continue to buy IKEA furniture. Why? We have a certain sense of pride in and an emotional attachment to products that we've assembled ourselves, even unnecessarily. "Human beings respond more positively to things they themselves have created or influenced,"

Ariely writes. "An investment of labor is also an important investment of emotional capital."

Emotional capital matters. I'd encourage you to take a few minutes to watch the Bobbie "Our Story" video. After you watch it, ask yourself this question: At any point did the CEO talk about the price of her formula compared to the competition? The ingredients? The buying experience? The convenience of at-home shipping?

The answer is no, no, no, and no.

When given the spotlight, CEOs like Laura Modi or Box's Aaron Levie (as discussed in Chapter 2) don't waste the opportunity. That may sound counterintuitive and opposite to what most people have been trained to do. When I was with CNBC, I watched CEOs come on a show and avoid answering the host's questions, instead pivoting the whole interview to tout their latest product development. These CEOs were not invited back.

"One of the things that many of the best storytelling CEOs I've worked with have in common is that they rarely talk about their products head-on," said Ashley Mayer, a former head of communications for companies including Box and Glossier. "People pay attention to what they have to say because they're interesting and articulate, and a by-product of that is they want to know more about the companies."

When Lindsay Kaplan ran communications at Casper, she could tell you about every layer of foam in the mattress—but she purposely didn't. She knew it wouldn't move a sale. "Many companies confuse product specs with consumer love," she explained. "Being creative and weird and unexpected is the emotional piece that truly drives a brand forward. . . . You can get someone to feel that they really want this [product], but they can't explain why." Casper experimented with that in many ways, including with its "Snooze Bar," a multicity pop-up experience for people to drop in and take a nap or sip coffee while enjoying a chat about how to get better sleep.

This doesn't mean you should never talk about the product. Sometimes you might be asked about it directly, and in those cases it's important to discuss the user experience as simply and clearly as possible. But don't assume that people will want to buy whatever you're selling because of a cool new feature.

The magic formula for story-driven brands that can go the distance? It's to tap into people's emotions before prompting them to make a purchase.

"Emotional decisions are the best ways to drive revenue and sales and growth," said Kaplan. "You can only grow logically so far without the emotional component."

CHAPTER 7

You Are Not Everyone's Protagonist

> You are a function of what the whole universe is
> doing in the same way that a wave is a function of
> what the whole ocean is doing.
>
> —Alan Watts, author and speaker

The entrepreneur Sara Mauskopf has a big voice on X but not in real life. Tens of thousands of people follow her account, where she goes by @sm. Outside social media, she is an introvert who prefers to stay in with her husband and three kids, only attending industry happy hours when she feels it's critical for her business.

It might seem counterintuitive, but Mauskopf gravitates to social media because she doesn't crave the spotlight in her personal life. For her, it would take a lot of mingling at cocktail parties to reach 50,000 people. But on X, she can pull that off multiple times per day—without the social anxiety brought by big crowds. X gives her the reach, improves her confidence, and helps draw attention to her business. Mauskopf is the CEO of Winnie, a website for parents to find day-care and other child-care centers online. On X, she weaves posts about her company with relatable anecdotes about life with her three kids. A classic Mauskopf tweet? "Just spent the morning chaperoning a preschool field trip and let me tell you, preschool teachers should be paid more than CEOs." *So true.*

Allow me to bust the myth, which I have heard repeated by peers and colleagues throughout my working life. The myth? To build a following as a storyteller, you have to be self-centered, self-promoting, or extroverted. In reality, it's often the opposite. Self-effacing, witty introverts like Mauskopf are far more commonly found on the internet than you might think. And yet, you wouldn't believe how often an executive tells me that they aren't on social media because they're "not interested in drawing attention to themselves." By implication, that means they don't want to be like those performative, ego-driven types who are. That sounds a bit like sour grapes to me.

In truth, you can be thoughtful and low-key yet still find success as a storyteller. Many of the people I interviewed for this book who had the largest followings online were also the humblest. I sum up people like Mauskopf with the term "quiet influencer." These are people who aren't trying to draw attention to themselves but can find a following online because of their ability to listen and absorb information. When they do share, it's to educate, inform, or entertain others, not to build up their egos. Another example of a quiet influencer is Jenny Fielding, a tech investor with a large social media following, who described herself to me as an "extreme introvert." She notes that entrepreneurs she meets often view storytelling—and social media as an extension of that—as little more than "fluff," but she views this tool set as incredibly valuable for leaders. "Anyone can learn it, and I genuinely believe that," she said. "I'm living proof."

In fact, having an outsized ego can be negatively correlated with being a good storyteller. Storytellers recognize that they are not the center of everyone's universe, so they need to work extra hard to hold attention and captivate people. (Unless you're Taylor Swift or Kim Kardashian, in which case everyone cares . . . probably a little too much.)

There's a phenomenon in our society, referred to by psychologists as the "spotlight effect," whereby people think others are noticing them much more than they really are and that everyone is hanging on their every word. That's another myth—because nobody has time for that! Just think about how many people you pass on the street each day, how many updates you scroll past on LinkedIn, X, Instagram, and Facebook, and how many emails you receive. You can't possibly pay close attention to most of it. And even when we do pay attention, we generally spend a second or two before mentally moving on.

What's more, and this may sound harsh: Most of the things we do (including what we post on social media) are not interesting to most other people.

I'll give you an example. I recently browsed LinkedIn and saw a post from an acquaintance notifying his contacts that he would be speaking imminently about the future of automation, and he included a selfie from the conference room floor. My response was this: "Okay, cool?" He made no mention of what he'd be speaking about or with whom. He also gave no indication of who might be the ideal target audience for this speech and whether they'd find value in it. He assumed that the mere fact that he was speaking somewhere meant that we all should line up to witness it, no context necessary. Or perhaps he was simply looking for likes because he thought he looked good in that selfie. The result was that no one cared all that much, and his post received very little engagement.

Likewise, I find myself constantly prompting friends in the industry to stop sharing links to press releases stating that they're "thrilled" by some announcement they're featured in. We assume that people are naturally intrigued by our every win. But the truth is that no one who's not a close friend or family member really cares. The real work to make a post like this relevant to the average person in an extended professional network lies in answering questions like "What does this mean for the industry?" or "Is there a great story I can share about how this all came together?" or "What does the article say that's relevant to the work that I or others do?" Bottom line: Consider the audience, particularly if you're looking to reach a broader group than your immediate family. What about this announcement would interest them? This chapter explores all of these questions and provides practical examples.

One helpful prompt I often share is "How would you explain this to a total stranger on the street?" If you can do that successfully, then you're probably on the right track.

Why Is Most Business Content Boring?

Author and internet personality Gary Vaynerchuk has spent years writing about why corporate content on social media doesn't land with most people. One might argue it's the noise; there's just so much of it these days. There's been a veritable explosion of content across blogging platforms like Medium, as well as sponsored posts on media websites that rely on them for revenue. However, Vaynerchuk doesn't think that's the problem, because audiences are still finding *good* content (his example of what good looks like is *Game of Thrones*—and I'd largely agree with that, outside the final season). Even amid the noise, people will pay attention when the content is truly riveting.

You may think that the comparison with *Game of Thrones* is a little unfair—after all, the whole point of a big-budget television series is to entertain (computer-generated dragons, anyone?). Corporate content aims at a different target: Getting people to pay attention is secondary. The real goal is to convince them to make a purchase. However, Vaynerchuk maintains that the big problem is that most corporate content is simply not very good. If no one is reading, then it's not translating into sales.

Vaynerchuk is not alone. Even the people creating marketing content for a living agree with him. When the marketing firm WMH surveyed decision makers for products that businesses sell to other businesses (versus consumers), about half said they find the advertising for these sorts of "B2B" companies "boring," and almost 80 percent said it doesn't prompt them to make a purchase. In a UK survey, 82 percent of marketers echoed that, saying they find B2B marketing "boring and repetitive."

Think about that for a minute: Billions of dollars every year are spent on corporate content that bores everyone to tears, including the people producing it.

To understand this better, I spoke with dozens of marketers and asked them point-blank how it could be this way. I heard a lot of fascinating responses, and I'll summarize the most common. One major problem, particularly with B2B companies, is that CEOs often hold marketing teams to the same metrics and timelines associated with sales. Rather than pursuing long-term outcomes, which have enormous payoffs, like building a company's brand, short-term thinking forces marketing teams to pursue metrics like monthly web traffic. Short-term metrics give them something to put in front of the CEO to say, "Look, our web traffic is up." Unfortunately, that might be a meaningless statistic, because it doesn't matter whether web traffic is up or down if no one is interested in buying the product. And that leads to a bunch of crappy content, which is cheap to manufacture and thrown like spaghetti against a wall.

Instead, according to Nick Zeckets, the founder of Air Traffic Control, which builds marketing software, B2B companies should focus their time and resources on creating truly valuable and original content, along with helping their leadership teams to be well recognized for their expertise in the industry. These efforts can take months without immediate payoff, said Zeckets, because building a following, writing content that people read, and creating a respected brand is hard. That's why this kind of effort is often on the back burner at companies, even today.

Aside from the obsession with data and short-term wins, a handful of other factors came up repeatedly in my conversations with marketing experts. These include the spotlight effect, which we discussed previously, and executive teams' desire to preserve "optionality," meaning the option to change course down the road when it comes to the product or business model or some other aspect of the business. This results in a defensive mentality that is overly concerned with risk versus upside. Let's start by discussing how the spotlight effect applies to companies.

When building a business, leadership teams can often get super focused on micro problems without pulling their heads up to look at the big picture. So, one hazard of the job involves CEOs getting it into their heads that everyone is paying attention to those same minor details, even down to the level of everything they say and do. That creates problems sharing the story, which requires a broader perspective, and an inflated sense of risk. Many companies don't have anyone tasked with providing that broad view. In fact, at bigger companies in particular, a lot of people are employed to say no to any request that carries with it any perceived risk, even if there's potential upside. Lawyers and communications professionals who are constantly looking for ways to avoid negative blowback drive some of this excessive caution. Occasionally the C-suite also takes a risk-averse stance that winds up curtailing their storytelling effectiveness.

This risk aversion goes beyond storytelling, and it is pervasive. In reality most corporations struggle to assess true risk—across every function. When Syracuse University professor Ralph O. Swalm presented the results of a landmark study of risk among 100 executives, he found that decision makers quashed new and creative ideas to grow a new business line in favor of cost cutting and making investments that they considered "safe." In a *Harvard Business Review* article, he summarized that these results "do not portray the risk-takers we hear so much of in industrial folklore. They portray decision-makers quite unwilling to take what, for the company, would seem to be rather attractive risks."

Companies claim to be pioneering, creative, and innovative but rarely behave that way in practice.[1]

Economists have likewise done many studies on the fear of loss as it pertains to financial investment and spending for research and development. Storytelling is a far less studied area, but I suspect the answer isn't all that different. The level of storytelling risk that most companies are willing to take is extremely low, even when there's a clear potential payoff in the form of delighting or surprising customers who will then buy the product. In a communications context, this fear is often rooted in the idea that people are paying extremely close attention and are ready to be offended or put off: If what you're saying doesn't land well, the company could lose business. So, the belief goes, it's better to be boring and say nothing even remotely controversial, despite rewards associated with being noticed. Those rewards feel less tangible to CEOs, so they stick with the messaging that feels safest.

"As a marketer, I spent a lot of my day having to remind everyone that no one really cares about us," said Anthony Modano, an executive who's worked at start-ups as well as big companies like Aetna. Modano doesn't mean that no one will ever care; he means that building an audience is hard work. "The reality is that to be noticed, you need to have a point of view, and ideally a provocative one."

We often forget that there are also risks associated with *not* having a point of view. Falling into obscurity could mean customers and consumers stop remembering that you exist. That's rarely the right strategy unless the company is thriving even without any awareness (that is rare) or there's been some controversy at the company making it wise to keep things a little dull for a while. A good example of the former is the post–Travis Kalanick years at Uber, following his resignation after a series of privacy scandals and complaints about discrimination, which became the subject of a Showtime drama. The new CEO, Dara Khosrowshahi, didn't want to make himself or the company the subject of a second drama series, so he laid low and focused on the fundamentals of the business. Most of the time though, there are real downsides to playing it too safe. And the good news is the bar is so low these days that being even a tad spicy can perk consumers up.

Take as an example Livongo, a company in the health-technology space, which sold for $18.5 billion to an incumbent, Teladoc, a massive transaction at the time. Livongo's CEO, longtime executive Glen Tullman, understood how to communicate. He aligned himself closely with the consumer and spoke out at every opportunity about how we all deserve a better, more affordable health-care experience. Tullman became known for warning large hospital systems, at conferences and in press interviews, that they would soon be disintermediated, meaning eliminated as a middleman (and likely had been already), unless they became more patient friendly. As a result, he became the person most associated with (the good kind of) "disruption" in the press. Most people would agree that US health care is far from perfect, so his voice felt like a breath of fresh air.

Years later, when I spoke to Tullman's former employees about the sale, many described his profile as a major contributing factor. If you're a CEO of a larger company and worried about a lack of innovation, wouldn't you want to buy the company known for being progressive? Rather than worrying about whom he might

183

upset, Tullman cared about being on the right side of history. And he took strategic, well-thought-out risks with his story that had a huge payoff.

Other factors contribute to our boring corporate content problem. The second one I heard consistently from marketing leaders is the idea of preserving a product's "optionality." Rather than being specific and descriptive, the language is kept vague so that the product's direction can change. The fear is this: If a marketer describes the company as a mattress seller, and then it starts selling pillows, how will anyone know about the pillows? The solution for many companies has been to just say that they sell "sleep solutions," because that could theoretically incorporate any future product line. The problem is that consumers do not buy "sleep solutions"—they buy pillows and mattresses. So, the company could miss the moment when an individual is making a purchase—all because of its pursuit of optionality. Isn't it better to be thought of for the mattress but then surprise customers by selling fluffy pillows too? Keeping options open shouldn't be the businesses' goal. Instead, companies should be known for a product so that it is top of mind for a consumer or buyer in the moment they are thinking about a purchase.

According to Modano, this is marketing 101: It's better to be known for something than for nothing, even if the something doesn't fully include every single product that a business plans to offer someday. Modano said he's seen corporations forget this constantly throughout his career.

Take Casper, a company that literally did get its start selling mattresses. It now has a line of many other sleep products, including pillows—but if you look at its website, it still emphasizes its mattresses because that's where it earns most of its revenue. One of its founders, Neil Parikh, told me this was a deliberate strategy from the outset: "We wanted people to think about us as a sleep brand because they only buy a mattress every seven to ten years," he said. "But we also knew that when they were in the market, and comparing mattresses, we needed to have the best product and make sure we were credible. So, it was essential that people thought of us for our mattresses, and that we won *Consumer Reports'* list of best mattresses, every year, even as we worked to align ourselves with bigger topics and themes."

The third factor? Aspects of stories that are fun and entertaining are at odds with the advice to CEOs from marketing departments, boards of directors, and elsewhere about how to best achieve their business goals. Here's a classic example: Stories have plots that typically include heroes and villains. To root for the hero, you need to get excited about their opportunity to make something right in the world. But many companies in the corporate world don't want to be the hero if it means creating an enemy, and many marketers I spoke to for this book will stress the importance of staying relentlessly positive and optimistic. Sometimes they don't even want to talk seriously about the problems that they solve. So corporate narratives instead try to please everyone and only talk about the positives. But if everything is golden, why do we need their solutions?

David Stillman, an expert on sales and marketing software who advises clients on effective storytelling strategies, often tells companies he works with to name the enemy, assuming a clear one exists. That might be a larger trend or a specific company. There's plenty of clever ways to do that.

One example he uses for a potential enemy is Salesforce, because it's one of the largest companies in the world of enterprise software. Most of Stillman's clients are start-ups that might someday compete with Salesforce, which means they'll need to convince customers to make a switch. Apologies to anyone reading this book who works at Salesforce, but I'm going to pick on the company for a minute! Given it's the 800-pound gorilla in the world of sales and marketing software, one could imagine a founder making the case with sales prospects that Salesforce was built decades ago and is no longer solving the business problems of today. That would be the ideal time to segue into showing off the actual product itself. "You acknowledge the resignation about the status quo," said Stillman. "And then you paint a picture about how it can be better."

Even if companies just take that first step—naming their enemy, whether it's Salesforce or any other company—they're making progress and will be ahead of most corporations today. Once people have a cause or company to rally around, ideally one with which they've already experienced negative interactions, the possibility of a better tomorrow has been opened. This powerful narrative is pervasive outside the business world—in books and movies. There's a simple reason why these sorts of stories—"slay the dragon and get to the promised land"—are still so popular. It's because they work. For more on narratives that work, cast your mind back to Christopher Booker's plots outlined in Chapter 2.

When selecting an enemy, however, it's vitally important to pick the right one. In my opinion, targeting groups or sectors is vastly preferable to picking on individual people. Companies or groups of companies can do bad things or build products that customers use resentfully, but good people with the best intentions usually still work there. The individual making negative remarks about other individuals might come off as a bully. There's something very distasteful about how we can be so disparaging about each other in our society. That's particularly true for public figures, whom many of us perceive to be fair game. But we're all human and can be affected by personal attacks.

So pick an enemy, even if it's as amorphous as the status quo, because relentless positivity is rarely the right tactic to engage an audience.

The Golden Ratio

Returning to Mauskopf, founder of Winnie, the key to building her audience involved staying humble and recognizing that she needed to go out of her way to inform people or offer something that resonates or makes them laugh. So in a world where it feels like everyone is sharing updates 24/7 about their personal and professional lives, how can you stand out? Those considering stepping up their game should ask the following questions: What's the right cadence? How much is too much? And what kinds of content are truly worthy of other people's attention?

Plenty of people on the internet constantly share their accomplishments with the world. But once you internalize the idea of the spotlight effect, you'll see that this strategy won't get you very far. These narcissistic oversharers might attract some followers, but for the most part people will ignore them—because they haven't given us a reason to pay attention. In fact, too much bragging without context or value is not only pointless but can have a harmful impact on a business leader's brand. Excessive self-promotion is extremely disturbing for most people in the digital world, as it is in the real world.

In 2014, a team of researchers from City University London asked a group of seventy-five people to remember a time they promoted themselves and to recall a time someone else bragged about their own achievements. They were then asked to rate how annoying these efforts at self-promotion were. Unsurprisingly, people found their own self-promotion to be less annoying than someone else's. The researchers also asked the participants to create a profile on social media. Half were told to be likable, and the other half weren't given any guidance from the researchers. People in the latter category were far less likely to self-promote, and therefore their profiles elicited more positive responses from the study participants than the profiles for people who were trying to be likable. The participants may have assumed that to be likable meant to self-promote, but in fact the opposite is true. The authors wrote, "In general, favorable impressions may be better accomplished by means of self-presentational modesty, or even self-denigration, than by outright bragging about one's positive qualities."

Bottom line: Many of us are not aware of when we're overdoing it and the impact it has. We might see that there are some likes on our posts, so people appear to be reacting favorably, but on a deeper level they tend to be put off. When two content and communications companies, Buzzstream and Fractl, surveyed 900 people, they found that the number one way to build a negative relationship with followers is to overly self-promote; 45 percent said they would be turned off enough to hit the unfollow button. The same is true for individuals.

I'll acknowledge that this idea may seem contradictory because many people assume the internet exists as a place to share our personal updates with the world: It's possible to overdo it and post far too often about one's accomplishments and achievements. But there's also far more appetite than we realize for insightful, informative posts, with a clear audience in mind, and far fewer downsides than we might think.

My personal pet peeve is those selfies that are now so pervasive on Facebook or LinkedIn with an attached quote intended to make the poster sound deep, like "Our greatest human adventure is the evolution of consciousness," when the clear intention was to share a photo next to a waterfall where they thought they looked hot. We can all get away with these non-self-aware moments occasionally, but why not own the intention? Perhaps we do just want some affirmation of a great outfit and hair day (I've been known to share an #ootd, or outfit of the day). And most of us do enjoy hearing when people in our network share brief updates about their new roles ("some personal news") because it can be helpful to know where they've chosen to land.

On the other hand, these announcements will almost always land better with context and an acknowledgment that people need a reason to care. If you make your network laugh, tell them something you learned, or share advice that might have taken them hours to figure out on their own, you're rewarding their attention with something useful. There's even something useful about an #ootd post, particularly if it includes a styling tip. Following street style and fashion accounts for many of us is a guilty pleasure.

We will have our best results with a less "me, me, me" attitude. Whenever we approach any kind of external presence, as opposed to heads-down operational work, that involves storytelling, we should assume two things: No one is already thinking about us, and no one will start thinking about us unless we find ways to be helpful or valuable or to share something that brings joy. It's a give-and-take.

This brings us to the "golden ratio" of social posts: the 9:1 rule. I came up with this formula early in my career, when I was starting out on social media. I haven't changed it in over a decade, simply because it works, and I share it with companies I advise daily.

So here goes: *For every one braggy post related to an accomplishment, milestone, or achievement, share nine that are useful contributions.* Think of the contributions—things that are interesting, valuable, entertaining—as *earning* the brags. Sometimes it is helpful to share something positive that happened on a personal or professional level—I totally understand that—but this lets you do it without it coming off as self-absorbed or generic. Companies are guilty of this too—have you ever scrolled a CEO's LinkedIn profile and viewed nothing but updates about funding milestones, customer wins, and key hires? These are important to share every once in a while, for the purposes of company morale and external validation, but a big opportunity for "contribution" content has been missed.

If there's anything to remember from this chapter, it's this: To be a successful storyteller, both online and offline, it's important to think about what the audience wants and needs. Many of us, as we move through our lives, welcome helpful information that we wouldn't get elsewhere—information that helps us do our jobs better, learn something new, or feel less alone with the challenges we face. If you can meet that need, you'll be a much more engaging storyteller.

Contributions in this vein might include

- A hilarious personal anecdote that will make someone laugh when they need a little bit of levity in their day
- An insight about what is *really* going on in the news beyond the headlines—something people in the industry would find helpful
- A piece of analysis that explains a complicated topic in an accessible way or provides a step-by-step for how to accomplish something that others find challenging

One example: When the Joe Biden administration highlighted Kaitlin Christine, a CEO in my network, for her company's work in breast cancer detection, I helped her share the news with her community. She initially wrote that it was an important milestone, and she described how honored she was without going into much detail. Because I knew a little about her story, I prompted her to share a little bit about how she felt in the moment when the White House reached out and what it meant to her. Christine's company, Gabbi, builds breast cancer risk detection software. She started it after losing her mother to the disease at a young age. After getting screened herself, Christine ended up getting a double mastectomy given her profile (genetics, family history, and so forth). So, to hear from the Biden administration felt like her life's goals were being realized and her mother would have been truly proud. Once reframed to talk about how personal the experience was for her, her post hit a nerve with her following.

The beauty of reframing content in this way is that even something promotional, like an important new milestone or new hire, can become a useful contribution and/or a moment to truly connect with an extended network. That turns the viewer from a passive "liker" into a true believer or ally. Likes become comments and reshares and, more importantly, offers of support.

I genuinely appreciate when CEOs talk about not just the great things they've accomplished in their roles and daily activities but how they got there. Some people refer to this trend as "building in the open." Imagine a scenario where a CEO doesn't just post something bland on LinkedIn about the stellar new chief technology officer they just hired. How about sharing instead how they found this amazing candidate? What tools did they use? Did they retain a recruiter—and if so, who? What kinds of interview questions did they produce to assess each candidate's technical prowess? What geographies did they focus on? Perhaps this information could even be viewable to anyone via an open document like Google Docs or Notion. Likewise, rather than announcing a venture capital funding round, a leadership team could talk instead about how they were able to raise money in a difficult funding environment. In Chapter 3, we touched on the value of authenticity—it works because it shows vulnerability or provides others with a potential lesson they can use in their own professional pursuits.

If you follow the 9:1 golden ratio, no one will begrudge you the odd self-promotional post that highlights your fantastic accomplishments. Those are important to share occasionally, because the industry may want to know what you're up to. The important thing is to use your voice to give back to your community *most of the time.* If you are a resource to others, they will follow you, and you will build influence.

The Power of Repetition

What if you lack the time to constantly think up original content and ideas to share? Well, that's understandable. We all have busy lives, and time for reflection is scarce. But if you've stumbled upon something brilliant that deserves its moment in the sun, here's an idea. Share it more than once.

This accomplishes a few goals: It keeps your content more frequent and relevant—a regular cadence is valuable to grow a following—and it ensures that your target audience sees it. It's perfectly acceptable to repeat the same idea, especially if you're sharing it in a new way. If you watch powerful storytellers like Mark Cuban or Steve Jobs, or really any politician, you will notice that they make a few points and use the same phrases again and again and again. I've also seen some of the most admired and well-respected influencers, like the child-development expert Dr. Becky Kennedy or the longevity expert Dr. Peter Attia, create a single piece of content and splice it in many ways to share across all the major social platforms. It may involve repetition but maximizes reach. The content still feels fresh, even if it's a new take on an old idea.

The reason this works goes back to the spotlight effect. Don't assume that people are hanging on your every word. If they're hearing you make a point, it's probably the first time—even if you've said it many times before. Perhaps they've heard you say it already somewhere but zoned out or forgot. More likely, they've never heard you say it before at all.

Researchers have found that repetition is associated with memory formation, meaning the information is more likely to stick in someone's mind the more they hear it. Good stories and the important points within them are meant to be repeated and remembered. There's a reason that we repeatedly return to our favorite books and movies. That's true in real life, and it's true on social media. Again, you don't have to repeat yourself verbatim: If you're highlighting an article you published recently or a podcast you appeared on, look for opportunities to make the same point or share the same link, but with a twist. Could you highlight a different quote this time? Or make a comment about the most powerful or surprising thing you learned while writing the piece or recording the podcast?

This aligns with a related point: Don't assume prior knowledge. As you think about what you want to say—and ideally, you're going to say it many times—consider that most of us live in a bubble. There's a lot we don't know. A few people might be experts on your topic, but don't avoid saying things that will seem obvious to the experts. The rest of us will appreciate what you're sharing if it provides value to us. I learned this firsthand in my own work. I have been involved in the health-care industry for about fifteen years. When I've shared accessible information, it has generated the most reshares and comments. The more esoteric the information, the less it resonates.

That might sound obvious, but we all harbor an impulse to seem like we're experts. I like to remind myself that while *some* of the people in my network also live and breathe the US health-care system like I do, most do not. Don't let the chance of one person making a catty remark—like "We already know that"—put you off an opportunity to share something important with the outside world. Even the experts have blind spots and gaps in their knowledge. On a personal note, I've received plenty of those remarks over the past decade, so I'm aware of the highly active contingent of mansplainers on the internet. But when someone says something like this to me, I typically shrug it off and respond politely, saying, "Why yes, but it still matters and it hasn't changed, so it bears repeating."

The other benefit to sharing seemingly obvious but important things, ideally at a regular cadence, has to do with *recency bias*, the idea that people give more weight to events of the recent past than historical ones. An example might be a manager giving a promotion to an employee who completed a high-profile project successfully, while forgetting about another individual who might have been more consistent in their track record for longer. Research has found that we are all culpable. The human brain tends to remember the last thing we read or the last person we interacted with—and, more literally, the last piece of information on a list.

So, when you log into a site like LinkedIn to check messages or scroll Facebook mindlessly, stumble upon someone's recent post, and think to check in with them—that's recency bias at work. Recency links closely to the idea of relevancy—as a journalist, I found myself not choosing to interview the expert I had to track down. Instead, I went to the person I had most recently seen an update from, who might have a few thoughts to share on a subject I was writing about. Likewise, many of the reporters I worked with would search for individuals posting about a topic and decide whether to interview them based on whether they had a relevant or unique take. That's another reason why posting regularly is beneficial.

The Sixth-Grader Test

As I look across the internet at different companies, I find myself regularly stumped trying to decode what they do. What in the world is "sales-enablement software"? Or a "one-stop shop portal for providers"? This is very real messaging from very real companies—companies with vast marketing budgets. And if you have a clue what these phrases mean, you're smarter than me.

This is why my favorite prompt for companies is the "sixth-grader test," which is not dissimilar from the "stranger on the street" test. It goes something like this: Could you explain what your business does to someone who is eleven or twelve years old? And if not, why not?

Even if you are writing for a technical audience, it is still helpful to work through exercises like this one. And if you can get your hands on an actual twelve-year-old and figure out a way to get them to sit still for a few minutes to test it out, that is even better! In that process, you'll learn that it's helpful not only to use simple language but to make your explanations shorter. Remember, a twelve-year-old's attention span is not that long.

As Mark Twain famously put it, "I didn't have time to write a short letter, so I wrote a long one instead." Communicating efficiently, concisely, and simply is hard and often takes a lot more time than being verbose. I've learned from editors I've worked with over the years that if you can find a simpler way to say something ("use" versus "utilize"; "give" versus "empower"), do it. There shouldn't be a difference between how you talk to people in the real world and how you communicate in a business context. Just because you're speaking to a customer or colleague doesn't give you license to sound like an AI chatbot.

Once we realize that the eyes and ears of the world are not directed at us, the journey into being a more effective storyteller begins. To walk that fine line between being braggy and being a contributor, keep in mind the golden ratio. And for those looking to reach a broader audience, keep it simple, say seemingly obvious things, find ways to be valuable to your community, and don't fear repetition! Above all, experiment. Content doesn't need to be perfect. Try new ways of communicating with your growing base of followers in simple language that even a twelve-year-old could understand, and you'll be surprised how much engagement you get.

PART 3
HOW WE RECEIVE STORIES

CHAPTER 8

For Good or Evil

With great power comes great responsibility.

—A proverb popularized by Spiderman

Here's a controversial take: Sam Bankman-Fried probably really was a genius. Before he was sentenced to twenty-five years in prison, he pitched himself as one of the good guys on a quest to save the world with his cryptocurrency fortune. And we, the public, ate it up. Bankman-Fried was a media sensation for a few years, appearing on the front pages of *Forbes* and *Fortune* because of his company, FTX. He was also a fixture on the gossip pages of the tabloids, hobnobbing with celebrities like Kate Hudson, Katy Perry, and Orlando Bloom. Who could forget that "You In?" ad with Tom Brady and his then-wife, Gisele Bündchen, encouraging us to use cryptocurrency to send payments to friends. The pair reportedly received up to $30 million in cryptocurrency and FTX stock as part of their agreement to promote the company.

Then it all came crashing down. In late 2023, Bankman-Fried was found guilty of stealing from customers in one of the largest financial crimes in history. For those who don't recall the details, he misappropriated billions of dollars of customer funds deposited with FTX, defrauded investors in FTX, and defrauded lenders to Alemeda, his crypto trading firm, of more than $1.3 billion, according to the Department of Justice. Later, in the spring of 2024, he was asked to forfeit $11 billion of his fortune. The prosecution argued during the trial—and the jury agreed—that Bankman-Fried's crypto exchange company, FTX, was essentially a scheme to siphon off vast amounts of customers' money and put it toward real estate, venture investments, and political donations.

How could this have happened? It all started when Bankman-Fried raised money in 2021 from some of the top funds in the world, including Tiger Global and Sequoia Capital, trading on his own credentials as a graduate of the Massachusetts Institute of Technology (MIT) with well-respected Stanford law professors as his parents. He made sure to be seen alongside political leaders and celebrities, further reinforcing the idea that his businesses were legitimate. He pitched to venture capital firms, getting them excited about the investment potential, a financial exchange that could be used by anyone, anywhere in the world, in any currency. Sequoia even published a long feature story speculating that Bankman-Fried had a good shot at becoming the world's first trillionaire. (They later pulled it down—more on that in a moment.)

As more details came to light in 2022, public sentiment about Bankman-Fried turned quickly negative. Accusations whirled about the company, its team, and its board, as many wondered how Bankman-Fried could have pulled off such a giant scam without his investors, key associates, and employees knowing. Bankman-Fried had raised tens of millions of dollars from some of the world's most elite financial institutions. Were they asleep at the wheel? Many of us rightfully wondered if Silicon Valley had failed to learn anything from the scandal not even a decade earlier, when CEO Elizabeth Holmes famously defrauded Theranos investors by propagating lies about her company's blood-testing technology.

In my view, all the hand-wringing and finger-pointing missed something: Bankman-Fried managed to pull off something quite spectacular. He may have been a crook, but he was a brilliant storyteller, and he'll go down in the history books for that. He convinced a lot of smart people to get behind him, largely on the strength of the stories he was telling them, his lifestyle, and the cast of characters around him. Upon further analysis, it's clear that Bankman-Fried leaned into classic storytelling tropes by casting himself as a protagonist we've all learned to love through books and movies. J. K. Rowling's Harry Potter (at least in the early years at Hogwarts, before he became a Quidditch jock) taught us never to underestimate the quiet, disheveled nerd on a preordained path to greatness.

Bankman-Fried leaned into that character at every opportunity he got, and he played the part flawlessly. Aside from his love of video games, he was so likable due to his support for charitable causes. While living in the Bahamas, for instance, he openly discussed paying off the country's $11 billion national debt. He courted policymakers by donating to political campaigns and arguing in front of Congress for more regulation of cryptocurrency. The whole FTX saga underscores that no great story will stand the test of time without relatable characters who make us want to root for their success.

"It was a package that [Bankman-Fried] presented to the world, an extremely cultivated image," said Susanna Kislenko, an Oxford, UK–based researcher who studies founder leadership, including the highest-profile cases of fraud. "And he, in particular, was very consistent about it."

So how did he do it? Well, let me pose a hypothetical question to kick us off: If you're a CEO and can only have one of these tools to succeed, which would you rather have?

An incredible story or an incredible product?

Early in my career, I'd have opted for the second, hands down: The incredible product surely is the most indispensable thing for a company's success. But after a few years of studying the world's best storytellers, I'd now flip my answer. I'd go with the incredible story, and I'd use all the momentum behind me to build out a product that would be worthy of the hype. I've seen too many examples where the winner who emerges in a category is not the one with the most capital or the greatest product. It's the company with the best story—and a *good-enough* product.

In the ideal scenario, a leader will have both. There is no faster trajectory to success than a great story *and* the goods to back it up. That is the dream for most companies, and rightfully so. "The best kinds of entrepreneurs ground themselves in the numbers and relate that to the story," said Steve Kraus, a venture capitalist with the firm Bessemer Venture Partners. "The worst kind tell the story and the numbers fundamentally don't match that, and then we look for [the business's true state] as we do our diligence."

Simply put, and to borrow a term from the investor and popular musician D. A. Wallach, "The best companies have both substance and sex appeal."

And yet I see a tendency to underestimate the power of the story in many circles—or worse, to rewrite history and pretend that the product sold itself. Helen Min, the tech marketing executive who worked at Dropbox as well as other technology companies like Facebook and Quora, has convincingly argued that many people in Silicon Valley view one of its most successful companies, Google, as being engineering first, extremely unconcerned with marketing or communications. Google has been an enormous success, becoming one of the largest companies in the world. And if Google didn't care about stories and was incredibly successful, why should anyone else?

That couldn't be further from the truth.

David Krane was one of the first 100 employees hired by Google, now Alphabet. He was also the first communications leader, personally brought in by Larry Page and Sergey Brin *because* they were so convinced Google would only win against competitors like Yahoo and Microsoft with a powerful story. Before Google, Krane was a journalism major who honed his chops by working with technology companies like Qualcomm and Apple. He quickly became the "voice of Google," helping shape all of its communications with the outside world.

Krane told me the two founders knew that a good story would be critical to the company's success, both in beating the competition and in having staying power. One classic example is Google's S-1, referring to the financial paperwork that companies put together during an IPO. Page and Brin had the novel idea of writing a letter about the mission of the business, addressed to Google's shareholders. The first sentence, "Google is not a conventional company," signaled that the founders were looking to attract long-term believers who understood the potential. They shared in the document that from the beginning they had intended to build a company that would help as many people as possible and have a real impact on the world. They acknowledged they would not steer Google to make short-term, predictable revenue. Another value? They made clear they would not hesitate to make high-risk, high-reward bets, both in funding projects with a 10 percent chance of earning $1 billion over the long term and encouraging employees to spend 20 percent of their time working on ideas that would benefit Google.

The letter was so successful in attracting the right kind of investor because it openly stated that not everyone would be a good fit for Google—but those who were willing to think big and take risks would be welcomed into the fold. That was a smart and calculated bet, because most investors would like to think of themselves as motivated by a bigger upside. And it gave Google some cover, at least from a communications perspective, if it chose to take a big gamble that didn't pan out. This letter was unconventional at the time, but many more executive teams today court Wall Street well before the IPO, sharing stories about the business to drum up enthusiasm among value investors versus those looking for short-term gains.

"These guys gave disproportionate time and commitment to supporting the storytelling and the brand," said Krane. "So when I would hear people on the outside saying these are just engineering companies, I would violently disagree with that analysis."

What the Google founders did to elevate the company's brand story was truly remarkable, down to the smallest details. Krane said that the founders even chose the word "Google" intentionally, knowing it was a misspelling of the word "Googol" (which refers to a very large number, in mathematical terms the number one followed by 100 zeroes). Larry Page and Sergey Brin knew that this would provoke conversation, which would make the name easy to remember, and that at some point people wouldn't even notice it anymore. And that's exactly what happened. Google was one of the first companies to have a name that eventually became a verb, referring to the idea of using the internet to search for information. That helped the company become the dominant player in the space, as it became such a natural, almost automatic human behavior to "google" information. And Google also delivered on the product and user experience—most of us have come to rely on Google because we know it works as advertised.

Having a powerful story can do wonders for any business. And Sam Bankman-Fried seemed to understand that better than anyone.

So here's the most important lesson from the FTX debacle: A great story can get you very far, but not all the way. If you are a fraud, no matter how good your story is, that will catch up to you. At some point, the product needs to deliver on its promise. It needs to be a Google, not an FTX. Otherwise, it's little better than a house of cards, meaning a strong gust of wind will bring the whole thing crashing down.

Playing the Part

We know that Steve Jobs referred to storytellers as the most "powerful people in the world." Historical figures like Mother Teresa and Mahatma Gandhi used their narrative gifts to do a lot of good for humanity, and their most famous teachings and sayings have now become known throughout the world. But as Nathan Baugh, author of *World Builders*, a popular newsletter on the intersection of technology and storytelling, reminds us, talented storytellers can also be "dictators, frauds and cheats." So let's return to FTX, because there's a lot we can learn from his storytelling technique. Baugh went deep on analyzing the company and came to the conclusion that Bankman-Fried's whole shtick worked for a few reasons.

First of all, he was relatable in terms of his appearance and his communication. He was genuinely smart about crypto and could explain complicated topics in a way that most people could understand. That made him a popular guest for cable television bookers—and really appealing to anyone trying to figure out if they should buy crypto.

What else worked? Well, according to Baugh, he played the part of the "unlikely hero," resisting his path to riches. Yet again, we see a popular storytelling trope in action: the hero facing a struggle, taking us back to several of Christopher Booker's story plots, including Overcoming the Monster and the Quest. Bankman-Fried represented his own battle as an internal one. He gave the impression of not really needing or wanting all the money he was amassing and of feeling uncomfortable about his resources. Despite all the evidence to the contrary (the lavish lifestyle in the Bahamas, for example), this impression of reluctant wealth seemed believable, particularly when he went as far as lending lines of credit to his competitors, investing in struggling businesses via his crypto fund, and donating large sums of money to charity.

As Baugh puts it, Bankman-Fried very intentionally played into stereotypes by "resisting the call." The heroes we admire most in fables and novels are predestined for a certain fate but struggle with their specialness. That reluctance makes them vulnerable and relatable. Again, I'm reminded of one of our favorite protagonists of all time, Harry Potter, who struggled with his own destiny as the "chosen one." These protagonists resist and resist until it's no longer possible to deny their calling, at which time they lean into their fate to become the heroes they were meant to be. Sometimes that occurs at great personal cost.

Did Bankman-Fried know what he was doing in aligning himself with a character? Well, after his conviction, he revealed something astonishing. In an interview with a journalist, he seemed to be aware that he was playing a game the entire time. In a fascinating late-night exchange over direct messaging with *Vox* reporter Kelsey Piper, Bankman-Fried suggested that he had a masterful skill for telling people what they wanted to hear even if it was totally fabricated. "Man, all the dumb shit I said," he wrote in a series of messages with the reporter. "It's not true, not really. . . . Everyone goes around pretending that perception reflects reality."

None of this is surprising to Kislenko, a postdoctoral fellow at the Skoll Centre for Social Entrepreneurship at the University of Oxford, who studies what she calls "founder syndrome." She defines this as the unhealthy obsession that some individuals have with their businesses, which often results in an unwill-ingness to let go even when things go off the rails. It becomes easy to see how someone can get caught up in and eventually start to believe their own lies. This can jeopardize the business's long-term health, and it alienates customers, employees, and boards of directors.

Kislenko, after attending countless pitch events, is convinced that founders must become adept at telling the version of the story that most appeals to investors, because raising capital is so critical for many companies to scale. Bankman-Fried, who raised close to $2 billion, is among the greatest players of this game. These entrepreneurs then get addicted to the rush of raising cap-ital, which then leads them to neglect their true mission. There's a huge ego boost associated with getting term sheet after term sheet from investors, particularly from some of the world's most elite funds. These founders can become very wealthy, very fast, which can blunt their sense of purpose. If all the focus is on rais-ing money and not on operating the business, it's easy to see how problems will arise.

The Power of FOMO

The way Bankman-Fried captivated Sequoia, one of the most important venture capital firms of all time, is an HBO docuseries waiting to happen. Unlike with most interactions between entre-preneurs and their investment firm backers, which occur behind closed doors, we know exactly what went down in this case. And that's because of Sequoia. After investing more than $200 mil-lion in the company, the firm commissioned a lengthy profile on Bankman-Fried that now lives on in perpetuity on the internet.

Somewhere during 2022, during Bankman-Fried's peak, Sequoia asked the journalist and private historian Adam Fisher to write about him (Fisher refers to him by his initials, "SBF") and his efforts to upend the banking system. Fisher had unprecedented access to many of the key players, including Bankman-Fried, Sequoia, and many of SBF's close friends and associates. Presumably Fisher also had some creative license. In the wake of those interactions, he seemed captivated by FTX and its quirky CEO. Here's an excerpt from the piece, which has now been taken down from Sequoia's website but still lives on in the Internet Archive:

> After my interview with SBF, I was convinced: I was talking to a future trillionaire. Whatever mojo he worked on the partners at Sequoia—who fell for him after one Zoom—had worked on me, too. For me, it was simply a gut feeling. I've been talking to founders and doing deep dives into technology companies for decades. It's been my entire professional life as a writer. And because of that experience, there must be a pattern-matching algorithm churning away somewhere in my subconscious. I don't know how I know, I just do. SBF is a winner.

In fairness to Fisher, most people who have been in the media long enough have at some point been taken in by a great storyteller. I've certainly been overly impressed by one or two who blew up their companies. If we're honest with ourselves, we've all been there with someone in our lives who overpromises and underdelivers. This may have been Fisher's turn, and it happens.

And yet I still couldn't wrap my head around it.

Any journalist, particularly an experienced one, knows the consequences of putting their professional reputation and credibility on the line. I'm sure the reporters who wrote glowing profiles about Elizabeth Holmes still haven't lived it down. After reading Fisher's piece, I got the sense that the author harbored a deep understanding of the risks. Fisher clearly understood crypto and the whole world of entrepreneurs much more deeply than most of us probably ever will. Crypto is still fraught with challenges and remains largely unregulated. It's still a Wild, Wild West, and plenty of people are manipulating aspects of the system to get rich. Despite all that, Fisher—and, more importantly because of the investment they made, Sequoia's partners—chose to believe. So, what about SBF might have gotten them there to thinking of Bankman-Fried as a winner? And beyond that, what captivated Bankman-Fried's investors to jump on board? The signal from them added major credibility to the company, particularly because Sequoia is considered one of the most elite firms in Silicon Valley.

The interaction that led to Sequoia's decision to invest in Bankman-Fried is striking. First, Bankman-Fried kept his cool during the pitch meeting, even feigning ambivalence at various moments. He gave the impression that he did not need the money, even though it's now very clear that he did. He seems to have innately understood that when you're raising capital, it is never a good idea to come across as desperate. The less you need the money, the better. This is not too dissimilar to the world of dating or the early stages of a friendship. There's often a delicate dance where neither party wants to seem too eager for fear of chasing the other off.

Bankman-Fried took it to an extreme. The profile tells us that he was playing video games throughout the pitch (you'll notice a running theme throughout this book related to an obsession with multiplayer gaming, which I absolutely believe is a decent practice ground for storytelling skills). Yep, you read that correctly: Bankman-Fried was playing *League of Legends* while he was in a pitch meeting with the top partners at the world's most well-respected venture capital firm—the very same one that has invested in Apple, Airbnb, Zoom, and Google.

Entrepreneurs are well aware of this need to give off an air of not needing the money. Dozens of articles have been written on how to generate FOMO—fear of missing out—among the investor set. Much of the advice boils down to a few things:

- Create a sense of urgency by insinuating that other funds are eager to do the deal.
- Be willing to walk away.
- Act like you're doing so well that you don't need the money.

By all accounts, Facebook's Mark Zuckerberg was an early pioneer when it came to FOMO. He once showed up to Sequoia Capital late, in pajamas, with a pitch deck titled the "Top Ten Reasons You Should Not Invest."

Actual competing offers can crank up the FOMO. In Bankman-Fried's case, there *were* a lot of interested investors. Plenty of other firms (whether they'll admit it or not) were circling around him at the same time, hoping to get their shot at making a life-changing investment in the next big thing.

Another major reason behind investor FOMO is our ingrained human instinct. As behavioral economist Daniel Kahneman has

The Storyteller's Advantage

concluded, the pain of missing an opportunity is psychologically more powerful to us humans than the pleasure of gaining one. Sequoia didn't invest in Zuckerberg, and a firm like that must have known how dire the consequences would be for not investing in the next transformational company (but don't feel too bad for Sequoia because the firm *did* invest in WhatsApp, which later sold to Facebook for $19 billion). Losses can also be emotional for other reasons too. Imagine you're a VC who misses an incredible deal, and you get a call from your own backers to ask why you've been asleep at the wheel when that company has a huge exit.

FOMO creates another problem, one that serves people who are out to take advantage of us, like Bankman-Fried. In our rush to avoid missing out on something hot, we don't do all the research we should. We might skimp on "due diligence" and fail to engage our critical-thinking skills fully. FOMO is an emotional response that tricks us into behaving recklessly, and that's a major reason why we should be hyperaware of it hijacking us. We should always have our guard up around people who like to share how much they don't care about or need money. If they're in our office trying to sell a product or raise capital, they almost certainly do.

The Desire to Believe

When you look at some of the highest-profile cases of founders behaving badly, it's clear that the people who rallied around them, providing funds or credibility in other ways, *wanted* to believe in them. I see a potentially optimistic takeaway here. In a world that is sometimes cruel and thoughtless, where bad things happen to good people every day, I can empathize with people who gravitate toward real-life heroes. Why do you think we continue to churn out Marvel movies year after year? We love the idea of the savior who will turn the parade of never-ending wrongs into rights.

Elizabeth Holmes, the would-be savior of the biotech industry, ticked a lot of boxes for investors, particularly those who lacked health-care knowledge or experience. A Stanford dropout who modeled herself after Steve Jobs, one of the most successful innovators in history, Holmes had a vision for revolutionizing lab testing and transforming the user experience of giving blood. She was also a female CEO in Silicon Valley, which remains male dominated to this day.

Like SBF, Holmes played a character. She was a chameleon, capable of transforming her identity to meet the needs of her business. When Holmes couldn't successfully raise capital from biotech investors in Boston, she pivoted to Washington, DC, and looked for high-net-worth individuals with backgrounds in business and policy. She decided to stay away from biotech experts, presumably to avoid answering tough questions about her scientific method or the technology. Around that time, she started pitching her voice a little lower, and she began to wear her trademark turtleneck sweaters, in an overt sartorial emulation of Steve Jobs.[1]

After speaking with several early Theranos employees in my network, several of whom have removed that particular job experience from their résumés, I now believe that many of her investors and her team supported her because they desperately wanted a version of the world to exist where Holmes could be the next Steve Jobs—not just so they would make even more money but for the sense of progress her success would signify. Holmes's succeeding would have meant a young, passionate woman with enough guts and chutzpah could take on the behemoth that is our health-care system and win. Her supporters wanted that inspiring vision to be possible.

Like Holmes's backers, Bankman-Fried also had a grand purpose. He stood out in the founder community because of his support for a movement known as Effective Altruism (EA), a philosophy that focuses on how to help others as much as possible, often pursuing extremely quantitative ways of assessing what that might mean. The definition of "help" in this philosophy comes from a calculus around how large a quantity of financial aid can be provided to those in need, which makes it particularly appealing to high earners. Bankman-Fried made clear that he would disseminate whatever fortune he earned to altruistic causes around the world. He may have been living a flamboyant lifestyle himself, but he did also seem to be giving a lot of money to charities (although many of them, as it later turned out, never received the funds). So, if Bankman-Fried became a trillionaire, his investors could imagine a future where he was not just making them rich too but also helping millions of people in the process. There's a reason he was so often compared to Warren Buffett, who has given away a huge slice of his fortune to charity. By backing entrepreneurs like Holmes and SBF, investors could fulfill their fiduciary obligations *and* make the world a better place.

Bankman-Fried's reputation as an "unselfish billionaire" did wonders for his image and his ability to raise money. Business and storytelling coach John Millen noted that his affiliation with EA may also have "disarmed" his investors into doing less due diligence than usual and buying into his hype for longer; FOMO may not have been the only factor. As Millen wrote, "This purpose-story disarmed suspicion: Sure, he wants to make a ton of money, but it's for a heart-felt purpose. He's a giver." That purpose and strong mission may have served Bankman-Fried in two ways: It allowed him to rally both hearts and minds, and it may have allowed him to evade scrutiny for longer. The same may have been true for Holmes and plenty of other fraudsters out there.

Yet, for these founders, hype must be backed by substance. Without that, any crack in the facade could bring the whole edifice tumbling down.

Affiliation with Known Tropes

Bankman-Fried fits a type: the nerd genius. Who else fits that category? Household names like Mark Zuckerberg, Elon Musk, and Jeff Bezos. The lesson of the past three decades? Ignore the nerd genius at your own peril. He—and to be clear, it's typically a young, white male—is a worthy adversary for any incumbent, and when he's not in the boardroom, you'll find him deep in the code, building the next great product that will drive the business forward.

One could argue this pattern matching is entirely rational: If it has worked many times before, surely it'll work again. It's a big reason that investors have given so many young, white males a shot, providing them with capital, connections, and other resources, and why they still so rarely invest in more diverse founders—despite the evidence that this strategy is a failing one. But the problem with investing in "characters" is that they tend to be cultivated. In reality the nerd genius stereotype has been manufactured by some very brilliant people working in the background to make a subset of companies more successful. Jessi Hempel's *Wired* profile of Margit Wennmachers, the head of marketing at the investment firm Andreessen Horowitz, credited her as one of these master stereotype creators. That profile may have exaggerated her role as an individual contributor, but it demonstrates nonetheless how brilliant communicators can shift our thinking—and is worth reading for that reason. As Hempel writes, "We're all familiar with Silicon Valley's mythological image of the tech founder: brilliant, nerdy, eccentric, well-meaning. What you don't know is that, more than just about anyone else in tech, Wennmachers is the person responsible for harnessing that prototype to build the legend of Silicon Valley."[2]

According to Hempel, Wennmachers and other communications leaders working in Silicon Valley had the brilliant insight that the public could get behind the idea of the nerd proving their detractors wrong. The *Wired* piece describes in vivid detail how the communications team working at Facebook went about popularizing the idea of the brainy outcast. It wasn't a coincidence that the media began reporting details about Mark Zuckerberg, such as his dressing in the same clothes every day because he had no time to think about what to wear. That indicated to the public that Zuckerberg had other priorities, like spending his time really digging into the code. The movie *The Social Network* supported this narrative by featuring times when he stayed up all night in his dorm room building the first version of Facebook's website or turned on those who stood by him to retain greater control of his business.

These stereotypes about successful entrepreneurs have had a profound impact on our culture, in both positive and negative ways. They have certainly led more funds to give certain founder archetypes or characters a closer look, including those who are younger and more technical. But they have also perpetuated bias and gatekeeping, preventing other founders who don't fit the stereotype from raising money. They have glorified young white men with little to no professional experience over female or non-white individuals, even those who are much more prepared. In fact, plenty of studies have found that middle-aged entrepreneurs with more years of professional experience under their belt tend to be more successful founders.

So we should ask questions about whether individuals like these who fit the stereotype are equipped to run teams with hundreds, if not thousands, of employees. Are they thinking deeply about the implications of what they're building? How do they respond to criticism? And how can they balance the business's financial imperatives with its responsibilities to its users and society at large?

In short, some professionals should be in the room, particularly as the company grows. Bankman-Fried is a great example of that. He never got around to appointing a chief financial officer, no matter how much money he raised. That should have been a huge red flag for potential investors. In the aftermath, it's clear that the company lacked basic financial controls. For a currency exchange, that should have been a priority from day one. I've got nothing against investing in visionary founders, but their teams need people ready and willing to hold them accountable.

Recognizing the Bias Around Elite Institutions

Bankman-Fried was educated at elite institutions like MIT. Elizabeth Holmes benefited from her affiliation with Stanford, even though she dropped out. Jessica Richman and Zach Apte, founders of the fraudulent health-tech start-up uBiome, also leveraged their connections to well-respected universities like the University of California, San Francisco, and Oxford. The star of another fraud case, Outcome Health CEO Rishi Shah, was a Northwestern dropout.

According to data from Crunchbase, about 25 percent of US seed or preseed investments between 2020 and 2023 went to founders who are alumni of just three schools: MIT, Harvard, and Stanford. Stanford leads the pack, which isn't surprising given its proximity to Silicon Valley, but is closely followed by Boston-based Harvard and MIT.[3] Investors still select business school graduates to start companies above all. Globally, this is also the case, with companies and investors alike favoring people from the most elite institutions.

When you look at most of the high-profile cases of fraud or wrongdoing in the business world, particularly in venture-backed start-ups, most of the founders emphasized their credentials and education. Let me be clear: Just because someone went to Stanford does not mean they're likely to commit unlawful acts. But it also doesn't mean that we should skip over the due diligence and assume they've got everything it takes to start and run a company. Our society is obsessed with credentials—also known as "credentialism"—which sometimes causes us to overrely on a person's titles or schooling when determining their suitability for a particular role or task.

A subtler lesson here? Let's stop treating people differently just because they went to a certain school or have an advanced degree. How about giving other kinds of entrepreneurs and operators—who went to less elite and expensive schools—a shot? There's no evidence that these individuals will be any less successful at starting and leading companies, despite what Silicon Valley's track record may suggest.

It's Rarely a Fraud from the Start

I believe that the vast majority of guilty CEOs did not set out to commit fraud. More likely, that outcome resulted from a series of bad decisions coupled with a feeling that it was too late to turn back. A research paper from IESE Business School that attempts to build a "process model of deception and legitimacy loss" reveals how that can happen. And it all begins with a powerful story.

Here's a hypothetical case: A founder sets out with a vision to change the world, rallying top investors and other key supporters in the process. Their elite education and network add to their legitimacy and make others more likely to skip their due diligence. One respected venture capital firm agrees to write a check but doesn't do its homework as rigorously as usual due to FOMO. A second investor believes that the original firm did the work and moves ahead quickly without adequately digging in. Over time, the gap between the reality and the hype keeps getting wider. Perhaps the business can't make money, customers start complaining, or there's a breakdown in the culture so that employees leave within months of being hired. As former supporters and investors begin to ask tough questions about the business, the founder feels trapped. They create new deceptions to assuage their investors' concerns. The deceptions continue, until the founder feels it's too late to admit the truth. The entrepreneur may on some level believe in their own hype.

The researchers from IESE used hypothetical stories like this one to understand how the severest cases of fraud can occur. As they found, some founders will double down on the lie even after it becomes clear that a reckoning is coming. In one notable real case outside the tech industry, Fyre Festival organizer Billy McFarland began selling even more luxurious accommodations after he learned that he could not deliver the basics to his guests, like clean water and shelter.

What happens after the word gets out? By studying real cases that follow a similar trajectory, the researchers found that once the deception is revealed, the company's original supporters—including its investors and board—will often point the finger directly at the entrepreneur. That individual will become a laughingstock and a cautionary tale. And yet, as the researchers note, oftentimes a whole lot of people along the way will have turned a blind eye or been complicit in the lie. The prototypical case study is Enron, which got away with a massive accounting fraud for years by misleading investors and keeping its stock high.

So, is there anything we can and should do differently going forward?

It goes without saying that we need to scrutinize businesses appropriately, put the right controls in place, and avoid the temptation to skip the due diligence. If there is a deception or lie of any magnitude, the board and the investors should know about it. It is also the board's responsibility to take care of any emergent problems. In the case of FTX, the fraud should have been obvious to anyone who took a proper look. When, after it was revealed to the public, John J. Ray III was appointed as the new CEO to help recoup funds, he described the company as one of the worst business failures he had ever seen. Ray, a lawyer who specializes in restructuring companies, was best known for leading Enron through bankruptcy proceedings, so he's seen quite a lot.

My takeaway here is that we need to keep our guard up when we meet with powerful storytellers. These individuals may be using their skills for good—or for deception or even outright evil. If a story sounds too good to be true, it very well may be.

Some subtle signs to pay attention to include overselling and a refusal to share specifics. If a business leader can't articulate downside risk—what could go wrong—then they're probably lying to themselves. The vast majority of businesses will face some kind of existential threat. The best anyone can do is come up with ways to mitigate those risks, not to pretend they don't exist.

In my advisory work, I caution founders who are adept at telling their story to avoid letting the gap between reality and hype get too large. Eventually either the business works or it doesn't. If it doesn't, there's no shame in returning the money and starting over with something else. Admitting failure is never easy, but investors tend to be forgiving to those who have tried, given it their best shot, and failed honorably. I've personally seen that time and time again.

As Kislenko puts it, the most common crime in entrepreneurship is losing sight of the real business and its true mission. Over time, it becomes hard to remember why you started the company in the first place. "If you're a good leader and you've got storytelling chops and charisma, then you need to understand the power that comes with that," she said. "Use it responsibly."

CHAPTER 9

Using Storytelling to Raise Capital

Storytelling is the most powerful way to put ideas
into the world today.

—Robert McKee, author, lecturer, and story consultant

There's something you should know about Sequoia Capital, the
most prestigious venture capital firm in the world and an
investor in some of the most successful companies in the world—
FTX notwithstanding. One of its leading investors, Michael
Moritz, began his career as a journalist. We may think of investors as having more technical, business, or financial skill sets, but
Moritz proved to be one of the most successful of all time with
a career behind him as an author and interviewer. That curiosity and passion for storytelling helped him secure investments in
companies that changed the way we live and work, making him a
billionaire in the process.

Moritz's life began about as far from Silicon Valley as you could
possibly imagine. His father was rescued from Nazi Germany as
a young man and earned a place to study at Oxford University,

225

thanks to a scholarship program. He then relocated to Cardiff, Wales, to teach classics at the local university and start a family. His son Michael felt like an outsider growing up in Wales, as one of the very few Jewish children at his school. It was also a highly volatile time. Industrial action by miners and railway workers in the 1970s meant that Britain was beset with blackouts and constant strikes. Most people in those days couldn't count on regular electricity or hot showers.[1]

Moritz, who excelled in school, lived and breathed the news from a young age. He dreamed of growing up and working for a publication like *The Telegraph* or *The Times* on London's Fleet Street. However, a mentor advised him to come to America, which offered more opportunities than the United Kingdom at the time. After getting a history degree from Oxford, he enrolled in a business program at the Wharton School of the University of Pennsylvania. He then landed a job as a correspondent for *Time* magazine in Detroit, where he chronicled the trials and tribulations of the automobile industry. That was the inspiration for his first book, an inside take on charismatic Chrysler CEO Lee Iacocca, who had brought the company back from the brink of ruin. Moritz later described Iacocca's leadership style as the most "seductive and mesmerizing" he'd ever encountered, rivaled only by that of the subject of his next book: Apple cofounder and CEO Steve Jobs.[2]

In the 1980s, Moritz moved to San Francisco with *Time* and aligned himself with the burgeoning technology industry. He felt a strong draw to Jobs, who immediately impressed Moritz with his astonishing talent for marketing and sales. Moritz closely chronicled the company's early years for the magazine, including the development of key products such as the Mac.

Jobs gave him unprecedented access to the company. In return, Moritz wrote a critically acclaimed book about the company titled *The Little Kingdom*, with a focus on the colorful personalities in the executive ranks. Moritz and Jobs became close but had a falling out after Moritz penned a profile that included intimate details about Jobs's daughter, Lisa Brennan-Jobs. At the time, Jobs denied that he was her father. Moritz never repaired the rift with Jobs, but the experience of being in his circle for several years was profound, and he became obsessed with understanding the core qualities that made for a great leader. Moritz later professed that Jobs and Iacocca were the two most powerful storytellers he'd ever known.[3]

Moritz could have stayed at *Time* magazine, where he was offered the role of bureau chief for the San Francisco office. But he wanted to get closer to the start-ups that were popping up in the Bay Area like weeds. He decided that journalism was not an attractive long-term option, and after a brief stint as a media entrepreneur, he made a short list of venture capital firms that he knew from his reporting days and applied for jobs there. Most flatly rejected him because he didn't have the finance or engineering background typical of Silicon Valley's investors.

But Don Valentine, the notoriously conservative and intense founder of Sequoia Capital, one of the most promising new firms at the time, had a notion that he could shake up the firm's image by hiring its first history major. Valentine also wanted to introduce some much-needed diversity into Sequoia's ranks (that seems laughable now as Moritz is, of course, also a white male). And the two men had something—or, rather, someone—in common. Valentine was also a big believer in Apple and had made the fortuitous decision to back the company in the late 1970s with a $150,000 check. Jobs was a bit of a hippy and an oddball who lacked the "right" Ivy League pedigree, but Valentine was willing to look past that because he felt that he was in the presence of a true visionary. Valentine had learned a valuable lesson by making an early bet on Jobs: Don't build your team based on central casting, meaning the stereotypical definition of what a successful business leader should look like.

Moritz later described Sequoia's move to hire him back in 1986 as a "head-scratcher" for virtually every fund at the time. But in the decades that followed, Moritz knocked it out of the park. His track record in terms of financial returns would become the envy of every technology investor in Silicon Valley. Moritz-led investments include such internet monoliths as Google, Yahoo, Zappos, and PayPal. In both 2005 and 2006, the Midas List ranked him as the top investor, meaning that for a period of several years, he was regarded as the most successful venture capitalist in the world. He remains the richest Welshman, with billions of dollars to his name. To come full circle, he now funds *The San Francisco Standard*, a news publication with a mission to better share the story of San Francisco.

So how did Moritz do it, given his nontraditional background as an investor?

In his own estimation, Moritz was particularly good at two things: synthesizing information quickly about new technologies that he was unfamiliar with and having a nose for sniffing out great storytellers. His methods for rooting out the best founders are legendary, particularly within the walls of Sequoia's offices. One tactic, according to former Sequoia investors I spoke with, involved asking a founder questions about their life rather than their business, such as inviting them to talk about their childhood before the age of twelve. Moritz was known across the firm for doing that before delving into the intricacies of the product or being walked through a pitch deck. For Moritz, the tactic helped him understand the founder's psychology and connect with them emotionally. By asking questions, as a trained journalist would do, he could gauge whether they could tell a compelling story—and if they had the necessary determination to succeed.[4]

Moritz doesn't often speak in public, but he has made his inclinations toward storytellers known. Today, he describes storytelling as the most vital skill in any founder's arsenal. "If you had to pick one skill, weirdly, yes, outside of technical prowess, and understanding our domain, product and all, it's storytelling," he coached a roomful of entrepreneurs during a rare speaking appearance. As Moritz explained, it all begins when a founder has to convince a cofounder to join their "nutty enterprise." From there, the founder needs to motivate the cofounders and the early team to work super hard, often at the expense of everything else in their lives. At some point, a customer needs to come on board, despite the fact that no others have agreed to do so before. Once a founder crosses that chasm, they then have to sell the story to "gullible people like us," he said, referring to Silicon Valley's venture capital funds. Imagine for a minute what it would take to do all of the above, especially for young founders without much job experience. There's something so irrational about the whole thing that you can't help but admire it.

"If people can't tell stories," Moritz has said, "I don't think they succeed as leaders."

Why Funding Is So Psychological

Most venture capitalists believe that their industry sits squarely at the intersection of art and science, straddling the ethereal and the technical. A helpful way to think about it is that investors rely on both the rational and the emotional in making decisions. But in reality, they usually start with the emotional. It takes time to rigorously go through the numbers, a task that usually happens later in the process with early-stage businesses, once the investors have already made a gut-level decision that the start-up is promising enough to dig in. Some funds have even built algorithms to add some science to the undertaking, such as Sweden's EQT Ventures and California's Correlation Ventures. However, evidence is mixed that these approaches work well when leading deals and taking big ownership stakes versus making smaller investments in venture capital rounds where another firm has done the work to get conviction. That indicates that algorithms may be most helpful in steering funds to join investment rounds as "participants" or "follow-on" investors, which in theory is a lower-risk proposition but may also result in lower financial returns.

Google's venture fund, now called GV, once had an algorithm with a so-called spotlight system that could kill potential investment opportunities if their metrics weren't promising. Per reporting from *Axios*, after using the algorithm, the company shelved it in 2022, once its investors realized they were making better decisions without it.[5]

GV's experience is in line with research on this kind of investment algorithm, which indicates that computer-based approaches are mostly helpful for inexperienced investors rather than seasoned ones. For instance, when a group of researchers in Switzerland at the University of St. Gallen built an investment algorithm in 2020 and compared its performance with the returns of 255 angel investors of varying experience levels, the results were striking. They found that the experienced investors fared far better than the algorithm, but the novices did not. The algorithm also made biased decisions, even when it wasn't fed race or gender-related data (which the researchers had access to but didn't share). It simply reproduced the same social inequities that were inherent in the training data, noting in its own conclusions that women founders tended to get funded less in follow-on rounds and should therefore be deprioritized. Meanwhile, when the experienced investors chose to invest in women and nonwhite founders or in nonconsensus ideas, they tended to dramatically outperform the algorithm.

So making purely analytical decisions doesn't remove bias, and it doesn't lead to better investment returns. There *has* to be more to an investment decision than rational arbitration. "Funding is very emotional, and it is very psychological," stresses Laura Huang, a Harvard Business School associate professor who's made studying VCs and their investments the focus of her decade-long research. For a recent study published in the *Academy of Management Journal*, Huang surveyed hundreds of venture capitalists about why they choose to spend more time with certain companies over others. Investors would often tell her about the superior product or the big market. But most of them, when pressed about what really drew them in, also acknowledged the importance of their "gut instinct." It wasn't uncommon for investors to tell Huang that they essentially made decisions within ten or fifteen seconds of meeting an entrepreneur based on a "feeling in their tummy."

That may sound random, like throwing darts blindfolded to see what hits the target. However, Huang found that the gut feeling was often based on a sense of connection, typically attributable to the founders' ability to both tell their personal stories and communicate their business plans (sometimes the two are intertwined). Sometimes the gut feeling arose because the investor could relate to the problem that the founder's business addressed. All of these dimensions, Huang argued, were helpful to investors in finding "home runs"—the biggest successes in the portfolio. She found that investors who weren't listening to their gut ended up playing it too safe to be successful, as the analytical side of their brains uncovered too many reasons why a potential funding opportunity might not succeed.

Huang's takeaway from all this research is that storytelling is an important way to forge a connection between a founder and an entrepreneur. This is particularly true for founders starting their first company or for those with little market traction.

I'll demonstrate that by way of an example. Close your eyes and think of yourself as a venture capitalist sitting in a San Francisco coffee shop. I'll give you a moment to imagine yourself in a Patagonia vest and Allbirds sneakers while you sip your oat milk cappuccino.

Founder 1 walks into the café and introduces themselves via their credentials, before reeling off a litany of data about the size of the market and the revenue opportunity ahead for their new ride-sharing mobile application.

Founder 2 walks in an hour later and shares a story about their recent experience standing in the rain waiting for a taxi at one o'clock in the morning. They then introduce an idea for an app that lets anyone with a smartphone grab a car in minutes—and they provide a quick demo to show how it might work. They ask you, the investor, to suspend disbelief and envision a world where no one has to shiver on a sidewalk corner on a winter night, desperately trying to flag down taxis filled with passengers. They close by walking you through the massive market opportunity and the chance to fundamentally transform the world of transportation as we know it.

Which of these pitches would be more memorable, especially if you had heard about ten others that same day?

I suspect the vast majority of us would pick Founder 2, assuming they did not have fundamentally dissimilar credentials to Founder 1.

And why is that? We learned in the introduction to this book that the human brain does not process data feeds very well. We process narrative. We aren't computers, and for that reason we are not hardwired to be logical in all circumstances or retain facts for very long. Feeling an emotion is a signal to our brains that we are experiencing something important. That makes us remember one pitch over another, even if the two businesses are identical.

David Krane, the CEO of GV and one of its first marketing and communications hires, remembers every detail of one of his favorite pitches of all time: the moment he heard Tony Fadell, the former senior vice president of Apple's iPod division, come in and share the vision for his top-secret new business. The pitch took place in 2011, but Krane described the encounter almost a decade and a half later as if it had happened yesterday. He recalled how Fadell got his firm to sign a confidentiality agreement, which remains uncommon for venture firms to agree to. Once they settled on a time, Fadell then asked to use one of the conference rooms for an hour prior to the pitch, another unusual ask.

Only a few of the partners were allowed to join the pitch at Fadell's request, so Krane recalled which of his colleagues walked in with him. He remembered that one of his fellow investors made an audible sigh the moment that they realized what Krane would be pitching after so much suspense. It wasn't some kind of new competitor to the iPhone or another kind of fancy gadget—it was a thermostat. Of all things, a thermostat?

By the end of the pitch, the investment partners were all completely and utterly sold. In Krane's own words, here's how Fadell used his storytelling superpowers to win:

We noticed there were several piles covered in black velvet drop cloth that were lined up in a runway down the center of the pitch table. As much as I had the urge to yank the drapery off, it was clear to me he wanted to take off the cloth himself. So that's what he did. When we finally got to what he was building, the drop cloth came off and it was a thermostat. There was that sigh from one of my colleagues, likely audible. Most of us were doing a version of this sigh internally because we were surprised, he had picked a thermostat, and honestly, we were a little disappointed. We let him finish his founder-led storytelling, though. *It was amazing.* He told us to look around the room right now. Fadell asked us to hold up our fingers and point at the beige devices that protruded from the walls. I remember thinking, "They all suck. I see them all, but no consumer can interact with them really. None are wireless and none are on the network." After we had made that observation, Tony [Fadell] told us to imagine we transformed these *unloved computers* into something interoperable, something accessible. He prompted us to consider that they could even work for us behind-the-scenes, something that could make our lives better.

The word that Fadell used multiple times, which Krane scrawled over his notebook and underlined, was "unloved."

He still remembers it because it activated him emotionally to hear that word, and it surprised him, given Fadell used it to refer to everyday products that most people rarely think about. Suddenly, he wanted to join Fadell and build a device that consumers could genuinely love and appreciate. He had fully bought into the vision of creating a new kind of thermostat that could learn people's schedules, including what temperature they liked and if they were in the home or not. Krane, off the back of that one pitch in that conference room, decided to lead the company's Series B and Series C rounds. He also did everything he could to guide it to a successful landing at Google.

Fadell's company was acquired for $3.2 billion three years later, making it one of the most successful hardware acquisitions of all time. Raising capital for hardware companies remains far more challenging than for software companies because of how challenging it can be to manufacture and commercialize devices. But Fadell succeeded because he cared about storytelling. He was trained by Steve Jobs, one of the master orators of all time, who instilled in him that customers didn't want to hear about what the product did. First, they had to understand why they needed it. Jobs made it look natural and easy, even as he would show up to presentations deeply prepared. Fadell, when pitching GV, convinced Krane and his team that he had learned at the foot of the master.

Foundational Storytelling

Sequoia, the firm that launched Moritz's career, retains its commitment to storytelling. From day one, it grounds its founders in skills that they wouldn't get elsewhere. In 2022, the firm launched an exclusive storytelling and product-development boot camp called Arc, led by one of its partners, Jess Lee.[6]

Much of the program is remote, but in-person elements involve field trips and speaker presentations. The program starts at Sequoia's headquarters on Sand Hill Road, that tree-lined Silicon Valley arterial road that has the densest concentration of venture capital offices in the world. In the first week, the founders sit through sessions led by screenwriters and slam poets flown up from Los Angeles. That lineup has included "Rives" from the HBO show *Def Poetry Jam*, who shares tips with the founders on how to loosen up in front of a live audience, such as speaking with intention and leaving space for both humor and improvisation. In the past, the group has also visited the movie studio Lucasfilm to get a walk-through on how to storyboard a film.

James Buckhouse, a well-known designer and lecturer at Stanford University, oversees the storytelling portion of the program. Buckhouse previously worked in animation at DreamWorks, where he worked on the *Shrek* franchise, before making the jump to Twitter and later to Sequoia. Buckhouse is a partner at the fund, but he doesn't make the investment decisions himself. Instead, he leads a small team that supports the portfolio companies (the start-ups that Sequoia has invested in) with story-driven design. He's a big believer that the products the tech community creates should be grounded in human experience and connected to an overarching narrative, rather than a series of pixels or lines of code designed to drive behaviors. He also strongly feels that entrepreneurs need to leverage stories in how they talk about their businesses and themselves and avoid getting into the weeds with metrics alone. One of his taglines is "Persuade with emotion but justify with logic." He's also something of a renegade in the tech world because he preaches methods that can't easily be quantified. It's a bitter pill to swallow in Silicon Valley, which is overrun with data-obsessed engineers.

As Buckhouse once said, "There's no faster way to make people actively ignore you and hate you for no good reason than to tell them you're a storyteller. Yet, without a story, we have no mechanism by which to generate a machine inside the minds of others that does positive work on our behalf, and on behalf of the planet. The story is what motivates us. The story is what helps us find meaning in not just our momentary actions but in our long-term actions."[7]

Think about that for a second. If you're an entrepreneur trying to start something, is there anything more essential than motivating talented individuals to rally behind your vision? If you can't convince investors, users, key hires, and customers, your business won't get the vital liftoff it needs. The story is what leaves all of these stakeholders with the right impression. Once the story is in their minds, it starts doing all that positive work on your behalf, even after you've left the room.

Buckhouse kicked off Arc's inaugural year by walking the founders through one very powerful story in particular: the third installment of the *Matrix* franchise. Part of the genius of the *Matrix* is that it leverages so many traditional storytelling tropes but still feels fresh given its science-fiction backdrop. The whole plot revolves around a "chosen one" on a quest to liberate humanity from its imprisonment by machines. He chose it because it's such a classic example of a "hero's journey," a common story type identified by the academic Joseph Campbell in the late 1940s. The hero's journey essentially involves a departure from the ordinary world, followed by an initiation into a special world via a series of challenges, and, finally, a triumphant return.

The hero's journey is a device that authors and screenwriters frequently use, and it's deeply familiar to anyone who's watched *Star Wars*. But we've also seen versions of it succeed in business many times over, particularly in Silicon Valley. And it's particularly effective in fundraising, because it harmonizes well with the common entrepreneurial situation of founders taking on challenging problems that few believe they can solve. No one expects entrepreneurship to be easy, so we delight in tales where founders overcome insurmountable odds, unlocking an important set of insights in the process. This kind of story helps us believe that a founder really can start that once-in-a-decade business and that it might just work, despite the overwhelming odds.

For these reasons, the best storytelling CEOs have been leveraging the hero's journey for years. Ellen S. O'Connor and Denise M. Lucy from the Institute for Leadership Studies interviewed dozens of CEOs in Silicon Valley in the early 2000s about their path to success. They discovered that the vast majority shared a story featuring a "self-driving agent overcoming obstacles to reach a goal, like an epic hero." O'Connor, in earlier research, also demonstrated that founders who used this narrative had greater success than others in raising funding. In her view, it works so well because it justifies the founder's right to represent a company and its values. It gets the point across that they are the right person to run this business and are likely to succeed despite their lack of professional experience.

One Heroine's Journey

One of my favorite examples of a hero's journey story involves Kate Ryder, CEO of a company called Maven Clinic and a Brooklyn-based mother of three kids. I first heard Ryder pitch Maven almost a decade ago, while I was working as a journalist. At the time, Ryder didn't have much going for her except a good idea and a lot of belief in her own abilities (both necessary qualities for anyone starting a company but not always sufficient for success). She was also a masterful storyteller. That proved to be a big competitive advantage for her at every stage of the business, as newer and bigger challenges arose. Her overarching story is the perfect illustration of the hero's (or rather the heroine's) journey. So let's walk through it in detail, and we'll refer back to the typical plot points throughout. It doesn't map out perfectly, but it's close enough.

Before starting her company, Ryder worked as a journalist for a number of years. Eventually, she got the urge to give entrepreneurship a try. As she describes it, it was in her blood. Her father and grandparents on both sides of the family had started their own businesses, and their work left a big impression on the young Kate. She made the jump into venture capital to learn about how companies were getting funded and to explore some potential ideas, landing a coveted role at Index Ventures in London, where she worked with some of the most elite investors in the business, who took her under their wing.

While at Index, she noticed that several of her female colleagues were struggling, mostly in silence, with pregnancy, the birth experience, and the postpartum months. Some weren't returning to work as they had expected to, despite having promising careers ahead of them, because of struggles with depression, painful pelvic floor issues, a lack of child-care support, or ongoing challenges with breastfeeding. These women, for the most part, were privileged, with good salaries and paid time off. So this made her wonder how women without resources, including the millions living in maternal-care deserts who lacked access to a physician or midwife, were managing. That insight led her onto the path of building a company in maternal health, a sector that had received very little investment at the time. Most investors were male and hadn't struggled with pregnancy personally, so the problem didn't seem important.

Index believed in Ryder enough to write her a $50,000 check to get her idea off the ground, a promising start. From there, she almost immediately hit roadblocks. The biggest was her difficulty raising further financing rounds to get her business started. She didn't give up, leveraging her background as a reporter by interviewing all the new mothers and health-care providers she knew so that she could deeply understand all sides of the problem.

That led to her solution, which was truly innovative at the time: providing online access to care rather than requiring patients to be seen in person. She discovered that a lot of support could be made available online, enabling women who were miles away from a lactation consultant, therapist, or doula to get the help they needed.

But there was still a lot of skepticism about her idea. Male investors—clearly not even bothering to hide their biases—told Ryder that no man would ever come to work for her, that the women's health market was small, and that women did not need this kind of help, citing as evidence the fact that their own wives did not need such help. These objections seemed inane to Ryder, but she also knew that she would run out of money quickly without the support of these investors. So she took a different tack by leaning into the far smaller pool of female investors she knew and making her struggles to raise capital part of the narrative. This gave her an edge because Ryder's cold reception by male investors infuriated the women she was pitching. It also demonstrated how much grit Ryder had, because she hadn't turned her back on her business even after dozens of rejections in a row.

Once Ryder shared her insights and showed some early traction from potential customers, notably large employers, she secured financing for Maven Clinic from Spring Mountain Capital's Lauren Brueggen for the first round and Sequoia's Jess Lee for the second round, so her company could grow. Ryder subsequently had her own kids, and she used Maven Clinic each time to prepare for motherhood.

Ryder has become an inspiration to other women's health founders and female business leaders who have faced similar challenges. Ultimately, those who bet on Ryder were rewarded. In 2022, she broke through the glass ceiling in a big way when she became the first CEO of a women's health company to become a "unicorn," the Silicon Valley term for the elite group of companies that achieve a $1 billion valuation. Even in the market downturn that followed, Ryder's business continued to raise follow-on capital, becoming a true darling of the health-care sector.

Maven Clinic's success also proved to be a big turning point for the women's health industry. It's true that this sector still doesn't receive its fair share of investment, but the industry now benefits from having a few examples of success, including Ryder's company. That has led to a rising interest in women's health, after its being one of the most underfunded categories within health care for years. While not every story fits perfectly into the hero's journey—a stage or two may be missing—the idea is to follow the trajectory as closely as possible, without feeling the need to deviate too far from real life.

The hero's journey can be a neat storytelling device for any business, particularly with the benefit of hindsight following a satisfying resolution. There were moments of tension, breakthrough, and realization followed by success (although in Maven Clinic's case, the ending has yet to be written, because the company is still growing and evolving). In addition to leveraging this narrative, Ryder didn't forget to mention the fundamentals when she was pitching investors. She emphasized the potential size of the market—in this case, roughly $14 billion—and mentioned any similar or competing companies that were generating sizable revenues. There weren't many at the time, but she may have pointed to a company founded a few years prior called Progyny, which was having success in the adjacent fertility market. She also described how selling to large employers meant a shorter sales cycle than traditional health-care companies face. Selling to enterprises is far easier than selling to hospitals or insurance companies, and the contracts are often structured in ways that are highly favorable to vendors like Maven Clinic.

To succeed in pitching investors, founders should also include details about their long-term margins, their technological "moats," and the quality of their team. It's also helpful to elaborate any prior success the founders may have had and to exit with the suggestion that lightning could strike twice. All of this should emphasize the clear message that an investor can make a lot of money by investing early. Chapter 8 describes in detail the power of FOMO in the human psychology, particularly when it comes to deal making.

Not all companies bear a resemblance to Maven Clinic. But entrepreneurs, no matter the stage of the business, can embody the hero's journey in their own way. The struggle might involve a fight with a large competitor or a lack of believers in the idea. Ultimately, there must be some kind of revelation, which in the classic tale leads to a kind of rebirth and then a triumphant return with newfound knowledge, inspiration, wisdom, and, ultimately, success. These stories resonate because they make us believe in something and give us a sense of control in a chaotic world. They remind us that like Neo from the Matrix, Luke Skywalker from Star Wars, and countless other movie heroes, we have the power to change things for the better.

Some founders have gone as far as intentionally adopting the hero's journey in how they talk about their business.

One entrepreneur, Chris Myers, even penned a piece for *Forbes* describing how other entrepreneurs can best use it to make their company's story more interesting. As he wrote, "It makes an otherwise boring story seem interesting and helps people to connect with our mission on a deeper level." Many have found these plots to be transformational in ways that a traditional elevator pitch—referring to a founder's ability to share their pitch with a venture capitalist in a matter of minutes—is not.

CHAPTER 10

Storytelling and Bias

> Everyone is a prisoner of his own experiences. No
> one can eliminate prejudices—just recognize them.
>
> —Edward R. Murrow, broadcaster

Companies led by women CEOs tend to perform better on the stock market than those run by men, according to a report from S&P Global.[1] And yet, when there's significant media attention to the appointment of a female CEO to a publicly traded company, its stock drops in the short-term by 2 to 3 percent, a study by Kellogg School of Management showed. That indicates the dip is a direct reaction to the appointment.

The markets are supposed to be rational, so what explains this discrepancy?

Ned Smith, a late associate professor of management and organizations at Kellogg, assumed that women leaders are disadvantaged from the start due to sexism and gender discrimination in the workplace. But as Smith and his team dug deeper into the research, looking at the media mentions and accounting for any bias related to the tone of the announcements, they made a confusing discovery. Companies where women CEOs experienced less media attention saw no drop in stock prices compared to those whose appointees got much more buzz. And for appointments of male CEOs, the amount of media attention didn't seem to have much of an impact on stock price at all.

In other words, if women were appointed CEOs, Wall Street would only react favorably if they didn't draw too much attention to themselves or the media didn't pay much attention to them. Why is that? Smith hypothesized that when investors learn about female CEO appointments, they are capable of reacting rationally, knowing that female CEOs tend to be good for the company's long-term stock price. That's not the problem. Smith only learned about the real problem later. When the New York Stock Exchange analyzed a group of six companies led by women, they found that these companies didn't just outperform the broader stock market; they tended to "double its returns over the same period." One hypothesis is that women who have made it to CEO rank tend to be better performers because they've faced more adversity than men to get there.

Let's shift back to our (mostly male) financiers on Wall Street. When investors see a lot of news about the appointment of a female CEO, they might know that this company could actually perform better. But they may assume that other investors in the market are likely to react negatively because of their bias—and *that* drives the stock price down.

"It's one of those things that makes you realize just how depressing some of your findings can be," Smith shared after revealing his hypothesis. These investors themselves weren't inherently biased against female CEOs. But they believed each other to be biased. And that made them react in a way that perpetuated more biases.

The topic of bias is so complicated because there's the black-and-white kind and the kind that involves many shades of gray. Some is unconscious—as the example of how the stock market treats female CEO appointments demonstrates. We are making progress in some dimensions but have a long way to go in others.

A *long* way to go. Just look at the key statistics, which are oft cited but still bear repeating: In America, Black men and women make up more than 14.4 percent of the population but just 1.6 percent of Fortune 500 CEOs. Hispanic and Latino people comprise the largest ethnic minority at 19.1 percent but account for only about 9 percent of CEOs in the S&P 500 (back in 2018, it was just 3 percent). Age-related discrimination toward employees who are more senior, which is discussed far less than gender or racial discrimination, remains pervasive across most industries, notably in business, finance, and technology. AARP, the group that represents older Americans, has long studied this phenomenon against Americans aged fifty and older in the labor force. In annual surveys, participants consistently state that their age has made it harder for them to land a job. Meanwhile, there are *still* barely any CEOs in the Fortune 500 who publicly identify as LGBTQ+, with the most well-known exception being Apple CEO Tim Cook.

In this chapter, we'll dive into a few high-profile examples of double standards—but we'll end on a practical note. None of it is fair, but there are ways to mitigate bias and move forward on a more level playing field, even as a single individual without a platform. As Harvard Business School professor Laura Huang argues in her excellent book *Edge: Turning Adversity into Advantage*, there are ways to acknowledge the stereotypes for those impacted by biases and to guide the perceptions of others. Huang notes that we can take action to move others' perceptions in a new direction rather than being at their mercy. In other words, we can take control of the narrative.

Imagine, for example, a female CEO is being appointed to a publicly traded company. To avoid stock dips, she might choose to avoid media attention altogether. Or she could not only explicitly make clear that she is a female CEO but also tell a story that emphasizes the exceptional qualities (grit, determination, courage) that she needed to get to this position, with a series of specific examples. GM's Mary Barra is a fantastic example as she does recognize in media interviews that she is one of the few female CEOs in the Fortune 500. She is also inclined to share advice with other women when asked, including to remain action-oriented even in times of hardship. That is straight out of the Huang playbook and might actually work, even as we acknowledge how frustrating it is that anyone who isn't a white man has to formulate these kinds of strategies.

We're finally seeing a few signs of progress. Rather than stock dips, we see more companies' market caps jumping when they appoint Black CEOs. A group of management professors studied this phenomenon and concluded that the simple reason is that these CEOs tend to be more qualified than their white counterparts—and the market is *finally* recognizing that fact.

Double Standards and the Media

There was a golden era when it seemed like a group of female CEOs had broken through the glass ceiling. These women were building power on their own terms and creating the next generation of brands in the process. In the late 2010s and through the early 2020s, companies like The Wing, Calibrate, Outdoor Voices, Glossier, and Away—all led by prominent millennial women—were raising tens of millions of dollars from venture capitalists and sparking a movement in the process. Remember the term "Girl Boss"? When I was in my twenties and working in technology journalism, that defined the zeitgeist of the time.

For a few years, anyway. One after another, these female CEOs became targets of criticism and so-called takedowns in the popular business press. Targets included Mos (education), Spring Health (mental health), ThirdLove (consumer retail), Outdoor Voices (athleisure), The Wing (consumer), Cleo (health care), Away (consumer), Calibrate (medicine), Glossier (beauty), and the list goes on. All these companies were led by women CEOs. Some of the allegations proved legitimate—several of these companies, including The Wing, were accused of fostering a racist culture and mistreating staff—while other allegations seemed borderline petty, such as former employees complaining about remaining in the office until 6 p.m. It got to the point when technology investor Marc Andreessen in 2022 tweeted, "Get you a hobby you love as much as the press loves running hit pieces on aggressive, determined female founders."

By 2023, tensions were so high that two of the biggest names in journalism—Kara Swisher and Jessica Lessin—met for a

Zoom get-together to address the topic head-on. Both agreed that the press needed to take a hard look at the motivations of the employees who were speaking out against their current or former CEOs, typically anonymously. They also encouraged reporters to consider the implications when they use terms like "aggressive" or "toxic" to describe these female CEOs. Do reporters typically refer to male leaders in this way? For that matter, Swisher and Lessin wondered, why had the media overlooked the bad behavior of so many male CEOs, including notorious cases like Travis Kalanick at Uber, while zeroing in on women again and again for relatively minor infractions?

"I think, as reporters, we don't want to admit we get influenced like this . . . but maybe we should think about it," Swisher told Lessin. "I don't think we do . . . but instead of knee-jerk saying, 'That's not what's happening, it's not sexism,' it just is."

The most appropriate terminology here is "double standard." Boards expect women to perform at the same level as, or better than, their male peers. However, many employees also expect women to differ from typical male leaders, exhibiting warmer and more nurturing qualities. It is a high-wire balancing act where no one is satisfied. Studies have shown that investors, as well as the larger business community, tend to perceive women leaders as less suited to entrepreneurship, despite evidence to the contrary, because they lack the aggressive "cowboy" traits that men supposedly have. Among Fortune 500 companies, only 8.2 percent of CEOs are women. Women hold about 28 percent of corporate board seats, a big improvement over decades ago but still not remotely representative.

The result of all this bad press? There are fewer high-profile, women-led start-ups than there were just a few years ago. At Outdoor Voices, female founder Tyler Haney was replaced by male fashion executive Mickey Drexler, previously the CEO of J.Crew, in the wake of a series of news stories about the supposedly "toxic" work environment she created. Outdoor Voices is now reportedly shutting down its retail stores and is rumored to be headed toward bankruptcy. Isabelle Kenyon, founder of the obesity medicine company Calibrate, was also replaced with a white male executive. Calibrate, after raising tens of millions of dollars from venture capitalists to ride one of the biggest tailwinds in history with the rise of the GLP-1 drugs, was later acquired by a private equity firm, reportedly for a fraction of its former valuation.

One could argue that these businesses struggled or failed for other reasons, related to market conditions or poor performance. And that may well be true. But there's no doubt the negative press and double standards accelerated the demise of these businesses and their CEOs. As former HP executive turned politician Carly Fiorina described it, women are either "the bimbo" or "the bitch," meaning they're either too soft or too hard. Rarely can they be anything in between—let alone simply be themselves.

Age-Related Bias: Both "Hard" and "Soft"

Researchers and sociologists Justyna Stypińska and Konrad Turek found that age-related discrimination is extremely common across workplaces today, most notably in industries like technology, media, and finance that prioritize younger employees who in theory can pull off an insane workload. But the bias doesn't just affect senior-level staff. In many industries, it also impacts the youngest employees who are entering the workforce and are perceived to have fewer marketable skill sets. Much of that occurs because of the way that these companies are set up, differentiating between lower-level workers, middle managers, and senior executives. Those who are over the age of forty benefit from laws on the books to protect them from discrimination, but only a few states have laws to protect younger employees.

The research uncovered that this type of discrimination can take two forms: hard and soft. Hard discrimination is the illegal kind that can get you fired and in deep trouble, like denying someone a promotion because of their age. The soft kind might include an off-color comment or joke and is rooted in stereotypes. The law doesn't explicitly prohibit that unless it results in an adverse employment decision. Nonetheless, it can still affect an individual's self-esteem and confidence, and it remains a major problem everywhere I look.

Bias Against Marginalized and Underrepresented People

Even as corporate America spouts diversity, equity, and inclusion (DE&I) committees (most companies now have some form of a group dedicated to DE&I), that hasn't stopped discrimination against Black and Latino workers. According to a 2021 poll, one in four say they have experienced some form of discrimination at work, far higher than the percentage of white respondents. Plenty of studies have shown that DE&I programs are worthy, but they aren't translating into real impact. That may be because so many of the problems that people experience day to day are cultural, and research has found that the problems are often based on white employees' assumption that they lack common ground with their coworkers. Important research from Harvard Business School zeroed in on a few common problems. Black employees reported that they weren't asked about their social lives by their peers or invited to social gatherings like lunches or after-work happy hours. They also reported that they couldn't express their true selves at work, including moments of genuine frustration or anger. All of this adds up to a lack of confidence and a feeling of merely surviving, rather than thriving, at work.

In studies on workplace discrimination, LGBTQ+ employees have also reported experiencing unfair treatment at work, and this is particularly pronounced for LGBTQ+ employees of color. That experience can negatively impact well-being and reduce job commitment and satisfaction. According to a 2021 poll, 45 percent of LGBTQ+ workers reported experiencing unfair treatment at work, including being fired or harassed because of their sexual orientation or gender identity. About 31 percent said this was still ongoing or that they had experienced it within the past five years.

Indeed, despite our efforts to combat it, including five decades of federal legislation designed to protect employees, discrimination is still alive and well in workplaces today. And the first step to doing something about it is to acknowledge that it exists.

How We Receive Stories

As you may have gleaned, this chapter isn't just about telling a story effectively. Instead, it prompts us to step into the role of the audience and think deeply about how we *receive* stories. If a young, handsome, Ivy League–educated white man is sharing an ambitious vision for his business, do we hear what he says differently than we do if a woman, Asian American, or older person is telling the same story? Do we have divergent expectations? Even if we believe that we are not biased and do not hold common stereotypes, the research tells us that we do.

Despite the strides we've made in equity and inclusion, we still live in a world where a person's looks, gender, accent, age, and race, in addition to a multitude of other factors, matter more than what they have to say. So much so that we even make judgment calls about people's abilities before they've even uttered a word. As an example, researchers from the University of the West of Scotland analyzed the eye gazes of people looking at social media profiles for prospective job candidates. They found that females were judged by their appearance, including their profile pictures, while men were judged on the basis of their profile's content, such as their interests and posts. All of that impacted people's ability to get the job.

In the world of entrepreneurship and venture capital, where I worked for years, the problem is particularly bad. Think of Silicon Valley as "ground zero" for this kind of bias because the tech world so clearly favors young, college-educated white men (bonus points for being good-looking). White men control an astounding 93 percent of venture capital dollars. Most of the large firms only had one female partner, if any. Very few had any Black or Hispanic check writers. So it is perhaps unsurprising, given our bias for investing in people who look and sound like us, that all-female founding teams receive just 2.3 percent of venture funding. Black entrepreneurs fare even worse, receiving less than 1 percent of available funding.

And yet none of this makes any logical sense: 70 percent of the so-called unicorns, meaning companies with a valuation of more than $1 billion, have founders who are immigrants, women, or people of color.

Laura Huang, the Harvard Business School professor who wrote the book on countering adversity, has spent years studying bias and venture capital. In one particularly sobering study, she lined up a group of men and women to deliver the exact same start-up pitch to an audience, which evaluated them and rated how likely they would be to invest. She also asked a separate study group to rate the men and the women on their looks ("attractive" versus "unattractive").

Which group do you think got the most positive response?

Resoundingly, it was the attractive men. Next came the unattractive men, and in last place, the women. With women, physical attractiveness did not seem to make much of a difference to how the audience perceived the pitch. It is not entirely clear why that is, but one compelling theory is that our society often assumes attractive women have only achieved success because of their looks. So, in that sense, their achievements are somehow less deserving than a man's.

People with accents, whether male or female, also fared less well across the board, proving how much bias we still have against immigrants or anyone from a different culture.

Our preference for men, and particularly for white, attractive men, comes down to the qualities that we give them unconsciously, which in our minds will make them more likely to succeed. Huang found that the men were more likely to be assigned positive qualities, including assertiveness or courage. Those same attributes are far less likely to be associated with women or people of color—and when they are, it is in a negative way. This is why, for example, people tend to view men and women of color as bossy, domineering, or overconfident.

This makes it extremely difficult for CEOs who are not white men to navigate expectations from their board, their employees, and other key stakeholders. Take a recent piece in *Vox*, targeting the retail start-up ThirdLove, which we first encountered in Chapter 3. The reporting included criticisms targeting CEO Heidi Zak from former employees related to the late hours they were expected to work (until 6 p.m.) and the pressure to join after-work happy hours. They also claimed Zak had not done enough to protect employees from her co-CEO and husband, Dave Spector, who was described as intimidating. Toward the bottom of the article, the writer included a few quotes from employees who said their team left at 5 p.m., that they were happy at work, and that they were indeed able to take time off to take care of personal matters.

While reading the piece, I couldn't help thinking to myself that ThirdLove is a venture-backed start-up with a board of directors and immense pressure to hit its targets, just like any other company. That's not easy for any CEO, let alone a female CEO held to near-impossible standards. How do you run an early-stage company that's *more* employee-friendly than any company run by a man, while also beating competitors on key metrics that investors care about, like capital efficiency and revenue growth? Again, I'm reminded of the dichotomy and the double standard. Women somehow need to be aggressive when it comes to making their companies successful—on par with a man—and yet they also must be warm and cuddly and nice.

Another rising-star CEO, April Koh from Spring Health, was admonished in the media for helming a culture where employees felt they needed to work too much, leading some to tell reporters they felt burned out. Koh was a hard worker, which sent a message to employees that they needed to be too. But why are the CEO's long hours considered an example of "burnout culture"? By contrast, I recently listened to a podcast episode with three men (investor Keith Rabois, founder Mike Shebat, and investor Harry Stabbings) who discussed in detail Shebat's commitment to what he calls an "Olympian work ethic" at his start-up. In this case, the company was held up as a model for what to do when it comes to making a start-up successful. Nobody on the podcast seemed to pay much attention to the risk of burnout or seemed concerned about that aspect of the start-up's culture. Instead, the resounding message was, if you can't hack it and keep up with the pace, then don't join the company. And that's perfectly fine. Even if the company is treating its employees unpleasantly in some ways, male-led companies aren't being criticized for that—even if some parties may consider those criticisms to be legitimate. Because female-led companies are being criticized publicly for not meeting lofty standards and male-led companies aren't being held to really any standards at all, the gap grows even larger.

As we listen to women and nonwhite CEOs tell their stories, how we react to what we hear reveals another way in which our bias comes out. The questions we ask often indicate that we seem to be rooting for women to fail, while we are more inclined to believe that men will succeed.

Huang has revealed this by studying the follow-up questions that men and women founders receive during popular start-up pitch competitions, like at *TechCrunch* Disrupt. She found that male founders are more likely to get questions about how they will win—"promotion-focused questions"—allowing them to play up their positive attributes as they respond to each question. Women are more likely to be peppered with questions from investors about how they'll avoid downside risk—what she calls "prevention-focused questions"—that put them on the defensive. Huang argues that promotion-focused questions typically lead to promotion-focused answers, while prevention-focused questions lead to prevention-focused answers.

After studying 140 interactions between investors and founders at 189 pitch competitions, Huang found that entrepreneurs who were asked prevention-focused questions—predominantly women and minorities—raised an average of $563,000. Those who received promotion-focused questions—mostly white men—went on to get an average of $7.9 million in funding. The bias here may not be evident at once, but it exists because the questions that men receive are more likely to set them up for success.

This Happens Every Day

Venture capital may be a particularly biased corner of the business world, but this problem occurs every day at companies worldwide, including those that are publicly traded household names.

Consider this case study: Rosalind Brewer, one of the most powerful Black women in America and the former CEO of Sam's Club, was referred to as a "racist" by her own employees when she made a comment on television about the importance of diversity and inclusion. Some people even took to social media to threaten to boycott her business. If you're wondering what prompted that, here's what she said to Poppy Harlow, a journalist with CNN, in a television interview:

> My executive team is very diverse, and I make that a priority. I demand it of my team and within the structure. *And then, every now and then, you have to nudge your partners, and you have to speak up and speak out.* And I try to use my platform for that. . . . I try to set an example. I try to mentor many women inside my company and outside the company because I think it's import-ant. Just today, we met with a supplier and the entire other side of the table was all Caucasian males. That was interesting. I decided not to talk about it directly with [the supplier's] folks in the room because there were actually no females, like, levels down. So I'm going to place a call to him.

Reading between the lines, Brewer seems committed to diversity at her business, and she's willing to look for opportunities for improvement, including making discreet calls to suppliers who she thinks could do better as well. Diversity is more than just an empty corporate value for her—it's a real, everyday concern. Her critics interpreted these remarks as Brewer calling for her company to stop hiring white men altogether. Meanwhile, at the time that she made the comments, four out of the eight members of her own executive team were white men, showing how these accusations were made in bad faith.

Yet white male leaders can make statements like this without repercussions. Here's just a small sampling of white male CEOs who have made public comments about diversity being good for business or supported legislative efforts to ban discrimination, all without backlash: Salesforce's Marc Benioff, Starbucks' Kevin Johnson, and Techstars' David Cohen. If anything, these CEOs have been championed and praised for their commitment to fostering more inclusive work environments.

We know that one of the most important qualities that great storytellers share is their authenticity. Those who are authentic have an edge over those who need to be careful and coached. And yet, another way in which we hold women and people of color back is by punishing them when they are authentic, effectively preventing them from leaning into the issues they care about.

"We seem to fascinate people because there are so few of us," said Zak, CEO of ThirdLove. "But the more you're out there, the more people seem to be looking for something to criticize."

Social Media and the Impact of the Parasocial

If you are nonwhite or female, how do you avoid being criticized and losing your position or your company? Well, one solution might be to stay out of the press altogether. If you're not visible and don't tell your story, then no one will come after you, right?

I disagree with this assessment because it is not connected to reality. Brands like Glossier only had breakout success in the first place *because* the CEO had a high profile. Without the CEO's brand, the company would probably be nowhere. Likewise, take Bevel founder Tristan Walker, who realized he needed to be visible in the media *because* he was selling a consumer product specifically for people of color. Without that attention, how could he reach his target audience? For these CEOs, it's a catch-22. Being in the press and building their profiles on social media will move the business forward in key ways, including in sales and marketing, but will also invite negative feedback.

Sarah Frier, the author of *No Filter*, a book about Instagram's origins and its impact, believes that for these female and non-white founders, "it's a can't-win situation." Building a brand comes with all sorts of risks and challenges. But it also helps these founders attract the kind of attention that most brands and founders could not dream of, at least without massive resources. Glossier CEO Emily Weiss has been extremely clear about that in interviews on the topic. She understands the pros and cons but has been deliberate in courting a large following because of the clear business benefits. "I really can't think of another beauty brand, and I can actually think of very few lifestyle brands, that attract as much attention as Glossier does," Weiss acknowledged in a candid interview with *Elle*.[2]

When Frier studied how brands and CEOs leverage Instagram, she discovered something crucial. Frier looked at the companies that had become successful through Instagram, which included Outdoor Voices and Glossier. She learned that these (mostly female) executives are expected to personify their brands not just in their carefully curated social media profiles but also in their everyday, real lives. At home, in the office, walking their dogs, at the coffee shop, and basically anytime they encounter a stranger on the street, they have to present the same flawless brand. That makes their "entire personality and presentation up for critique because it's part of the brand," Frier explained.

On a conscious level, we are smart enough to know that the profiles with big followings on Instagram and other social apps are heavily edited. But we also have exceedingly high expectations for the people we follow on Instagram, particularly if we encounter them in real life. We feel that we've "known" them on some level for years; we treat them as part of our extended friend network, even though the friendship is nonreciprocal.

Scientists have known about the power of these "parasocial relationships" since the 1950s. Back in those days, before the advent of social media, we tended to fixate more on movie stars, sitcom actors, and athletes. More recently, parasocial relationships have started to extend to CEOs, particularly those with big brands and followings on apps like Instagram. For executives like Weiss, who has an online following of millions, that is a lot of "friendships" to maintain. So how can CEOs get away with the sin of simply being in a bad mood and having a crappy day?

For Weiss, the problem only got worse when people who had followed her for years came to work for her company. They were employees, but they already felt they knew who she was because of her Instagram profile. One former Glossier employee told the press that many incoming employees viewed Weiss as some kind of "messiah" and felt personally stung when she wasn't friendly enough. Running a business is not easy, particularly for those who are doing it for the first time. It's not always smiles and warm handshakes. Start-up CEOs tend to be even more inexperienced and have never run a company at scale before. So, from that perspective, there are a lot of employees to potentially disappoint, any one of whom might call a friendly contact in the media.

"I don't think the majority of those hit piece stories are made up or even particularly exaggerated," suggested Jacquelyn Miller, a communications executive who has closely watched the female founder takedowns. "But I also think they'd be much less likely to be written about men because our expectations for their behavior are lower, and people are less likely to 'tell' on them."

That brings me to a potential solution, at least until we figure out how to fix bias in the workplace for good (if that ever happens). A thorough read of the hit pieces on CEOs across a variety of publications suggests that one of the big problems is the gap between reality and expectation. Some of this can't be helped. Weiss is never going to live up to the godlike figure in her employees' minds, no matter how perfect she attempts to be. But there are ways to reduce the risk.

Mitigating Risk and Staying Focused

We've heard a lot about the problem. So let's talk about the possible solutions. We may not be able to fix discrimination and bias overnight, but we can be aware of how we act on an individual level. We can check ourselves and try to do better personally, as well as hold those in our networks accountable. This is true for anyone, no matter where they sit in the organization. But leaders reading this book should be thinking most deeply about these issues, finding ways to improve their own organizations while also putting some protections in place. That is particularly necessary for employees who come from marginalized backgrounds and may be underrepresented in the workforce.

CEOs and other business leaders should feel comfortable sharing their stories in public forums, including the press, given the benefits of doing so. But to protect themselves, they should be very wary of hype. My first piece of advice is for entrepreneurs to recognize a universal truth: What goes up must come down. Again, I am all for engaging with the press, particularly as more newsrooms look to incorporate diverse voices and perspectives. But I would caution leaders to be very careful about their participation in what we refer to in the industry as "puff" pieces. Being vaunted in the media may feel good. But with too much of this type of exposure, the gap between external perception and reality can get too big—and that is dangerous. CEOs in general should avoid projecting exponential success and infallibility ("We're changing the world! We're crushing it!"). That will only lead to disappointment among employees and other stakeholders, as well as brewing resentment. Most companies are not crushing it; they're learning as they go. Instead, I suggest being more open and transparent about some of the struggles that have arisen and avoiding giving the impression of linear success. In Chapter 3, we discussed how business leaders can use transparency as a way to endear themselves to their employees and build trust with external stakeholders. There's no reason why that transparency—within limits—shouldn't also apply to the press.

Alternatively, it makes sense to wait to engage with these sorts of glowing feature stories until there are meaningful data points or customer anecdotes to share, so it's not all pie-in-the-sky vision. Reporters rarely want to write puff pieces but end up doing so if they're not given the full picture. CEOs who are up front about their challenges can create a more balanced view and a more realistic set of expectations surrounding the business. And their honesty takes the wind out of the sails of any potential criticism because they have already owned the issue. So there's no potential for a "gotcha" moment.

We may aspire to be featured on the front cover of a magazine and lauded for our brilliance. But I'll caution you that coverage like that is a double-edged sword. Selling a dream will invariably lead to disappointment. Bottom line: It's important to avoid letting the reality-versus-expectation gap get too wide. Businesses can reduce the risk of blowback in the media if they don't get too far ahead of their skis.

In practical terms, how big should the gap be between reality and hype? Some hype is usually necessary—but how much is too much? Well, there's no exact formula for that, but I'd recommend sussing it out by asking this set of questions:

- If someone joined our company after reading recent glowing coverage, would they be extremely disappointed by the culture or the internal organization as it really exists?
- Is there a major disconnect between the expectations (dollars raised, hype generated in the media) and the reality of the business (dollars made, goals met)?
- Is there a cult of personality at the company to the extent that if the CEO left, there wouldn't be much left?
- Is the company projecting success and nonstop positive momentum for no other business purpose than because it makes the leaders at the company feel good to read the headlines?

If the answer to any of these questions is yes, then it's worth taking a beat to figure out how to right-size the business, so that the story the CEO tells will be consistent with the operations.

Another good rule of thumb: Leaders should avoid appearing on stage, sitting on panels, or engaging with the media when the sole line of questioning is aimed at making an issue of their race or gender. A question or two about how to make it as a Black woman in the corporate world might be helpful to audiences, but it's deeply troubling (not to mention unfair to the executive) if that appearance turns into diversity theater. Such discussions should always come back to business metrics or customer examples to demonstrate how the business is doing and not relate only to the leader's gender or race.

Zak, the ThirdLove CEO, told me she tends to agree to most, but not all, press requests. She typically says no to opportunities where she's only invited to speak *because* she's a female CEO and not because of her business or anything else that she's achieved. She's doesn't see a benefit to her business if she will only be asked how she juggles her family life with her kids at home and her professional responsibilities (a question men are not asked). Other CEOs have taken similar steps to ensure they don't become a target. I spoke with one communications expert, Kyle Arteaga, who worked closely for years with Aicha Evans, CEO of Zoox, Amazon's self-driving-car subsidiary. Arteaga said Evans was invited to speak to the press daily because she's a powerful Black woman at the helm of an important company. Nevertheless, Evans was thoughtful about what she agreed to. Her reaction to Arteaga: Would the interview cover a substantive issue related to her work?

Another good case study here is Jane Fraser, who's one of the most powerful women in financial services. She's the CEO of Citi. But I bet you haven't heard of her unless you're in the banking or financial services industry. Fraser hasn't made it a priority to lean into the fact that she's one of the most powerful women in finance (a male-dominated industry). Instead, her press interviews have focused more on the transformation underway at Citi because that's the job she was hired to do.

Owning the Edge

In some cases, the right approach is to act like a Jane Fraser and maintain a relentless focus on the job to be done. In others, a successful strategy involves leaning into what makes you different or unique. Leaders can own that edge—what makes them different from everyone else—and then divert attention back to the work. Huang's important book describes how women and minority CEOs can turn their differences into superpowers by owning the bias up front and making it into an empowering part of the story—in other words, by flipping the stereotypes on their heads.

Here's a concrete example of how that could work. We know that individuals with accents may struggle to get hired into roles or to raise money. So, someone with a noticeable accent might look the individual or group they're talking to in the eye and say, "You can probably tell from my accent that I'm from the South. Allow me to tell you about where I come from and all the ways that it has contributed to my success."

The same is true for those who look young—these individuals might be taken less seriously in professional settings. Huang, when she teaches, recognizes that she might not fit the template of a typical professor in the eyes of her students. Instead of brushing past it, she acknowledges it up front, with humor: "I know it may look like I'm here to sell you Girl Scout cookies," she often jokes. Then she shifts the conversation to focus on her professional credentials and accomplishments, which drive home the point that she has something of value to share with the class, so they better pay attention.

Likewise, this same idea could work for more experienced, older folks. There's plenty of value in being up-front about having deep ability in a specific field due to years of relevant industry experience.

Here's another concrete example. My friend Deena Shakir has risen to become one of the few Arab American women in venture capital and has earned the respect of the (mostly white and male) investor class through her shrewd investments. But her path wasn't straightforward. Her family emigrated from Iraq, and when she was a child, her home was vandalized after the 9/11 attacks, with racial slurs painted across her driveway. After graduating from Harvard, she took a job in public policy and later at Google. She made her way into venture capital through a lot of hustle, landing a role at the fund Lux Capital. Her first months were a major struggle because she had to learn the industry from scratch while juggling having young children at home.

As a venture capitalist, she's succeeded by positioning herself as an underdog, becoming obsessed with finding other underdogs to invest in. That's been a huge benefit to her, both in how she shares her own story of getting into the industry and in how she describes the companies she invests in.

She links her own experiences to her investment decisions. And she turns bias into a strength that will make her a more successful investor. "Investing in women, but also in underrepresented founding teams, is actually better for the bottom line," she told me. For Shakir, who invested in the women-led Maven Clinic as it became a unicorn, it's already paying off.

With whatever strategy you take, it's important to recognize that the process has multiple steps. The best place to start is with ourselves. Most of us carry some form of bias in how we perceive those we work with. It may be as subtle as judging someone who doesn't speak up in meetings, without recognizing they may be contributing behind the scenes. Or the bias might show up in an assumption that someone's lack of degrees or certifications means they won't be as competent as others on the team who have Ivy League educations.

The first step is to acknowledge our own biases up front, which is easier said than done. Then we can educate ourselves, ask questions of others, and take steps to empathize with the people we work with and in our personal lives. Once we've come clean with ourselves, the work begins in addressing the biases that others may feel toward us—and, as Huang reminds us, in turning our adversity into our advantage.

CHAPTER 11

Storytelling and AI

Some people call this artificial intelligence, but the reality is this technology will enhance us. So instead of artificial intelligence, I think we'll augment our intelligence.

—Ginni Rometty, former CEO of IBM

Lex didn't write this chapter on my behalf. But Lex did have suggestions about how to make my prose crisper, my questions more pointed, and my sentences more concise—feedback I appreciated along the way. What I most valued about Lex, an editor I started working with while writing this book, was its lack of concern for my feelings. Lex didn't seem to care about my deep insecurities, the tender and vulnerable emotions that most writers feel about their work. Lex's only focus involved improving the quality of my content. Within seconds of my request for help on a revision, Lex would provide an alternate version of my prose, mostly without any structural issues, passive voice, or spelling mistakes.

Lex, if you haven't already surmised, is not a human editor but an AI chatbot embedded within a word-processing program in the cloud. By the time you're reading this, Lex may have made some major strides forward. By 2030, Lex may have composed the next great American novel and invented a whole new kind of story plot. Or the total opposite might have happened. Lex might no longer be relevant, having given way to better, faster, and cheaper AI products.

Alternatively, in a far less popular future scenario, we may realize in a few years that the large language models (LLMs) powering many AI companies reached their zenith in 2024 before running into limits in computational capacity, electrical power, or even the availability of fresh water. In other words, maybe we have bought into the hype just a little too much, and perhaps this is the best that Lex is ever going to get. Some people are already starting to warn that we may be in an AI bubble, but those skeptics seem few and far between as I write in 2024.

The reality today is that no one knows. I once heard an AI researcher say that mocking the technology in 2024 is like being disappointed that a nine-month-old baby can't play sports because all it does is "soil itself and scream." It's just way too early to evaluate AI's potential at this stage of its development. This is one of the inherent problems with assessing the quality of AI products. We can claim to be experts or thought leaders, and there seems to be an ample number of those, but this technology's direction and its real applications remain very unclear at this point. AI is also advancing quickly, so any offering today may seem stale in just a few years or even months.

Also in 2024, fearmongers are spreading concerns about AI's role in the destruction of humanity. Elon Musk, an early investor in OpenAI, has been talking about the sinister potential of AI for years, noting on Joe Rogan's podcast that "AI will probably be smarter than any single human next year."[1] (You'll know by the time you're reading this whether his prediction was right or not.) Sam Altman, OpenAI's CEO, has also shared fears about AI ending the world and making specific human jobs redundant, saying that he expects AI will replace 95 percent of the work that creative and marketing agencies do.[2] But I've also heard far more skeptical and credible takes on the technology's true potential. Dr. Angus Fletcher, a story scientist with advanced degrees in both neuroscience and literature, thinks that AI can do a limited set of things and has been overhyped for its near-term usefulness by people like Musk, who want to "float stock prices."

Bottom line: AI remains murky and mysterious, even as we begin to understand both its opportunities and its limitations. I am particularly intrigued by whether AI will replace human storytellers or, more broadly, whether it will impact our ability to imagine, invent, and create—all of which is important to consider as storytelling becomes more important in the world of business. I've heard experts in the field say that AI is coming for the jobs of knowledge workers, which means it's going to have massive impacts on the way we work. But what about creative workers, like playwrights and authors? Producing brilliant works of art is one of the capabilities that makes us human, and if AI diminishes or changes that, what does that mean for the future of humanity? Can this technology ever create the next Shakespearean tragedy or even outpace the greatest writers of all time by ingesting every important piece of text ever produced and creating the ultimate novel? Or will it always lack imagination, leaving pursuits like creative writing and narrative formation firmly in our lane?

"These generative AI models are creating copy that sounds plausible based on iterative statistical analysis of the way language works," said Dylan Tweney, a former journalist and content strategist, who has studied the impact that AI will have in creative fields. "The copy will sound great, and may even be imaginatively inspiring, but don't be fooled into thinking it has any connection to the truth because that's not how AI works." AI is notorious for fabricating information that comes off as entirely plausible. Tweney said we should think of LLMs as "confabulation machines": they're useful in writing as a partner in creation, not as a substitute. For example, AI would come in handy in brainstorming ideas for an article or rewriting copy without spelling mistakes, not in generating the first draft.

Tweney has managed teams of content writers and doesn't think this role is in jeopardy *if the goal is to create truthful content that is interesting to read.* A lot of people don't understand that, however, so he suspects that a lot of AI-generated content, which very few people will read, will likely be dumped onto the internet for many years to come.

Despite that, Tweney is optimistic about the future of storytelling because "real human authenticity will stand out like a lighthouse," he said, in an ocean of AI-generated content. The bottom line, in his view: Just because the computer can sound like a human being and has an unrivaled capacity for research, that doesn't mean it's a replacement for storytellers. Most of us have a gut instinct for when content is not AI-generated, although that may change over time as the technology gets more sophisticated.

When I posed that same question about AI's limitations to Uri Hasson, the neuroscientist and psychologist, he shared a prompt with me:

"What is the word that comes to mind first? 'I think today it's going to . . .'"

Rain, right?

In his studies of generative AI, the computer also says rain. Every single time. That's because, as Hasson puts it, "it goes with the statistics." A good storyteller, however, would know that the element of surprise is critical and would find ways to vary the response. The computer would not be able to do that, unless it was programmed to do so, ensuring it will most often come up with boring and predictable stories.

We see AI most effectively summarizing and imitating. As I write this in 2024, one can prompt a generative AI tool to create a text "in the style of Shakespeare," and the result isn't so bad. It seems able to mimic the voices of popular celebrities, such as the actress Scarlett Johansson.[3] Johansson said the company OpenAI had done so without her permission, provoking a media frenzy and even concerns from regulators about the potential harms associated with so-called deep fakes. But the thing about human-made art is that it doesn't just imitate. It pushes boundaries and provokes us to think and connect in new ways.

Furthermore, many of the greatest writers of all time are associated with multiple genres, making it almost impossible to replicate their style. They didn't merely create "in the style of" one of their predecessors. They subverted or reinterpreted existing literary styles, creating something radically new, often in response to factors like their health, traumas, or personal relationships. To offer a simplified example: The author James Joyce was known for his realistic stories in *Dubliners* and *A Portrait of the Artist as a Young Man*, before he branched out into a far more experimental work with *Ulysses*, and then embraced an even more revolutionary style with *Finnegans Wake*. Sometimes life circumstances have provoked artists to branch out in entirely new directions. Joyce, for example, struggled with chronic eye troubles and prolonged anxiety related to his daughter's mental health. Can we say that these issues "caused" him to become a great writer or to embrace ever more experimental styles? Of course not—but these are factors in his literary development. His life as a human being is inseparable from the work he created.

Likewise, think about why we still find the works of Ernest Hemingway so compelling. We are drawn not just to the words but to his style—those trademark short, concise sentences, in which no single word feels extraneous—and worldview. His prose may be spare but is marked by vulnerability and deep feeling. Hemingway showed us that we don't need flowery, long sentences to convey strong emotion. His style of writing was radical and novel at the time and therefore required a human to do it. It may be entirely possible for AI to mimic his voice today—but, as luddite as this may sound, there is still something special about the real thing. We may also feel drawn to Hemingway because we know something of his own story and his trauma, particularly his years as an ambulance driver during World War I, where he was witness to horrific war injuries and fatalities.

Jane Austen is another example of a writer who has only become more popular with time and now has a certain timeless quality, because she writes about how humans interact with one another in society. Austen writes so beautifully about the human desire to learn and change as we meet people who move through our lives. Her characters elicit a strong emotional response: We laugh alongside them, and we feel deeply for them, even though our own society is so profoundly different from Austen's. Her stories are about who shows empathy: who can deepen their ability for it and who cannot. Many of her works show that humans can change, particularly when faced with people in their lives who encourage them to become better versions of themselves. Could AI draft a novel like this, showing distinctly human emotions and capacities like empathy? The jury is still out on that.

"When it comes to art, it's not just about the story," said Trung Phan, a former financier turned screenwriter and AI researcher. Phan sees a lot of storytelling potential in these AI tools but also recognizes their limitations after studying them for years. "People want to know about the flawed individual behind the story," he noted. The beauty of stories is that they're intrinsically linked to their storytellers—that's what makes them powerful and resonant versus purely abstract.

Compelling art allows us to peer into the mindset of a human being from a different time and get a sense of what that person might have been like. With AI-generated stories, assuming the content is accurate, something is often missing that we can't pinpoint. The output may be technically fine; it may even seem to have been produced by someone who is empathetic or a good listener. But it doesn't provoke an emotional response (at least not for me). I think that's because I know there's no human behind it to be curious about or to try to relate to. Some people, however, may feel differently, and companies like Woebot, maker of an AI therapy chatbot, find that their users feel more comfortable with a nonhuman in the loop. Some users even prefer it, considering it easier to share their deepest secrets with an entity that is not human and therefore doesn't judge. Overall though, the experts I spoke to were skeptical that AI alone could replace any company's content marketing team anytime soon. "People will not form relationships with the AI that is generating the content," said Tweney. "If the goal is to move the business forward and achieve tangible results with content, then we need humans communicating with other humans."

I don't think I'm alone in feeling that AI-generated stories lack a certain humanlike quality, although the technology is improving at a terrifying pace. When the public relations firm Highwire put AI-generated content to the test, analysts concluded that it didn't really move the needle. The content didn't lead to much engagement and ranked extremely low in search engines. Human-drafted content outperformed AI-generated content across every metric that mattered.

Where we are today: Yes, human-generated content can be generic, but it is still orders of magnitude better than any AI-generated copy. That says a lot! I believe it's because while AI can create factually accurate content (although there's no guarantee of that, given its predilection for fabricating), it struggles with narrative, which I'd argue requires a human connection to be fully effective.

Fletcher, the story scientist, is firmly in the "no" camp on AI's ability to overtake us as storytellers and creatives, even over time. You can train an AI to fix a copy error in a piece of text, Fletcher says, but AI does not have the ability to sense people's emotional responses, which means it cannot be empathetic with other beings in the ways that humans can. He describes AI as capable, at best, of producing "not bad writing."[4]

Fletcher, a Renaissance scholar at Ohio State University, who has been educated in both science and the humanities, has written extensively and powerfully about literature's true power and potential. He argues that narrative itself is a technology to help humans resolve complicated thoughts and become better at being human. And for that reason, it's been part of our experience since the beginning, going all the way back to cave paintings from tens of thousands of years ago. AI will never be able to produce "good writing," he thinks, which may be why Highwire's AI-driven content failed to result in engagement. When he refers to skillful writing, he is harkening back to some of the great literary works mentioned in this chapter.

As he explains, large language models, a subset of AI, use neural networks (a method that teaches computers to process data in a way inspired by the animal brain) to process and identify trends in the data they ingest and, based on users' prompts, to convert those into "stories" in text, video, or audio format. In theory, LLMs can "learn" over time to make connections between different types of writing, essentially matching patterns of language, and deliver results that seem strikingly intelligent. Human creativity doesn't rely on that kind of pattern matching alone, because we generate our best ideas through our interactions with others and through our emotional experiences.

Studies have also found that computers can struggle with correlation and causation. Today, an AI can learn, for instance, that smoking is correlated with cancer. But it will struggle to understand that cancer does not cause smoking. That may change, given the emerging field of so-called causal AI, which aims to learn cause-and-effect relationships within data. Likewise, there's been a slew of well-reported problems related to the computer making stuff up, which has the potential to cause real harm. In the spring of 2023, AI gave outdated advice to a patient about breast cancer and then invented health organizations to back up its claims, and researchers have also found indications that AI was more likely to wrongly indicate breast cancer in Black women.[5]

Still, there may be something useful in AI's ability to summarize complex information quickly and provide feedback on how to improve prose. I've been astounded by its ability to pull up relevant results as I've searched for advice on a travel destination or even a medical issue. Even so, I've become more convinced by the model of a human writing the prose and the AI editing it, versus the other way around. Already, we're seeing AI applications in software where this kind of technology speeds up editors' ability to review copy with tools like Grammarly. So we may be headed toward a future where most of us will write fiction, memos, journal entries, homework assignments, and news articles with an AI-based companion of some kind. Writing without an AI chatbot or assistant might be the equivalent of penning a handwritten letter today: quaint enough to be charming.

How that will impact us as storytellers in the future is still unknown. Perhaps having a helpful editor in the background correcting our mistakes will make us better writers. Or it could do the opposite, becoming a crutch that stifles our creativity. The fear is that AI will lead to a future where we all get lazy along the way, with most forms of text resembling how email increasingly looks today: short, lacking emotion, and functional. Or we might just endlessly copy each other's styles and work, prompting the AI to generate text for a content-writing project in the style of a human who seemed creative to us 100 years ago when people were still doing their own work.

The Impact on Humanities Education

Of most concern to many of the researchers I spoke with is the ongoing decline of the humanities. It's not directly attributable to AI, but some US colleges focused on the liberal arts have seen a 50 percent drop in applications in recent years as more students gravitate to science, technology, engineering, and mathematics (STEM), including computer science.[6] The United Kingdom and Europe are reporting similar trends: along with seeing declining enrollment, universities are shrinking their budgets for teachers' salaries in non-STEM subjects.

In business, we may feel that science and engineering are producing more valuable future job applicants, so many business leaders think it's important to prioritize STEM regardless of where AI is headed. And yet, that thesis may mean that we are committing ourselves to a path where young people no longer see value in reading and writing. Humanities education teaches us skills like creativity, imagination, critical thinking, and reasoning. (Full disclosure: I'm biased here because I have advanced degrees in history and journalism.) Reading literature is like training for the brain, and research shows that it makes us both smarter and kinder. Studies published in 2006 and 2009 by the University of Toronto found that people who read fiction appear to be better able to empathize with others and to view the world from others' perspectives.[7]

Nathan Baschez, the engineer behind Lex, told me he built the technology *because* of his fascination with human creativity. In his view, AI can make us more efficient, but it can't turn us into the next Shakespeare. That takes practice, trial and error, luck, and a lot of talent. There's a reason there hasn't (arguably) been an equivalent to Shakespeare in the hundreds of years since he wrote *Hamlet* and *Macbeth*.

There's also value for the human brain in trying to become the next Shakespeare, even if there's little chance of that. Not only is both reading and writing works of fiction enjoyable, but doing so is also good for us. It reduces stress, promotes relaxation, and enhances connectivity in the brain, which is particularly important as we age. One of my favorite ways to get to know new people in my life is to ask them their favorite novel and then to read it. That is like opening a window into their soul. If you're curious, mine is *Of Human Bondage* by W. Somerset Maugham. Once you start it, you can't put it down.

We may be losing something critical in our race to build the smartest computers. Fletcher fears that we've forgotten the very reason we built computers in the first place: They are supposed to be tools that make our lives easier and better, not the other way around, because we are only building skills to communicate with them (and not each other). If we educate our kids to grow up responding to AI and designing their lives around what AI can do, then we've gotten it backward. How can we instead use AI to free up time so that we can do what we do best? It's our very humanity, in Fletcher's view, that makes us such fantastic storytellers. AI, even if it ingests all the literature ever written, will never be able to tell stories in the way that human beings can.

Augment or Replace Jobs?

As AI continues its march into our lives, technologists and philosophers alike are continuing to ask questions about whether these tools will outpace us, replace us, or merely augment our abilities. A lot of that, of course, depends on the role that we're discussing. Some roles, it seems obvious, will soon be replaced by AI; others seem like they can only ever be the purview of a human being. In some cases, the individual whose job has been replaced by AI may be able to retrain to perform a different role. Many experts have theorized that we may be headed into a future where a three- or four-day workweek is the norm, simply because AI is going to make us so much more productive. In 1930, John Maynard Keynes, in an essay titled "Economic Possibilities for Our Grandchildren," famously predicted that his grandchildren might work only fifteen hours a week due to technological improvements. And as a result, we will reach a much higher standard of living. It remains unclear, however, once AI does automate tasks and replace the human workforce, what societies around the world will do with their newly unemployed populations.

So, what can AI do best? In theory, it is simply more effective than us at ingesting vast quantities of information and spitting out answers to a targeted set of questions. It has vast potential for information gathering, sifting through data, and identifying patterns—perhaps even suggesting medical diagnoses. But AI's capabilities also have limitations and pose outright dangers, including the fabrications and hallucinations that are already notorious in the press. LLMs seem to be confidently sharing plausible-sounding but utterly incorrect results—and that is already having consequences because humans (especially those who aren't paying close attention) sometimes can't spot the errors. This could become even more of a problem as the fabrications seem increasingly real.

And yet, even skeptics agree that there is undoubtedly potential for AI to remove some of the drudgery from our work lives—the rote memorization, the data entry, the documentation—and allow us to focus on whatever sparks our imagination and brings us joy. The team behind Lex designed their tool for that very purpose. In their view, the human writer remains in charge but is assisted in the process by "asking Lex" whenever they get stumped or need help. This AI is not writing the text on anyone's behalf.

For most professions, I'd argue that AI will do at least some of the heavy lifting. I can see full-fledged replacement by AI in jobs that involve manual entry or require a human to perform a very consistent task for hours on end, like driving a truck across the country or inputting data into a spreadsheet. Other jobs likely to be impacted by AI include basic customer service, scheduling, and other administrative roles that involve rote processes.

Goldman Sachs, the global investment bank, estimates that AI could replace up to 300 million full-time jobs worldwide while also increasing global GDP by increasing productivity growth.[8] Health care will be hit hard, particularly in America, where the number of health-care administrators has risen by more than 3,000 percent since 1970.

This could open up more opportunities for humans to shine by doing tasks that only they can do, specifically in areas where AI is limited. Remember that a computer can be trained to have a conversation that shows the appearance of emotion or empathy, but an AI has not experienced those moments in life that truly connect us to others and prompt us to reflect deeply and evolve our thinking. That is the fundamental constraint.

Creativity Within Constraints

I see a lot of potential for AI in helping writers with story plots, structures, and formulas. Sometimes an outline alone can get a writer going, especially if the human author needs only to fill in the gaps with their idiosyncratic knowledge, experiences, and feelings. Information without structure can feel like a stream of consciousness that our brains can't handle well, so we tune out. That's the reason that we gravitate to the same plots over and over, such as Joseph Campbell's hero's journey or the seven Booker plots from Chapter 2, which are broken down into a series of stages to hold our attention.

AI might also be helpful in prompting us to realize when our stories don't work because they lack a compelling structure. Most great stories, for instance, should contain a true setback, a moment when our hero might not win. There should also be a satisfying ending, and ideally there's also some kind of surprise or revelation to keep the audience on their toes.

There are, of course, great works of art that follow none of these conventions. There's an entire genre of film, for instance, with deeply unsatisfying endings. Titles that spring to mind for me: *There Will Be Blood*, *Atonement*, and *Dr. Strangelove*. But these kinds of challenging works are the exception that proves the rule. Most of the time, most of us find story structure a great aid to focusing our attention. Stories that lack structure are more likely to be experienced as boring or pointless rather than as great works of genius.

We tend to gravitate to formulaic plots, even as we try to invent new ones. Per the experts I spoke to, ChatGPT, Open-AI's chatbot based on large language models, will continue to incorporate more narrative and character arcs, as well as different structures. Some of these mechanical elements will be helpful. Imagine you have to write a script: You could prompt ChatGPT to come up with a sample script or template with all the key elements, and you would fill in the details to add human touches and personalization.

We could even imagine a world in which this kind of support with structure helps us create new kinds of art rather than holding us back. Developer and storyteller Aytekin Tank writes about how constraints, rules, and boundaries can spark rather than limit creativity.[9] Imagine you're provided a sheet of paper and told to write anything down. The result may be far less imaginative than a prompt that begins with a specific question: "Write about your first memory." AI could provide those prompts and then supply the beginnings of an outline based on what you write.

AI could also be particularly helpful for other kinds of writing, like nonfiction. With this genre, readers and publishers have certain expectations, including word count, form, and so on. Such "constraints [allow] for deeper focus without the distraction of endless possibilities," said Tank.

Finding Authenticity

We need to be most careful in not relying too heavily on AI to write for us. It may have a grasp on the literal meanings behind words but not understand how humans talk in the real world. Paul Graham, the prominent technology investor, told a funny story on X about how a stranger sent him a cold email regarding a novel project. "Then I noticed the word 'delve,'" he wrote. Graham doesn't have anything against the word, but he ran an analysis and found a huge spike in titles or abstracts using the word "delve" in 2022—the year that ChatGPT launched. Conclusion: The email was almost certainly generated by a chatbot and, Graham concluded, not worth reading as a result. Clearly, "delve" is a word that AI favors, although it's fallen out of favor with most (but not all) humans.

On the other hand, Graham's conclusion proved controversial: Nigerian Twitter exploded with comments about how not everyone writes and speaks in the same way, so Graham might be jumping to the wrong conclusion.

That said, there do seem to be certain words preferred by chatbots and increasingly less so by humans. Per software developer Shivangi Jain, some words are a dead giveaway that an AI and not a human is behind a text; these include "transformative," "foster," and "tapestry." Here's my test: Would you use a given word in real life when talking with someone over coffee? If so, by all means, write like you speak—I'm all for authenticity in whatever form it takes. If you would not, do us all a favor and take it out of the text.

Most experts agree that AI can write content quickly and that it will get better over time at generating clicks and attention. All the fake content on the web today is already highly programmatic, generated by humans at so-called content farms, churning out words that they know have a good chance of catching fire on social sites like Facebook. With the introduction of AI, content could get even better at attracting web traffic and the advertising dollars associated with it ("A thing happened, and you'll never believe what came next!"). If web business models continue to value quantity over quality, it's not hard to imagine that AI can fuel all of the marketing copy businesses generate going forward—perhaps leading to a massive increase in the quantity of crummy clickbait content. A sobering thought. And the opposite of what will make companies successful at telling their story in the next few decades.

AI and Newsrooms

It remains unclear how much AI will make its way into fields like publishing, fiction writing, and playwriting, as well as the outlets known for producing high-impact journalism, like *The New York Times* and *The Wall Street Journal*. And in doing so, will it replace the jobs of human writers, authors, and editors employed today? This is not the same issue as the content farms; these writers are among the best at what they do, and they're producing work that requires years of practice and training.

The media industry is clearly bracing for a hit, particularly at the junior levels. AI is going to have a massive impact on junior journalists, just as it will on early-career lawyers and paralegals. These are jobs that require people to do information gathering and research, then compile their findings into briefs and similar documents. I recently sat among a group of lawyers at a conference who described feeling utterly conflicted about the whole topic.

On the one hand they could imagine junior lawyers, who still bill at hundreds of dollars an hour despite being a few years out of law school, being utterly replaced by AI. The technology will be superior at gathering information for briefs, they suspect. That could be a good thing, particularly if it saves their clients money. On the other hand, they recalled the days in which they had to do that painstaking work themselves, and most of them were grateful for it in hindsight, even if it was expensive for their clients. They all agreed this kind of work was essential in making them into the lawyers they are today, with the skills and real-world experience to justify their high price tags. As a former journalist, I feel the same way about my years of digging through and summarizing financial filings, even if I resented it at the time.

That said, we have seen similar technological advancements that haven't made us more stupid because we've simply evolved around them. "It's similar to, say, the introduction of a tool like Excel in the finance world," said Phan. "There was a time when you couldn't just dump data into a spreadsheet," Phan added— you had to do numerical analysis much more painstakingly. Phan said it's possible, but not necessarily the case, that junior lawyers and journalists will never get the training they need because they've been replaced by AI researchers and reporters. But just as a financial analyst is freed up by Excel and doesn't need to spend time doing manual work crunching numbers, maybe a paralegal or a reporter could be freed up by AI-powered research. Wouldn't that enable them to cover more ground? Phan believes it's also possible that people will find different, but potentially more efficient, ways to learn their crafts.

Newsrooms everywhere are deeply conflicted and confused about how to harness this new technology. A 2023 report from JournalismAI via the Polis think tank at the London School of Economics and Political Science found that 75 percent of newsrooms used AI somewhere in the process of gathering information to report the news. These newsrooms were integrating AI despite the fact that more than 60 percent described having concerns about the ethical implications of doing so. And in 2024, for the first time, two winners of the Pulitzer Prize for journalism revealed that they'd used AI tools in their writing: in one case, to browse through thousands of files documenting police misconduct and, in another case, to identify bomb craters in Gaza. (Previous years' winners may have used AI, but this was the first year the Pulitzer committee asked about it.)

However, there are high-profile examples of generative AI use in newsrooms to generate not just text but coverage—and it's not good coverage. In one notable incident, the magazine *Sports Illustrated* was accused of publishing poorly written AI-generated articles with fake bylines of reporters who did not exist. It all came out after readers noticed the decline in quality, and staff expressed frustration and anger following the revelations. *Sports Illustrated* maintained that the news articles were written by humans but acknowledged that the writers used pseudonyms and that the headshots were AI generated.[10]

The Columbia Journalism School, which is studying the dissemination of AI, has issued articles arguing that AI will lead to a fundamental transformation in newsrooms, even while recognizing that it's no panacea. There's a lot that AI will never be able to do. AI technology will not solve the crisis of trust that global newsrooms face, and it will not be a viable alternative to actual humans uncovering information, sifting it, and packaging it into readable news. That work requires judgment and critical thinking, which even humans with decades of experience struggle with at times. There's also unlikely to be an AI fix to the pervasive problem of bias in journalism because the data sets that train the models are themselves biased.

Still, with the economic pressures that many newsrooms are facing, the prospect of using AI will likely be too enticing for media companies to turn down completely, as the London School of Economics' research shows. Many of them might race to incorporate it without thinking through all the problems that remain. That might bring about some efficiency and productivity improvements but create new problems, just as *Sports Illustrated* discovered.

Could there be a silver lining in all this? If AI can quickly generate stories that take very little human oversight, like rewrites of news or quick updates based on earnings reports, could that leave humans to do more investigations or analyses? I recall how these types of stories took up a lot of my time while I was working at newsrooms like Reuters, covering big companies like Apple and Amazon. I would have been thrilled to have an AI "colleague" to take these tedious but important stories off my plate. That's long been the most optimistic view of where this technology is headed: AI will take away the grunt work and allow us all more creative freedom to flourish.

My most optimistic vision of the future is that humans will realize what makes us special and lean into that versus trying to be more like computers. We'll abandon our obsession with data and metrics and realize the true potential that stories can have in our lives. Computers will handle the tedious work, unleashing us to become our truest and most authentic selves.

Or perhaps the exact opposite will happen. Perhaps the chatbot writing my next book will "delve" into it.

Imagination Unleashed

My three-year-old son's favorite book is *Goodnight Moon*. The pages are worn out and peeling after endless nights with him curled up in his bed reading the book. It relaxes him because it's become part of our nightly routine. There will always be a place for the classics, and children of every generation will bid goodnight to their socks, clock, mouse, house, air, and noises everywhere.

The next evolution of storytelling in our household came in the month before my son met his new sibling. A friend sent us a book, from a company called Wonderbly, about my son and his soon-to-be sister, with the illustrated characters designed to look just like my children, with their wavy brunette hair and brown eyes. It's not a classic like Margaret Wise Brown's lovely *Goodnight Moon*, but my children gravitate to it far more often because it's *about them*.

In the near future, I'm sure that my children will watch television shows based on characters they create, with preprogrammed story arcs and emotional experiences that are customized based on their demographic information and their interests. We may already be there, thanks to companies like Charisma, based out of Oxford in the United Kingdom.[11] With Charisma, game developers can create characters with backstories and emotions, who then freestyle conversations with AI-generated dialogue. Watching a few of these videos, I found the characters eerily humanlike, but in that AI style that we've become so accustomed to: They're impressively real, but there's something ever so slightly off about them.

We have this tendency to want to believe that progress is linear. We'll either be living in a world dominated by AI, or not. I have come to believe that our experience will be multidimensional. I'll wager that our children will be reading *Goodnight Moon* and creating AI characters for games and television shows that are deeply personalized—or, taking the opposite tack, intentionally fictionalized so our imaginations can flourish in some novel ways.

The AI-generated stories will likely improve to the extent that the avatars will resemble humans so closely that we won't be able to notice the difference. Indeed, if you want to experience something creepy, search for AI-generated videos of the late rapper Tupac Shakur reflecting on his life. For a second, it's possible to believe the video is real until you remember he died in 1996. (Speaking of Tupac, the rapper's estate is now threatening to sue Drake over a track that featured an AI-generated version of Tupac's voice.)[12]

There's no doubt in my mind that AI will be used to create personalized video content for kids or to create fake videos of long-dead historical figures. This content will increasingly flood our social media channels. And as parents, we'll need to be prepared for that (good luck to us!).

But while the avatars will improve, the stories will never capture everything that we turn to human-created stories for. None of this AI content is a form of storytelling or imagination at all. Humans are the ones supplying the creativity, creating the prompts, and telling the AI program what to do. But this content could provoke new forms of art, I'd argue, that could be just as groundbreaking as the moment that Picasso moved from the classical style to an entirely new one that reflected modern life.

Ultimately, AI is a tool—an extremely cool and occasionally scary one. But it is still just a tool. Humans have been using tools for millions of years, and as we've used them, they have changed us. It remains up to us whether we continue to use this new technology we created, recognizing its limitations (the hallucinations, the fabrications, and the tendency toward the banal) while carving out specific use cases where it excels. Or we may choose to let it make us lazy and replace our human creativity with formulaic content rooted in patterns, trends, and data. I hope our grand experiment with AI leads us to a place where we recognize how totally unique the human brain is. Before my son goes to bed at night, after he reads *Goodnight Moon*, he likes to tell me stories about his day. I am regularly astounded by his sheer creativity. His narrative feats involve everything from exploring deep questions about where dinosaurs came from to telling tales about the creatures he encountered on his walk home. These are magical conversations that I'll never have with a computer, and I'm okay with that.

Conclusion

"The default bias within companies these days is saying something by not saying anything," said Donald Trigg, a longtime health executive who has run both publicly traded and private companies. Trigg has witnessed tremendous change in corporate culture over the past twenty years. Teams have become fully remote or hybrid, and cultures have become flatter than ever before. Even the style of the office has changed, as companies have moved from cubicles to open doors and glass walls where everyone can peer into each other's intimate workspaces.

"Cultures are less hierarchical than ever," he said. "You really need to win the inside, by which I mean your own employees, to win the outside." The outside, according to Trigg, is everything else, ranging from customers to media to financial markets. In today's world, companies succeed by winning both the inside and the outside. There's no other way.

The most progressive CEOs recognize these changes. But storytelling has not yet cemented its place in the corporate world as the most important skill set any leader can possess to stay relevant in our times. Stories, as discussed throughout the pages of this book, are a powerful tool for growth that leaders can use to recruit talent, sell to customers, raise capital, and win. As we learned by example, through conversations with executives like Aaron Levie, Laura Modi, and Alexis Ohanian, storytelling can be used in a variety of ways for businesses to keep employee morale high, grow, and stay ahead of the competition.

For those who aren't yet in leadership roles or starting companies, I hope that *The Storyteller's Advantage* has provided a set of actionable tips to start telling more stories. Even the most introverted people in my network have found success in mediums that feel authentic to them. Becoming an effective storyteller does not mean self-promoting, and it doesn't mean having a big ego. None of us need to see another series of cringeworthy LinkedIn posts replete with hashtags and outdated memes. For anyone who needs a chuckle, there's even a dedicated "LinkedIn lunatics" subreddit filled with examples of some of the worst offenders. Please peruse at your leisure and avoid doing anything that resembles those posts. This kind of approach falls flat because the posters are trying way too hard, crafting content to fit into tropes that tend to be successful on LinkedIn rather than sharing any authentic thoughts or feelings. Scrolling through, it's hard to know whether to laugh or cry.

Good storytelling means staying true to yourself. If it feels unnatural and uncomfortable, it's probably not going to work. Those who take it too seriously and agonize over how the outside world perceives them will come off as robotic and stiff. Remember the cardinal rule: There is no invisible committee of people obsessively waiting for you to fail or to criticize you publicly. No one is paying that close attention to anyone else. Most of us are all too wrapped up in our own lives. So take more risks, be bold, and get creative. Say yes, because stories are what give our lives meaning, purpose, and joy. The corporate world could sure use more of that.

Acknowledgments

I once shared a Twitter poll asking if most people would find it more challenging to have a baby, start a company, or draft a book. The result? Easily, the book. There is an exhaustive list of people I'm indebted to who stood by me in this process, through endless revisions and late-night writing sessions. Thank you to my agent, Julia Eagleton from Janklow & Nesbit, who first reached out to me and encouraged me to become an author, well before I had even considered it as a possibility. Thank you to my editors, Colleen Lawrie, Geraldine Collard, and Kristen Kim, for believing in the project and for all the ways—big and small—that you made it better. This book gave me the opportunity to work once again with my very first editor, Dylan Tweney, who gave me my start in journalism and kept me out of the depths of the writing doldrums. Thank you to my cousin Elsie Ramsey, who sat alongside me painstakingly fixing punctuation in the summer of 2024 while sipping her trademark Coke Zeros, and to my mother, Laurie Farr, who first instilled in me my love of writing and editing (there is no one more adept at spotting punctuation mistakes in the wild). To my dear friends and collaborators Jacquelyn Miller, Alyssa Jaffee, Ellen Leanse, Sarah Frier, and Leslie Schrock for supporting me through this process in more ways than you can know. I'm grateful to Amanda Ashford, Jennifer

Janson, and Michael Yang from OMERS Ventures for the early encouragement and for the digital health team at Manatt.

To my husband, Jarred Colli, my partner in life, I am grateful to you for keeping me going through everything. This book would not have been possible without you. Thank you to my kids, Thea and Miles, for giving me an excuse to revisit children's stories and for your insistence that I keep reading them to you well past your bedtime.

Lastly, thank you to everyone who contributed their stories to this book. It has been my privilege to share them.

Notes

Introduction

1. Yonego Joris Toonders, "Data Is the New Oil of the Digital Economy," *Wired*, August 4, 2015, https://www.wired.com/insights/2014/07/data-new-oil-digital-economy.

2. Beth Stackpole, "The Next Chapter in Analytics: Data Storytelling," MIT Sloan, May 20, 2020, https://mitsloan.mit.edu/ideas-made-to-matter/next-chapter-analytics-data-storytelling.

3. "Creating a Narrative with Reports and Data Graphics," University of North Carolina Wilmington, September 6, 2023, https://onlinedegree.uncw.edu/programs/business/ms-business-analytics/creating-a-narrative-with-reports.

4. Doug Sundheim, "How Patagonia Became the Most Reputable Brand in the United States," *Forbes*, December 12, 2023, https://www.forbes.com/sites/dougsundheim/2023/12/12/how-patagonia-became-the-most-reputable-brand-in-the-united-states.

5. "Why Storytelling Is Your Business's Secret Weapon," *New York Times*, https://nytlicensing.com/latest/marketing/storytelling-is-your-secret-weapon (accessed June 11, 2024).

6. Guest Contributor, "Opinion: Why Those Who Tell the Best Stories Rule Society," Cision (Gorkana), March 16, 2018, https://www.gorkana.com/2018/03/pat-southwell-opinion-those-who-tell-stories-rule-society.

7. "How to Manage Your Company like an Improv Group: Twitter CEO Dick Costolo," video posted to YouTube by Bloomberg Originals, May 22, 2013, https://www.youtube.com/watch?v=xstzSihSu44.

8. Dick Costolo, "How to Run Your Company like an Improv Group, by Twitter CEO Dick Costolo," *Bloomberg*, April 11, 2013, https://www.bloomberg.com/news/articles/2013-04-11/how-to-run-your-company-like-an-improv-group-by-twitter-ceo-dick-costolo.

9. Christine Lagorio-Chafkin, "A 'Holy Shit' Moment: How Steve Huffman and Alexis Ohanian Built Reddit, the 'Front Page of the Internet,'" *Vanity Fair*, September 24, 2018, https://www.vanityfair.com/news/2018/09/how-steve-huffman-and-alexis-ohanian-built-reddit.

10. Kerry Hannon, "A Nation of Quitters: US Workers Aren't Staying at Jobs for as Long as They Used To," Yahoo! Finance, updated June 3, 2023, https://finance.yahoo.com/news/a-nation-of-quitters-us-workers-arent-staying-at-jobs-for-as-long-as-they-used-to-114100476.html.

11. "The Science of Storytelling, with Paula Croxson and Uri Hasson," *This Is Your Brain*, February 25, 2022, https://thisisyourbrain.com/2022/02/the-science-of-storytelling-with-paula-croxson-and-uri-hasson-s3-ep5.

12. Paul J. Zak, "Why Your Brain Loves Good Storytelling," *Harvard Business Review*, October 28, 2014, https://hbr.org/2014/10/why-your-brain-loves-good-storytelling.

Chapter 1: The Founder as Chief Storyteller

1. Mason Walker, "U.S. Newsroom Employment Has Fallen 26% Since 2008," Pew Research Center, July 13, 2021, https://www.pewresearch.org/short-reads/2021/07/13/u-s-newsroom-employment-has-fallen-26-since-2008.

Chapter 2: Plot Lines

1. Anna Mazarakis and Alyson Shontell, "How Box CEO Aaron Levie Got Mark Cuban to Invest in Their Startup While They Were Still in College—Without Ever Meeting Him," *Business Insider*, July 17, 2017, https://www.businessinsider.com/how-box-ceo-aaron-levie-got-mark-cuban-to-invest-2017-7#.

2. L. Jon Wertheim and Sam Sommers, "The Eternal Appeal of the Underdog," *New York Times*, March 15, 2016, https://www.nytimes.com/2016/03/15/opinion/the-eternal-appeal-of-the-underdog.html.

3. "How Box Created and Led the Cloud Content Management Category," Decibel, https://www.decibel.vc/articles/how-box-created-and-led-the-cloud-content-management-category (accessed June 11, 2024).

4. Amy Ingram and William Gartner, "What Do Entrepreneurs Talk About When They Talk About Failure?," Research Gate, January 2013, https://www.researchgate.net/publication/261175279_What_do_entrepreneurs_talk_about_when_they_talk_about_failure.

5. Tom Clynes, "How to Raise a Genius: Lessons from a 45-Year Study of Supersmart Children," *Scientific American*, September 7, 2016, https://www.scientificamerican.com/article/how-to-raise-a-genius-lessons-from-a-45-year-study-of-supersmart-children.

6. Tom Eisenmann, "Why Start-Ups Fail," *Harvard Business Review*, May 2021, https://hbr.org/2021/05/why-start-ups-fail.

7. Robert McKee, "Story-in-Business: Why Story Works, Overcoming Negaphobia, and Authoring the Future," McKee Story, https://mckeestory .com/wp-content/uploads/story-in-business-white-paper.pdf.

Chapter 3: The Big Four Storytelling Secrets

1. Gabriel Perna, "Jonathan Bush on Founding Zus Health, Lessons from Athenahealth and Hospital Cafeteria Food," Health Evolution, July 28, 2021, https://www.healthevolution.com/insider/jonathan-bush-on-founding -zus-health-lessons-from-athenahealth-and-hospital-cafeteria-food.

2. Heidi Zak, "An Open Letter to Victoria's Secret," ThirdLove, November 19, 2018, https://www.thirdlove.com/blogs/learn/an-open-letter-to-victorias-secret.

3. Elizabeth Segran, "Victoria's Secret Threw Shade at ThirdLove, and CEO Heidi Zak Had the Perfect Response," *Fast Company*, November 19, 2018, https://www.fastcompany.com/90270034/victorias-secret-threw-shade -at-thirdlove-and-ceo-heidi-zak-had-the-perfect-response.

4. Jacob Silverman, "Spies, Lies, and Stonewalling: What It's Like to Report on Facebook," *Columbia Journalism Review*, July 1, 2020, https://www .cjr.org/special_report/reporting-on-facebook.php.

5. Silverman, "Spies, Lies, and Stonewalling."

6. "Unexpectedly Canine—Customers Can't Keep Their Paws Off TD Bank's One of a Kind Dog ATM," TD, May 15, 2024, https://stories.td.com /us/en/article/unexpectedly-canine-customers-cant-keep-their-paws-off -td-banks-one-of-a-kind-dog-atm.

7. "2024 Gen Z and Millennial Survey: Living and Working with Purpose in a Transforming World," Deloitte, 2024, https://www.deloitte.com/global /en/issues/work/content/genz-millennialsurvey.html.

Chapter 5: Management by Story

1. "Steve Jobs' 2005 Stanford Commencement Address," video posted to YouTube by Stanford, March 8, 2008, https://www.youtube.com/watch?v =UF8uR6Z6KLc.

2. "Our Credo," Johnson&Johnson, https://www.jnj.com/our-credo (accessed November 21, 2024).

3. Don Sull and Charlie Sull, "MIT SMR's Culture 500," MIT Sloan, https://sloanreview.mit.edu/culture500/research (accessed June 11, 2024).

4. Dan Bigman and Ted Bililies, "Benioff's Way: A Conversation with Salesforce Founder and 2022 CEO of the Year Marc Benioff," *Chief Executive*, October

20, 2022, https://chiefexecutive.net/benioffs-way-a-conversation-with-salesforce
-founder-and-2022-ceo-of-the-year-marc-benioff (emphasis added).

Chapter 6: Story-Driven Brands

1. Hubert Joly, "Creating a Meaningful Corporate Purpose," *Harvard Business Review*, October 28, 2021.

2. Reid Litman, "For Gen Z, Brand Is What You Share, Not What You Sell—Part I," Ogilvy, October 4, 2022, https://www.ogilvy.com/ideas/gen-z-brand-what-you-share-not-what-you-sell-part-i.

Chapter 7: You Are Not Everyone's Protagonist

1. Quoted in Dan Lovallo, Tim Koller, Robert Uhlaner, and Daniel Kahneman, "Your Company Is Too Risk-Averse: Here's Why and What to Do About It," *Harvard Business Review* (March–April 2020).

Chapter 8: For Good or Evil

1. John Carreyou, *Bad Blood: Secrets and Lies in a Silicon Valley Startup* (New York: Knopf, 2018).

2. Jessi Hempel, "How to Win Founders and Influence Everybody," *Wired*, January 21, 2018.

3. Joanna Glasner, "Stanford, Harvard, MIT Still Top the List of Schools Producing Funded Founders," Crunchbase News, May 17, 2022.

Chapter 9: Using Storytelling to Raise Capital

1. "Michael Moritz: Cardiff-Born Billionaire from 'Ordinary Comprehensive,'" *BBC News*, July 12, 2012, https://www.bbc.com/news/uk-wales-south-east-wales-18809606.

2. Ellen Florian, "Michael Moritz: The Best Advice I Ever Got," CNN, January 13, 2012, https://money.cnn.com/2011/12/21/technology/michael_mortiz_best_advice.fortune/index.htm.

3. Owen Thomas, "Mike Moritz Regrets: He Never Patched Things Up with Steve Jobs," *VentureBeat*, April 6, 2010, https://venturebeat.com/business/mike-moritz-return-to-the-little-kingdom-steve-jobs-apple.

4. "Why Storytelling Matters for Founders," video posted to YouTube by Peak XV, July 3, 2020, https://www.youtube.com/watch?v=mS06WYMjyD4.

5. Dan Primack, "Google Ventures Shelves Its Algorithm," *Axios*, September 28, 2022, https://www.axios.com/2022/09/28/google-ventures-shelves-its-algorithm.

6. "Arc," Sequoia Cap, https://www.sequoiacap.com/arc (accessed November 21, 2024).

7. Stewart Scott-Curran, "Sequoia's James Buckhouse on the Role of Story in Experience Design," Intercom, July 27, 2017, https://www.intercom.com /blog/podcasts/sequoia-james-buckhouse-experience-design.

Chapter 10: Storytelling and Bias

1. Christopher Helman, "Fracker Chris Wright, Trump's Energy Pick, Isn't a Climate Denier—He's a Pragmatist," *Forbes*, June 6, 2024, https:// www.forbes.com/sites/kimelsesser/2024/06/06/female-ceos-outearn-male -counterparts.

2. Véronique Hyland, "How Emily Weiss Influenced Everything," *Elle*, March 25, 2024, https://www.elle.com/beauty/a60112997/emily-weiss -women-of-impact-interview-2024.

Chapter 11: Storytelling and AI

1. "Elon Musk Freaks Out Joe Rogan About the Dangers of AI," video posted to YouTube by Enterprise Management 360, September 1, 2023, https://www.youtube.com/watch?v=VozVRnZaceo.

2. Anna Tong, Jeffrey Dastin, and Krystal Hu, "OpenAI Researchers Warned Board of AI Breakthrough Ahead of CEO Ouster, Sources Say," *Reuters*, November 23, 2022, https://www.reuters.com/technology /sam-altmans-ouster-openai-was-precipitated-by-letter-board-about-ai -breakthrough-2023-11-22.

3. Gene Maddaus, "After Scarlett Johansson Dustup, AI Lobbying Group Urges Congress to Outlaw Deepfakes," *Variety*, June 10, 2024, https:// variety.com/2024/biz/news/scarlett-johansson-ai-lobbying-deepfake -microsoft-openai-software-alliance-1236029583.

4. Angus Fletcher, "Why Storytelling Will Prevent AI Dominance," video posted to YouTube by Singularity University, March 9, 2023, https://www .youtube.com/watch?v=6VuVVDK83vk.

5. Edward Winstead, "Can Artificial Intelligence–Driven Chatbots Correctly Answer Questions About Cancer?," National Cancer Institute, October 3, 2023, https://www.cancer.gov/news-events/cancer-currents-blog/2023 /chatbots-answer-cancer-questions.

6. Nathan Heller, "The End of the English Major," *New Yorker*, February 27, 2023, https://www.newyorker.com/magazine/2023/03/06/the -end-of-the-english-major.

7. Annie Murphy Paul, "Reading Literature Makes Us Smarter and Nicer," *Time*, June 3, 2013, https://ideas.time.com/2013/06/03/why-we-should-read-literature.

8. Jack Kelly, "Goldman Sachs Predicts 300 Million Jobs Will Be Lost or Degraded by Artificial Intelligence," *Forbes*, March 31, 2023, https://www.forbes.com/sites/jackkelly/2023/03/31/goldman-sachs-predicts-300-million-jobs-will-be-lost-or-degraded-by-artificial-intelligence.

9. Aytekin Tank, "How Limitations Can Foster Innovation and Productivity," Jotform, https://www.jotform.com/blog/how-limitations-can-foster-innovation-and-productivity (accessed November 21, 2024).

10. Santul Nerkar and Kevin Draper, "For Sports Illustrated, Report About Fake Authors Is Latest Stumble," *New York Times*, November 28, 2023, https://www.nytimes.com/2023/11/28/business/sports-illustrated-artifical-intelligence.html.

11. Charisma, https://charisma.ai.

12. Bill Donahue, "Tupac Shakur's Estate Threatens to Sue Drake over Diss Track Featuring AI-Generated Tupac Voice," *Billboard*, April 24, 2024, https://www.billboard.com/pro/tupac-shakur-estate-drake-diss-track-ai-generated-voice.

Bibliography

Introduction

Costolo, Dick. "How to Run Your Company like an Improve Group, by Twitter CEO Dick Costolo." *Bloomberg*. April 11, 2013. https://www.bloomberg.com/news/articles/2013-04-11/how-to-run-your-company-like-an-improv-group-by-twitter-ceo-dick-costolo.

"Creating a Narrative with Reports and Data Graphics." University of North Carolina Wilmington. September 6, 2023. https://online degree.uncw.edu/programs/business/ms-business-analytics/creating-a-narrative-with-reports.

Hannon, Kerry. "A Nation of Quitters: US Workers Aren't Staying at Jobs for as Long as They Used To." Yahoo! Finance. Updated June 3, 2023. https://finance.yahoo.com/news/a-nation-of-quitters-us-workers-arent-staying-at-jobs-for-as-long-as-they-used-to-114100476.html.

"How to Manage Your Company like an Improv Group: Twitter CEO Dick Costolo." Video posted to YouTube by Bloomberg Originals. May 22, 2013. https://www.youtube.com/watch?v=xstzSihSu44.

Joris Toonders, Yonego. "Data Is the New Oil of the Digital Economy." *Wired*. August 4, 2015. https://www.wired.com/insights/2014/07/data-new-oil-digital-economy.

Lagorio-Chafkin, Christine. "A 'Holy Shit' Moment: How Steve Huffman and Alexis Ohanian Built Reddit, the 'Front Page of the Internet.'" *Vanity Fair*. September 24, 2018. https://www.vanityfair.com/news/2018/09/how-steve-huffman-and-alexis-ohanian-built-reddit.

"The Science of Storytelling, with Paula Croxson and Uri Hasson." *This Is Your Brain*. February 25, 2022. https://thisisyourbrain.com/2022/02/the-science-of-storytelling-with-paula-croxson-and-uri-hasson-s3-ep5.

"Why Storytelling Is Your Business's Secret Weapon." *New York Times*. https://nytlicensing.com/latest/marketing/storytelling-is-your-secret-weapon (accessed June 11, 2024).

Zak, Paul J. "Why Your Brain Loves Good Storytelling." *Harvard Business Review*. November 5, 2014. https://hbr.org/2014/10/why-your-brain-loves-good-storytelling.

Chapter 1: The Founder as Chief Storyteller

Lagorio-Chafkin, Christine. "A 'Holy Shit' Moment: How Steve Huffman and Alexis Ohanian Built Reddit." *Vanity Fair*. September 24, 2018. https://www.vanityfair.com/news/2018/09/how-steve-huffman-and-alexis-ohanian-built-reddit.

Zook, Chris. "Founder-Led Companies Outperform the Rest—Here's Why." *Harvard Business Review*. October 25, 2017. https://hbr.org/2016/03/founder-led-companies-outperform-the-rest-heres-why.

Chapter 2: Plot Lines

Clynes, Tom. "How to Raise a Genius: Lessons from a 45-Year Study of Supersmart Children." *Scientific American*. September 7, 2016. https://www.scientificamerican.com/article/how-to-raise-a-genius-lessons-from-a-45-year-study-of-supersmart-children.

Dufour, Francois. "How Box Created and Led the Cloud Content Management Category." *Decibel*. https://www.decibel.vc/articles/how-box-created-and-led-the-cloud-content-management-category (accessed June 11, 2024).

Eisenmann, Tom. "Why Start-Ups Fail." *Harvard Business Review*. May 2021. https://hbr.org/2021/05/why-start-ups-fail.

McKee, Robert. *Story: Substance, Structure, Style, and the Principles of Screenwriting*. New York: ReganBooks, 1997. Available at https://ia600101.us.archive.org/22/items/RobertMcKeeStorypdf/Robert%20McKee%20-%20Story%20%28pdf%29.pdf.

Chapter 3: The Big Four Storytelling Secrets

"#brandsgetreal: Social Media and the Evolution of Transparency." *Sprout Social*. January 26, 2024. https://sproutsocial.com/insights/data/social-media-transparency.

Frier, Sarah. *No Filter: The Inside Story of Instagram*. New York: Simon and Schuster, 2020.

Segran, Elizabeth. "Victoria's Secret Threw Shade at ThirdLove, and CEO Heidi Zak Had the Perfect Response." *Fast Company*. November 19, 2018. https://www.fastcompany.com/90270034/victorias-secret-threw-shade-at-thirdlove-and-ceo-heidi-zak-had-the-perfect-response.

Silverman, Jacob. "Spies, Lies, and Stonewalling: What It's Like to Report on Facebook." *Columbia Journalism Review*. July 1, 2020. https://www.cjr.org/special_report/reporting-on-facebook.php.

Summers, Juana, Jason Fuller, and Justine Kenin. "Why Customer Service Ratings Are Getting Worse." *NPR*. March 15, 2023. https://www.npr.org/2023/03/15/1163733421/why-customer-service-ratings-are-getting-worse.

"2024 Gen Z and Millennial Survey: Living and Working with Purpose in a Transforming World." Deloitte. 2024. https://www.deloitte.com/global/en/issues/work/content/genz-millennialsurvey.html.

"Unexpectedly Canine—Customers Can't Keep Their Paws Off TD Bank's One of a Kind Dog ATM." TD. May 15, 2024. https://stories.td.com/us/en/article/unexpectedly-canine-customers-cant-keep-their-paws-off-td-banks-one-of-a-kind-dog-atm.

Zak, Heidi. "An Open Letter to Victoria's Secret." ThirdLove. November 19, 2018. https://www.thirdlove.com/blogs/learn/an-open-letter-to-victorias-secret.

Chapter 5: Management by Story

Bigman, Dan, and Ted Bililies. "Benioff's Way: A Conversation with Salesforce Founder and 2022 CEO of the Year Marc Benioff." *Chief Executive*. October 20, 2022. https://chiefexecutive.net/benioffs-way-a-conversation-with-salesforce-founder-and-2022-ceo-of-the-year-marc-benioff.

Gothelf, Jeff. "Use OKRs to Set Goals for Teams, Not Individuals." *Harvard Business Review*. December 17, 2020.

"Our Credo." Johnson&Johnson. https://www.jnj.com/our-credo (accessed January 10, 2025).

"Steve Jobs' 2005 Stanford Commencement Address." Video posted to YouTube by Stanford. March 8, 2008. https://www.youtube.com/watch?v=UF8uR6Z6KLc.

Sull, Don, and Charlie Sull. "MIT SMR's Culture 500." MIT Sloan. https://sloanreview.mit.edu/culture500/research (accessed June 11, 2024).

Chapter 6: Story-Driven Brands

Litman, Reid. "For Gen Z, Brand Is What You Share, Not What You Sell—Part I." Ogilvy. October 4, 2022. https://www.ogilvy.com/ideas/gen-z-brand-what-you-share-not-what-you-sell-part-i.

Chapter 8: For Good or Evil

Carreyrou, John. *Bad Blood: Secrets and Lies in a Silicon Valley Startup*. New York: Knopf, 2018.

Chapter 9: Using Storytelling to Raise Capital

Florian, Ellen. "Michael Moritz: The Best Advice I Ever Got." *CNN*. January 13, 2012. https://money.cnn.com/2011/12/21/technology/michael_mortiz_best_advice.fortune/index.htm.

Litman, Reid. "For Gen Z, Brand Is What You Share, Not What You Sell—Part I." Ogilvy. October 4, 2022. https://www.ogilvy.com/ideas/gen-z-brand-what-you-share-not-what-you-sell-part-i.

Primack, Dan. "Google Ventures Shelves Its Algorithm." *Axios*. September 28, 2022. https://www.axios.com/2022/09/28/google-ventures-shelves-its-algorithm.

Scott-Curran, Stewart. "Sequoia's James Buckhouse on the Role of Story in Experience Design." Intercom. July 27, 2017. https://www.intercom.com/blog/podcasts/sequoia-james-buckhouse-experience-design.

Thomas, Owen. "Mike Moritz Regrets: He Never Patched Things Up with Steve Jobs." *VentureBeat*. April 6, 2010. https://venturebeat.com/business/mike-moritz-return-to-the-little-kingdom-steve-jobs-apple.

"Why Storytelling Matters for Founders." Video posted to YouTube by Peak XV. July 3, 2020. https://www.youtube.com/watch?v=mS06WYMjyD4.

Chapter 10: Storytelling and Bias

Bever, Lindsay. "Sam's Club CEO Called 'Racist' for Remarks on Diversity." *Washington Post*. September 15, 2015. https://www.washingtonpost.com/news/morning-mix/wp/2015/12/15/sams-club-ceo-called-racist-for-remarks-on-diversity.

Bishop Smith, Edward, Jillian Chown, and Kevin Gaughan. "Better in the Shadows? Public Attention, Media Coverage, and Market Reactions to Female CEO Announcements." *Sociological Science*. May 17, 2021. https://sociologicalscience.com/articles-v8-7-119.

Dobbin, Frank, and Alexandra Kalev. "Why Diversity Programs Fail." *Harvard Business Review*. March 27, 2024. https://hbr.org/2016/07/why-diversity-programs-fail.

Elsesser, Kim. "Female CEOs Outearn Male Counterparts in S&P 500 Companies." *Forbes*. June 5, 2024, updated June 6, 2024. https://www.forbes.com/sites/kimelsesser/2024/06/05/female-ceos-outearn-male-counterparts-in-sp-500-companies.

Fleming, Olivia. "Are All These Female-Founder Takedowns Fair?" *The Helm*. June 24, 2020. https://thehelm.co/female-founder-takedowns-outdoor-voices-away-the-wing.

Gupta, Suraj. "Council Post: Diversity: The Holy Grail of Venture Capital." *Forbes*. August 12, 2024. https://www.forbes.com/councils/forbes businesscouncil/2022/05/26/diversity-the-holy-grail-of-venture-capital.

Hinchliffe, Emma. "Women CEOs Run 10.4% of Fortune 500 Companies. A Quarter of the 52 Leaders Became CEO in the Last Year." *Fortune*. June 5, 2023. https://fortune.com/2023/06/05/fortune -500-companies-2023-women-10-percent.

Huang, Laura. *Edge: Turning Adversity into Advantage*. New York: Portfolio, 2020.

Hyland, Véronique. "How Emily Weiss Influenced Everything." *Elle*. March 25, 2024. https://www.elle.com/beauty/a60112997/emily-weiss-women -of-impact-interview-2024.

Legault, Helena. "Parasocial Relationships with T.X. Watson." Pol Comm Tech Lab. March 28, 2024. https://www.polcommtech.com/post /parasocial-relationships-with-t-x-watson.

Lloyd, Camille. "One in Four Black Workers Report Discrimination at Work." Gallup. March 5, 2024. https://news.gallup.com/poll/328394/one-four -black-workers-report-discrimination-work.aspx.

Maddaus, Gene. "After Scarlett Johansson Dustup, AI Lobbying Group Urges Congress to Outlaw Deepfakes." *Variety*. June 10, 2024. https://variety .com/2024/biz/news/scarlett-johansson-ai-lobbying-deepfake-microsoft -openai-software-alliance-1236029583.

Russell, Melia. "April Koh Built a $2 Billion Mental-Health Startup by Age 29. Current and Former Employees Say She Led a Fast-Paced Culture That Created Panic and Fear." *Business Insider*. March 22, 2023. https://www.businessinsider.com/spring-health-april-koh-mental-health -startup-culture-burnout-quitting-2021-11.

Schiffer, Zoe. "ThirdLove Says It's by Women, for Women. But Women Who've Worked There Disagree." *Vox*. September 16, 2019. https:// www.vox.com/the-goods/2019/9/16/20864206/thirdlove-bra-company -women-employees-quit-ceo.

Sears, Brad. "LGBTQ People's Experiences of Workplace Discrimination and Harassment." Williams Institute. September 6, 2024. https://williams institute.law.ucla.edu/publications/lgbt-workplace-discrimination.

Sebbings, Harry. "Keith Rabois and Mike Shebat: Creating an Olympian Mindset to Work Ethic." Video posted to YouTube by 20VC with Harry Stebbings. November 27, 2023. https://www.youtube.com/watch ?v=flf81mI5yEU.

Stypińska, Justyna, and Konrad Turek. "Hard and Soft Age Discrimination: The Dual Nature of Workplace Discrimination." *European Journal of Ageing*. January 24, 2017. https://www.ncbi.nlm.nih.gov/pmc/articles/PMC5550623.

Umoh, Ruth. "154 Fortune 500 Companies Released Diversity Data Last Year. Here's What They Reveal About the State of DEI." *Fortune*. March 13, 2024. https://fortune.com/2024/03/13/fortune-500 -diversity-data-promotions-representation-legal.

Wong, Rose. "Stop Screening Job Candidates' Social Media." *Harvard Business Review*. September 2, 2021. https://hbr.org/2021/09/stop -screening-job-candidates-social-media.

Wood-Brooks, Allison, Laura Huang, Sarah Wood Kearney, and Fiona E. Murray. "Investors Prefer Entrepreneurial Ventures Pitched by Attractive Men." *PNAS*. March 10, 2014. https://www.pnas.org/doi/full/10.1073 /pnas.1321202111.

Chapter 11: Storytelling and AI

"Columbia Journalism School Explores 'AI in the Newsroom' with Events Through September." Columbia Journalism School. September 20, 2024. https://journalism.columbia.edu/news/ai-september-events-cjs.

"Elon Musk Freaks Out Joe Rogan About the Dangers of AI." Video posted to YouTube by Enterprise Management 360. September 1, 2023. https://www .youtube.com/watch?v=VozVRnZaceo.

Fletcher, Angus. "Why Storytelling Will Prevent AI Dominance." Video posted to YouTube by Singularity University. March 9, 2023. https://www .youtube.com/watch?v=6VuVVDK83vk.

Kelly, Jack. "Goldman Sachs Predicts 300 Million Jobs Will Be Lost or Degraded by Artificial Intelligence." *Forbes*. March 31, 2023. https:// www.forbes.com/sites/jackkelly/2023/03/31/goldman-sachs-predicts-300 -million-jobs-will-be-lost-or-degraded-by-artificial-intelligence.

Maddaus, Gene. "After Scarlett Johansson Dustup, AI Lobbying Group Urges Congress to Outlaw Deepfakes." *Variety*. June 10, 2024. https://variety .com/2024/biz/news/scarlett-johansson-ai-lobbying-deepfake-microsoft -openai-software-alliance-1236029583.

Nerkar, Santul, and Kevin Draper. "For Sports Illustrated, Report About Fake Authors Is Latest Stumble." *New York Times*. November 28, 2023. https://www.nytimes.com/2023/11/28/business/sports-illustrated-artifical -intelligence.html.

Tong, Anna, Jeffrey Dastin, and Krystal Hu. "OpenAI Researchers Warned Board of AI Breakthrough Ahead of CEO Ouster, Sources Say." *Reuters*.

November 23, 2023. https://www.reuters.com/technology/sam-altmans-ouster-openai-was-precipitated-by-letter-board-about-ai-breakthrough-2023-11-22.

Winstead, Edward. "Can Artificial Intelligence–Driven Chatbots Correctly Answer Questions About Cancer?" National Cancer Institute. October 3, 2023. https://www.cancer.gov/news-events/cancer-currents-blog/2023/chatbots-answer-cancer-questions.

Index

Christina Farr is a business journalist and venture capitalist. She is a managing director at Manatt, a general partner at Scrub Capital, and editor in chief of the popular industry newsletter *Second Opinion*. She was named a "rising star" in venture capital by *Business Insider* and *VC Journal*. She lives in New York with her husband and two children.

Credit: Sylvie Rosokoff